FAMILIES, DELINQUENCY, AND CRIME

Linking Society's Most Basic Institution to Antisocial Behavior

Ronald L. Simons
University of Georgia

Leslie Gordon Simons
University of Georgia

Lora Ebert Wallace
Western Illinois University

New York Oxford
OXFORD UNIVERSITY PRESS

Oxford University Press, Inc., publishes works that further Oxford University's objective of excellence in research, scholarship, and education.

Oxford New York
Auckland Cape Town Dar es Salaam Hong Kong Karachi
Kuala Lumpur Madrid Melbourne Mexico City Nairobi
New Delhi Shanghai Taipei Toronto

With offices in
Argentina Austria Brazil Chile Czech Republic France Greece
Guatemala Hungary Italy Japan Poland Portugal Singapore
South Korea Switzerland Thailand Turkey Ukraine Vietnam

Published by Oxford University Press, Inc.
198 Madison Avenue, New York, New York 10016
http://www.oup.com

ISBN 978-0-19-533042-7

The Roxbury Series in Crime, Justice, and Law

Series Coeditors:

Ronald L. Akers, University of Florida
Gary F. Jensen, Vanderbilt University

This new series features concisely and cogently written books on an array of important topics, including specific types of crime and central or emerging issues in criminology, justice, and law.

The books in this series are designed and written specifically for classroom use in criminology, sociology, deviance, delinquency, criminal justice, and related classes. The intent of the series is to provide both an introduction to the issues and the latest knowledge available—at a level accessible to undergraduate students. ✦

All of us have a mutual interest in the virtue of one another . . . for societies cannot exist if only a few have virtue. . . . Virtues such as justice and temperance can be taught. . . . Education and admonition (should) commence the first five years of childhood.

Plato
The Dialogues

You are the bows from which your children as living arrows are sent forth.

Kahlil Gibran
The Prophet

You need a license to catch a fish or drive a car but any *#@%!*&$ can be a parent.

Todd (Keanu Reeves)
The movie *Parenthood*

About This Book

Families, Delinquency, and Crime: Linking Society's Most Basic Institution to Antisocial Behavior explores the link between family life and antisocial behavior. In recent years, researchers from a variety of disciplines have investigated the relationship between society's most fundamental social institution—the family—and various forms of criminal behavior. Simons et al. fill a fundamental void in the literature by demonstrating how these seemingly disparate lines of research can be woven together using classic and contemporary theories of delinquency and crime.

Families, Delinquency, and Crime evaluates and explores popular explanations using the results of studies by sociologists, criminologists, and psychologists. Each chapter succinctly defines terminology, establishes a review of empirical literature, and provides an effective argument that families are a dynamic aspect of our social lives that are intricately related to delinquency and other problem behaviors. Clear examples of each situation are plentiful.

Part I explains child and adolescent antisocial behavior. The chapters review theory and research regarding the effect of family structure, marital conflict, parental antisocial behavior, and parents' childrearing practices on a child's risk for conduct problems and delinquency.

Part II focuses on adult antisocial behavior and shows how the various family socialization processes and childhood behavior problems discussed in Part I influence the probability of later adult crime. Explanations are provided for both the continuity and discontinuity of antisocial behavior across the life course. Consideration is given to the manner in which romantic partners often modify deviant life course trajectories. The book also explores the link between family experiences during childhood and adult risk for either perpetrating or becoming the victim of marital violence. ✦

Contents

Preface

This book was written in an attempt to fill an important gap in literature. It brings together research and theory from criminology, psychology, family science, and sociology regarding the role of family processes in the etiology of delinquent and criminal behavior. It is designed to be an aid to scholars interested in the link between family and deviance. In addition, we believe it will serve as a useful supplemental text in two very different sets of courses.

The first set includes juvenile delinquency, deviant behavior, and criminology courses taught in sociology and criminal justice departments. Increasingly, theory and research in the areas of crime and delinquency have emphasized the importance of family processes in explaining the development of deviant behavior. Hirschi's social control theory, Sampson and Laub's life course perspective, Akers' social learning model, and Gottfredson and Hirschi's general theory of crime, for example, all identify parental behavior as a cause of delinquent behavior. Further, criminologists have begun to focus on family-related issues such as marital violence, child abuse, and the manner in which romantic partners influence each other's involvement in antisocial behavior.

Textbooks on juvenile delinquency and criminology present a general overview of these theories. They do not, however, provide a detailed account of the similarities and differences between these frameworks regarding the theoretical processes and mechanisms whereby family interaction is linked to onset, maintenance, and desistance of deviant behavior. Also, very little information is included in these textbooks concerning the extent of research support for these theoretical positions. Finally, delinquency and criminology textbooks give scant attention to theoretical developments and research findings from family sociology and developmental psychology. This theory and research has much to say about the validity of criminological frameworks and can be used to elaborate and extend these theories. We have attempted to address each of these limitations.

The second set of courses consists of family and child development courses taught in departments of sociology, psychology, and family studies. These courses often include topics such as child conduct problems and delinquent behavior, child abuse and neglect, and marital violence. Family and child development textbooks usually limit their discussion of these issues to work completed by family scholars and developmental psychologists. There is little consideration of the extensive scholarship on these subjects by criminologists and social deviance researchers. We address this limitation by including studies by family and child development scientists and by criminologists. Further, we link the two bodies of literature to show how each might be used to augment the theoretical efforts of the other.

Over the past few years, we have had the good fortune of working at research institutes at Iowa State University and the University of Georgia concerned with the nexus of family processes and social deviance. Our research projects have been interdisciplinary efforts involving sociologists, psychologists, and family scientists. We have been challenged by our colleagues, who piqued our curiosity and forced us to consider alternative perspectives. This has been an incredibly exciting, stimulating, and liberating exercise. We hope that this enthusiasm for the subject matter is evident throughout the chapters of this book.

Finally, we need to recognize the various individuals who provided invaluable assistance in the preparation of this text. We thank the reviewers who offered insights and suggestions that dramatically improved the quality of the chapters: Charles Amissah (Hampton University), Candice Batton (University of Nebraska), Joseph R. Franco (Pace University), Hua-Lun Huang (University of Louisiana—LaFayette), Daniel Lee (Indiana University of Pennsylvania), David Myers (Indiana University—Purdue University Indianapolis), Everette Penn (Prairie View A&M), David Sanford (Northwood University), and Charles Vivona (SUNY College at Old Westbury). We also express our gratitude to the staff of Roxbury Publishing—especially Jim Ballinger and Claude Teweles—for their expert guidance and direction. Lastly, we want to acknowledge the numerous, often spirited, discussions with colleagues, family, and friends that helped sharpen our thoughts about many of the issues discussed in the book. ✦

Foreword

Ronald L. Akers
University of Florida

Family is a central, indeed, as the subtitle of this book states it, the "most basic" social institution in society. The family performs a number of critical functions, but among its most enduring and important is the responsibility for socialization of children. It is difficult to imagine a society with conforming, law-abiding members of society and citizens of the state in which there is no system of family-based child-rearing. Every society and political state leans heavily on the operation of informal social control in primary groups, especially family and kinship groups, to support conformity and counteract deviance. This centrality has long placed the nature and structure of the family, family relationships, parenting, and socialization practices at the forefront of theory and research on the causes and prevention of crime and delinquency. Although marriage and family as a field of study remains at the core of sociology and course offerings in sociology departments, the social structural and social psychological dimensions of the family have been the focus of research across many different disciplines. Similarly, as an interdisciplinary field of study, criminology must draw from those different disciplines to understand and explain the role of family in antisocial and deviant behavior, crime, and delinquency. But to be profitable, this must be done in ways that integrate the different strands into a theoretically coherent view of the processes by which the family has an impact on conforming and deviant behavior.

That is what Ronald L. Simons, Leslie Gordon Simons, and Lora Ebert Wallace have accomplished in a very impressive manner in

Families, Delinquency, and Crime: Linking Society's Most Basic Institution to Antisocial Behavior.

Simons, Simons, and Wallace recognize that family affects, here and now, the deviant and law-violating behavior of children and adolescents and also has longer-term effects over the life course. Therefore, they first direct their attention to the question of family processes nad variables in the behavior of children and adolescents focusing on the insights, implications, and applicability of control and social learning theories. While they recognize differences in relative emphasis in the two approaches, they avoid the trap of assuming that only theories in the control tradition are relevant to the family and only social learning theory is relevant to peers. They show that both traditions have something relevant to say about the family and the interaction of family variables with peer influences, work, and neighborhood conditions. The authors conclude that consistent discipline and monitoring by parents prevent or reduce deviant and antisocial behavior in their children, both directly and through impact on peer influences. Their analysis finds that corporal punishment of children, especially after they reach school age, is counterproductive in socialization in most families. But among families in high-crime neighborhoods tougher family socialization and disciplinary practices, including corporal punishment, may be needed to offset deviant peer influences and protect against the high-risk situations that children in these neighborhoods often encounter.

Next the authors turn to questions related to the links between childhood socialization and deviance later in life, focusing on life course perspectives but also weaving in aspects of control and learning theories. Their life course model starts with family practices and problem behavior among children at age 10 and younger, brings in peer and school influences in the teenage years, and then looks at how these factors earlier in life have an impact on and are conditioned by family, marital, and occupational variables in adulthood. There is, of course, both continuity and change in behavior patterns through the life course; the question is how much there is of each and what explains both. The authors find that childhood socialization can have an effect later in life and that early involvement in deviant and delinquent behavior is somewhat predictive of adult deviance. But most of the time it is not, and research shows that "the majority of delinquent children grow up to be conventional adults!" (p. 172). The question is why this would be true. Their analysis finds that socialization and social factors in adult life work to change previous deviant patterns and enhance conforming behavior. However, Simons, Simons, and Wallace admit that the answers to this question are not yet clear and unraveling the answers represent a challenge for future research.

In the popular view the answer to the question of the link between family and deviance is simple. It's the parents' fault. The family has no values and no control over the kids. In reviewing the policy implications of their work, Simons, Simons, and Wallace get beyond this blame-the-parents tendency. Rather, they advocate "social policies that strengthen families and enhance quality of child care" such as parenting classes, Head Start programs, financial support, and other "family-friendly policies" (p. 173).

The goal of the Roxbury Series, of which this book is part, is to provide both an introduction to and the latest knowledge on the subject in a way that is accessible to students and other nonexperts. It is clear that the authors have achieved that goal. Those for whom this is the first exposure to the subject will have no problem understanding it in this text. At the same time, those who are well acquainted with the subject will still learn something. After reading the book, I found myself better informed even about issues that I already knew well and had studied in depth. Simons, Simons, and Wallace are enthusiastic, engaged, and knowledgeable about the subject of family relationships and antisocial behavior. The content of the book is richly informed, not only by the most recent research and theory in the field but also by the findings from collaborative efforts in the authors' own high-quality research. All of this is presented in a concise and remarkably well-written manner. ✦

About the Authors

Ronald L. Simons is Professor of Sociology and Research Fellow with the Institute for Behavioral Research at the University of Georgia. He completed his graduate training at Florida State University and the University of Wisconsin. For the past several years he has been involved in longitudinal studies of the effect of family and community factors on child adjustment. These projects are funded by National Institutes of Health and have resulted in numerous articles and books.

Leslie Gordon Simons is Assistant Professor of Child and Family Development at the University of Georgia. She completed her doctorate in sociology at Iowa State University. Her research investigates the effect of child characteristics and parental behavior on adolescent risk for conduct problems, depression, and early sex.

Lora Ebert Wallace completed her doctorate in sociology at Iowa State University and is Assistant Professor of Sociology at Western Illinois University. Her research interests include models of stress, coping, and psychological well-being, as well as the examination of behaviors and conditions among adolescents and adults. ✦

Part I

Family Processes and the Deviant Behavior of Children and Adolescents

Chapter One

Defining Our Terms and Focus

Most people regard the family as a safe haven from the stress and turmoil of everyday life. For the majority of Americans, the cultural image of the family emphasizes affection, consensus, harmony, and mutual support. Consistent with this view, sociologists (Ambert, 2001; Cherlin, 2002) have described the many positive functions served by families. There is, however, another side to families. Although they often function as an important source of nurturance and support, many categories of criminal and antisocial behavior are rooted in family processes or directed toward family members.

Most people have some awareness of this fact. Indeed, if asked why some persons commit crimes, the average person is likely to provide an explanation that focuses on how the deviant individual was parented (Wilson and Herrnstein, 1985). Further, in the last two decades there has been an increase in the public's awareness of domestic violence. Most individuals recognize the fact that spouse and child abuse are a part of everyday life for many families. However, other connections between families and crime are less well understood. Few people are aware, for example, of the various ways a person's criminal behavior or involvement with the criminal justice system tends to disrupt the lives of family members, or of the role that marital partners often play in fostering or deterring their spouse's involvement in crime. This book is concerned with this darker side of families. It focuses on the various linkages that exist between types of deviant behavior and family life.

Social scientists have defined the terms *deviant behavior* and *family* in a variety of ways. This chapter considers the assumptions and difficulties associated with different definitions of these concepts, and then presents the definitions that will be used throughout the book. These definitions are important, as they specify the nature and range of topics to be considered. We begin by describing the relationship between social norms and deviant behavior.

Social norms tend to vary widely from one society to another, and this has given rise to the culturally relative definition of deviant behavior. The advantages and limitations of the culturally relative definition will be briefly discussed, and a case will be made for a restricted absolutist definition that specifies a class of antisocial behaviors thought to be morally unacceptable in virtually all cultures. Such infractions are often classified as crimes, and in modern, industrialized societies they are frequently considered to be evidence of a psychiatric disorder. A shoplifter, for example, might be labeled a kleptomaniac, or a patron of prostitutes might be labeled a sex addict.

Having identified the class of deviant and criminal behaviors with which we will be concerned, we will turn to the construct *family*. Although sociologists have found it difficult to identify the essential elements of a family, we will present a rough definition sufficient for our purposes. The final portion of the chapter provides an overview of the associations that exist between families and antisocial behavior. The subsequent chapters are organized around these associations.

Deviance and Social Norms

Social deviance is any thought, feeling, or behavior viewed as objectionable by a group of people (Liska and Messner, 1999). A cognition, emotion, or action is considered deviant because it violates the social norms that the group members share regarding how a person should behave. Therefore, a discussion of the nature of social deviance necessarily requires consideration of the importance and function of social norms.

Socially organized activity requires social norms. In the absence of shared norms, human interaction would be total chaos. A society or culture can be seen as a collection of routine situations or occasions, each with its set of governing norms (Goffman, 1963; Hewitt, 1991). U.S. culture, for example, includes situations such as watching a movie at the theater, eating in a restaurant, buying groceries, undergoing a dental exam, going out on a date, playing tennis, attending a university class, and watching TV with friends. The list of situations consists of any event or activity that members of the culture can name or recognize (Goffman, 1974). Each of these situations has its own set of social norms that participants rely on in interacting with each other. It is the shared meanings provided by social norms that enable individuals to coordinate their actions in a situation.

When a person violates the taken-for-granted norms associated with an occasion, the organized flow of activity is interrupted. This disruption prevents the parties from synchronizing their efforts in order to realize the goals or outcomes that are the *raison d'être* for the situation. Interaction breaks down as the parties no longer know what to expect or how to behave. This is the reason we tend to react to deviant behavior with shock, disapproval, and often hostility. Deviant behavior disrupts situations, causing the other participants to feel inconvenienced, frustrated, exploited, or abused. If the norm violation appears to be intentional, the perpetrator may be defined as mean-spirited, disgusting, or immoral; if the violation seems to be unintentional, the perpetrator is apt to be perceived as careless, naïve, insensitive, or emotionally disturbed (Immershein and Simons, 1976; Scheff, 1984).

Of course, societies consider certain norms to be much more important than others. Many social norms, for example, represent the simple social conventions of everyday life. We expect people to refrain from picking their nose or passing gas in public, to show up at appointments on time, to wear matching socks, to maintain a certain physical distance during interaction, and to keep their lawn mowed. Individuals who violate these and similar social norms are usually considered odd and eccentric, especially if they persistently engage in such behavior. Although their actions may elicit anger and disdain, such people are usually not considered immoral or mentally ill.

In contrast to these social conventions, some social norms are invested with great moral significance. They represent the most cherished principles of a people and are viewed as necessary in order to ensure a decent and orderly society. A male who walks through the mall wearing nothing on the top half of his body would be violating a social convention, whereas a man who walks through the mall wearing nothing on the lower half of his body would be violating one of society's important moral principles. The violated rule, in this case, is the injunction to cover one's genitals and buttocks in public. Other examples of morally significant norms would be laws prohibiting theft, murder, treason, child abuse, and the desecration of sacred religious symbols.

Although the violation of social conventions elicits disapproval and perhaps a mild reprimand, the violation of important moral principles is considered a much more serious matter. Offenders may be severely criticized, physically restrained or attacked, imprisoned, or committed to a psychiatric facility. Parties to a situation react more strongly to violations of moral principles because such behavior is seen as a threat to the safety and security of the group, whereas breaches of social convention are usually seen as less consequential acts that only temporarily interrupt the flow of interaction. Whereas social conventions serve as informal guides to social interaction, morally significant norms are often formalized into law, and violators are arrested as criminals.

Cultural Relativity and Antisocial Behavior

Sociologists who study deviant behavior note that social norms, and therefore what is considered deviant, vary across cultures. Having more than one wife, for example, is acceptable in several Middle Eastern societies, whereas this behavior is deviant and illegal in most Western societies. Although women routinely go topless in some societies, most cultures consider this mode of dress to be morally unacceptable. In addition to the many differences that exist between societies, what is considered normative often changes within a society over time. For instance, at the turn of the twentieth century women living in the United States did not have the right to vote. Prior to the civil rights movement of the late 1950s and early 1960s, people of color were excluded from many activities, facilities, and organizations, including several public universities. The individuals who first pressed for changes in these social norms and statutes were viewed as deviant. Today, however, any person who suggests that women should not have the right to vote, or that ethnic groups be segregated from mainstream society, is viewed as immoral or emotionally disturbed.

This variability in social norms argues against an absolutist definition of deviant behavior. An absolutist definition assumes that certain acts are inherently deviant or unacceptable by their very nature and that these acts are deviant now and forever, here and everywhere else (Goode, 2001). Religions, as well as the common man in most societies, tend to embrace an absolutist view of morality. Sociologists, on the other hand, find this view unworkable given vast cultural differences in what is considered deviant. Even within a particular religion, there are often differing views. Jerry Falwell and Jesse Jackson, for example, are both Christian ministers with huge constituencies. Even so, these two individuals hold opposing views regarding abortion rights, gender roles, premarital sex, divorce, homosexuality, and capital punishment. Similarly, mainstream Islamic practitioners hold very different views of jihad, women's rights, suicide, and religious freedom than adherents of extremist organizations like the Taliban of Afghanistan.

Sociologists possess no transcendent criteria that might be used to evaluate the legitimacy of what different groups consider to be right or wrong. Hence, in an effort to avoid ethnocentrism, we let the group that we are studying specify what is deviant. We then go on to investigate the various factors that lead some individuals to engage in this deviant behavior. This approach defines deviant behavior relative to the social norms of the group or collectivity that is being studied. Hence, is it usually referred to as the "culturally relative" definition of deviance. Most sociologists believe this to be the only reasonable perspective on deviant behavior, given the substantial variability between groups regarding what is considered social deviance.

Although the culturally relative definition of deviant behavior is widely accepted among sociologists, many view it as an oversimplification. Although social norms vary dramatically from one culture to another, certain norms tend to be present in virtually all societies. This fact has led some sociologists to append a limited absolutist perspective to the culturally relative definition of deviance. While granting that definitions of right and wrong vary dramatically from one society to another, they contend that there are certain categories of behavior that are rather universally condemned (Davis, 1949; Gottfredson and Hirschi, 1990; Kornhauser, 1978;

Newman, 1976). These actions are considered immoral and are punished in virtually all societies because they are inherently harmful. Any culture that would not define these behaviors as unacceptable would be seriously jeopardized.

Ruth Kornhauser (1978), for example, has argued this position in her classic work on theories of crime. She notes that human beings have needs such as economic sufficiency, health, and safety. Further, humans are social creatures who must cooperate with each other to satisfy these needs. Hence, people everywhere live in groups. Group life, or social organization, requires that people follow norms involving honesty and fairness. Conversely, social organization is impossible if individuals break these social rules and pursue their individual interests through the use of force and fraud.

Kornhauser (1978) points out that all groups, whether a family, a work organization, a university, or a friendship group, require a commitment to these norms. When members violate these norms, interaction breaks down. This is not only true of conventional organizations; it also holds true for delinquent and criminal groups. Ironically, even as criminal organizations pursue illegal ends through the use of force and fraud, they insist that their members be loyal, honest, and fair with each other. Indeed, there is severe condemnation of gang members who violate these norms. This condemnation is necessary because group life, even that of criminals, requires adherence to these norms. They are the sine qua non of organized social activity.

More recently, Michael Gottfredson and Travis Hirschi (1990) have argued for a similar point of view in their book, *A General Theory of Crime.* They contend that all groups, regardless of cultural heritage, endorse values such as fair play, honesty, long-range planning, and sensitivity to the rights and needs of others. And, conversely, the violation of these values is condemned in all social groups. Thus selfishness, dishonesty, fraud, coercion, and use of force are considered deviant and are negatively sanctioned in all societies.

The present book concentrates on deviance that involves the violation of these universal norms. Although we recognize that social norms and definitions of deviant behavior vary considerably across cultures, our focus will be largely limited to acts that are viewed as dysfunctional and are negatively sanctioned in virtually all societies. These acts include cheating, lying, stealing, and threatening or attacking others. Such actions involve using force or fraud to get one's way.

Our concern will be with the interface of family life with these serious forms of deviant behavior. Rather than focusing on culturally relative forms of deviance, such as learning disabilities, religious or political extremism, sexual orientation, or bigamy, we will examine deviant behavior considered seriously disruptive in most societies and often labeled crime or mental illness. Our discussion will focus on acts such as childhood aggression, adolescent delinquency, adult crime, and child and spouse abuse as they relate to family processes.

As we will see in the next chapter, past research has demonstrated that the above acts tend to be correlated. An individual who engages in one of these acts tends to engage in many of the others as well (Elliott, Huizinga, and Menard, 1989; Gottfredson and Hirschi, 1990; Jessor, Donovan, and Costa, 1991; Osgood et al., 1988; Patterson, Reid, and Dishion, 1992). Thus, for example, it is usually the case that adolescents who frequently get into fights have also engaged in other delinquent acts such as shoplifting, skipping school, or using illegal substances. Similarly, adults convicted of one type of crime have usually engaged in a wide variety of other types of crimes as well. Researchers often refer to persons who engage in such behavior as antisocial. Such actions stand in contradistinction to prosocial behavior. Prosocial behavior takes into account the needs and concerns of others, and thereby contributes to the welfare of the group. Antisocial behavior, on the other hand, is selfish, hostile, and disruptive, and threatens the integrity of the group.

Expressions of antisocial behavior tend to vary by age. Antisocial behavior during elementary school consists of actions such as bullying, lying, refusing to comply with adult requests, showing extreme anger and resentment, deliberately annoying others, and being spiteful and vindictive. Over the past 25 years, there has been a trend in the United States toward the medicalization of deviant behavior (Conrad and Schneider, 1992). Increasingly, deviant behavior is seen as evidence of a psychiatric disorder. As part of this trend, children who frequently and persistently engage in antisocial behavior are often diagnosed as suffering from oppositional/defiant disorder (Rey and Walter, 1999). We have reservations about this development, as it often involves prescribing psychotropic medication while ignoring social factors that contribute to the child's behavior. In the following chapters, we will often use the term *oppositional/defiant behavior* when describing the antisocial behavior of children. We do not assume, however, that children who display this pattern of behavior necessarily suffer from a psychiatric disorder.

Whereas antisocial behavior during adolescence often includes oppositional/defiant behavior, it is delinquent actions that are of most concern (Loeber et al., 1998). Delinquency consists of adolescent antisocial actions that are illegal (Steiner, 1997). These include initiating physical fights, shoplifting, stealing, setting fires, destroying property, and using illegal drugs. Adolescents who persist in such behaviors might be diagnosed as having a conduct disorder (Steiner and Wilson, 1999). In subsequent chapters, we will use the terms *delinquency* and *conduct problems* interchangably when referring to adolescent antisocial behavior. Again, we make no assumption that this pattern of conduct implies a psychiatric disorder.

Finally, there is the antisocial behavior displayed during adulthood. This can involve a wide variety of criminal behaviors, such as robbery, burglary, physical assault, fraud, sexual coercion, and domestic violence. Individuals who engage in such acts also often display various deviant behaviors that are antisocial but not illegal. These include actions such as lying, cheating, sexual promiscuity, substance abuse, and irresponsibility. Adults with a history of this pattern of criminal and deviant behavior are sometimes diagnosed as suffering from antisocial personality disorder (American Psychiatric Association, 1994). Throughout the following chapters, we will use the terms *antisocial* and *criminal* in discussing adult deviants, but we do not assume that these individuals suffer from psychiatric disorders.

What Are Families?

This book is concerned with the relationship between the family and the antisocial behavior of children, adolescents, and adults. We have identified the category of socially deviant actions denoted by the term *antisocial behavior.* Now we need to specify what we mean by *family*. As is evident in any undergraduate textbook, this is not an easy exercise.

The family is a core social institution that exists in all societies. A social institution is an organized area of social life that meets certain fundamental needs of the society and the people living in it. The religious, educational, economic, and political components of society represent other key social institutions. Although the family continues to be an important social institution, some of the functions that it served during the preindustrial era are no longer evident (Hareven, 1994). Preindustrial families operated as schools, workshops, churches, and welfare agencies for their children. Today, outside institutions have taken over many of these responsibilities.

This does not mean, however, that the family has become less important. In many respects it remains the most basic of social institutions. The family provides food and shelter to its members. It is the context within which children learn fundamental social skills and satisfy their affective needs. Family relationships offer children a context for learning moral values, self-control, and love and trust for others. Families also meet the emotional and companionship needs of adults. Adult family members play together, help each other solve problems, and provide each other with social, economic, and emotional support.

At several points in our discussion, we have referred to "the family." This reference should not be taken as an indication that all families are similar or that there is a prototypical type that most families approximate. Although the family is a basic social institution in all societies, its form varies considerably from one culture to another. For example, although most Western societies practice monogamy, polygamy is encouraged in other parts of the world. In some cultures, the majority of couples have children without legal marriage, and there are societies where husbands, wives, and children do not live together under the same roof. Thus, we refer to "the family" much as one might refer to "the economy" or "the government" (Skolnick and Skolnick, 2001). "The family" is an abstract term used to denote an array of forms and practices that serve a common set of social and psychological needs for a group of two or more people who share kinship or affective ties.

One does not have to leave the United States to encounter a variety of family forms. People often think of the American family as the traditional nuclear family consisting of a married couple with its offspring. But this is only one type of family, and it is actually in the minority (Teachman, Tedrow, and Crowder, 2000). Many individuals would agree that, in addition to the traditional nuclear family, childless married couples, as well as single parents and their children, are families. However, this still leaves out a number of other family types. For example, many cohabitating couples have lived together for years although they eschew legal marriage (Seltzer, 2000). It would be difficult to argue that these couples are not families. This is especially true of the thousands of cohabitating couples that have had children together. Similarly, many gay and lesbian couples live together in a committed relationship even though they cannot legally marry in most states. And, in some cases, these couples are raising children together. Such living arrangements would appear to constitute a family.

Given this wide variety of forms, how should we define the term *family* for purposes of this book? In an effort to reduce complexity and confusion, we have chosen not to emphasize family processes such as love, sex, childbearing, and the like. Rather, we believe the simplest and most straightforward approach to studying families is to focus on the two core relationships present in families: the parent-child relationship and the committed relationship between two adults (Jones, Tepperman, and Wilson, 1995). In other words, we consider the parent-child unit and the adult couple unit to be the fundamental components of a family. A particular family may have just one or both of these relational units.

The Focus of Subsequent Chapters

The chapters of this book follow directly from the definitions of family and deviance presented above. Generally stated, we will be concerned with the various ways parent-child and adult couple relationships influence, and are influenced by, child and adult antisocial behavior. The chapters are roughly organized according to stages of the life course: Part I is concerned with explaining the antisocial behavior of children and adolescents, and Part II focuses on the antisocial behavior of adults.

Part I begins with a review of both past and recent research findings regarding the impact of parenting on child and adolescent conduct problems. Social and self-control theories are utilized to organize the presentation of this information. In the next chapter, Chapter Three, social learning perspectives expand the focus to include the reciprocal relationship between parent and child behavior, and the mechanisms that account for these mutual influences. In addition, consideration is given to the manner in which parental behavior directly and indirectly influences the probability that a child will affiliate with a deviant peer group.

Chapter Four explores the controversy regarding a particular disciplinary strategy—corporal punishment. We discuss a variety of methodological issues relating to the study of this topic, and note the ways in which the effects of physical discipline appear to vary by age of child, severity of punishment, community/cultural context, and the nature of the parent-child relationship. The chapter also examines evidence regarding the contention that exposure to abusive parenting leads to delinquency and crime.

Divorce and single-parent families are often seen as important causes of delinquent behavior. Chapter Five reviews research regarding this contention. We investigate a variety of explanations for the association between family structure and child behavior problems, including the hypothesis that quality of parenting mediates this relationship.

Finally, having identified several avenues whereby parental behavior increases the chances of child antisocial behavior, Chapter Six broadens the focus to consider the manner in which work and community conditions influence the way parents interact with their children. We discuss topics such as the effect of work conditions and economic hardship on parental behavior, neighborhood differences in the effectiveness of various parenting practices, the adverse consequences of juvenile arrest on families, and the way parents often work together to provide for the "collective socialization" of the children living in their community.

Our primary aim in Part II is to show how the family socialization processes and childhood conduct problems discussed in Part I influence the probability of adult crime and deviance. Chapter Seven reviews data showing a tendency toward stability or continuity of antisocial behavior across the life course. Conversely, we also present evidence indicating that many antisocial individuals adopt a more conventional lifestyle during early adulthood. We discuss several theoretical explanations for these life course patterns. There is evidence, for example, that romantic partners can modify deviant life course trajectories. We review findings regarding a variety of avenues whereby spouses and cohabitating partners exert this effect.

Chapter Eight examines research on marital violence. We discuss gender differences in the incidence and prevalence of this behavior, distinguish between common couple violence and spouse abuse, and review various typologies of male batterers. Our discussion of these topics includes consideration of the extent to which domestic violence is part of a more general antisocial lifestyle fostered by exposure to dysfunctional parenting during childhood.

Abusive parenting is the focus of Chapter Nine. Although the chapter is largely concerned with physical abuse, sexual abuse is also briefly considered. We discuss the incidence, prevalence, and stability of child abuse, and examine the extent to which it is transmitted across generations. We review data indicating that physical abuse is often part of a more general antisocial lifestyle, whereas sexual abusers tend to be specialists who usually do not have a history of engaging in other antisocial behavior. Further, we explore the childhood antecedents of these abusive behaviors. We note, for example, that there appears to be a link between childhood exposure to harsh, rejecting parenting and growing up to become a physically abusive parent, whereas sexual abusers oftentimes report that they were victims of sexual abuse as children.

The final chapter of the book, Chapter Ten, summarizes and integrates the findings from the previous chapters. We note that there is strong support for the thesis that exposure to inept parenting increases an individual's risk for childhood conduct problems, adolescent delinquency, and adult antisocial behavior, including marital violence and child abuse. There is also evidence, however, that factors such as educational success, a conventional friendship network, a happy marriage, or a satisfying job can moderate the risk of these negative outcomes. We briefly discuss the components of competent parenting and review evidence suggesting that there has been an insidious drift in the past few decades toward less effective styles of parenting. The chapter ends by briefly considering social policies that might be pursued in an effort to strengthen families and thereby reduce antisocial behavior. ✦

Chapter Two

Linking Parenting and Delinquency: Theories of Social and Self-Control

According to opinion surveys, residents of the United States consider crime to be a major social problem. If asked what they believe to be the major cause of crime, the majority would probably cite lax and ineffective parenting of children (Wilson and Herrnstein, 1985). This chapter reviews the evidence in support of this contention. We will begin by reviewing studies showing that adult criminals usually have a history of antisocial behavior during childhood. Next, we will consider pioneering longitudinal research, conducted from the 1930s through the 1950s by the Gluecks and the McCords, showing an association between inept parenting and delinquency. We will then discuss social control theory's view of the parent-child relationship and the way this theory stimulated sociological research on the link between family processes and adolescent deviance. The results of this research will be briefly reviewed, and we will describe the manner in which self-control theory builds upon these findings. The chapter ends with a discussion of the limitations of control perspectives on the link between family processes and the deviant behavior of children and adolescents.

Criminal Careers Start Early

One of the most widely accepted findings in criminology and developmental psychology is that childhood conduct problems are a strong predictor of subsequent involvement in antisocial behavior. Results from a variety of longitudinal studies show that children who are aggressive and noncompliant during elementary school are at risk for adolescent delinquency and adult crime (Caspi and Moffitt, 1995; Conger and Simons, 1997; Loeber, 1982; Patterson, Reid, and Dishion, 1992; Sampson and Laub, 1993). This continuity of deviant behavior has been found in several countries, including Canada, England, Finland, New Zealand, Sweden, and the United States (Caspi and Moffitt, 1995). Indeed, the evidence for this continuity is so strong that the *Diagnostic and Statistical Manual of Mental Disorders* (American Psychiatric Association, 1994), the handbook psychiatrists use as a guide in making psychiatric diagnoses, asserts that oppositional/defiant disorder during childhood is a developmental antecedent to conduct disorder during adolescence. It also asserts that a diagnosis of adult antisocial personality requires that the person displayed conduct problems during adolescence. As Robbins has noted, "adult antisocial behavior virtually requires childhood antisocial behavior" (1978, 611). It is extremely rare that a person who was a model child and adolescent suddenly begins to engage in criminal behavior as an adult.

These findings indicate that antisocial tendencies tend to become manifest during childhood. The roots of an adult antisocial lifestyle appear to be planted during the person's formative years. Parents are generally seen as the primary agents of socialization in the early years of a child's life. Although inborn traits involving temperament and personality are considered important, most social scientists assume that a child's psychological and behavioral development is heavily influenced by the family environment provided by the parents. This leads to the hypothesis that ineffective parenting is an important cause of delinquent and criminal behavior. As we will see later in this chapter and in the following chapter, several contemporary theories of deviant behavior include this idea.

Early Evidence Linking Parenting and Delinquency

From the mid-1920s through the 1960s, the husband-and-wife team of Sheldon and Eleanor Glueck conducted research on crime and delinquency at Harvard University. They completed several large-scale studies in an attempt to identify the causes of juvenile delinquency and adult crime (see Laub and Sampson, 1988, 1991).

Compared with other studies completed during this period, the Gluecks' research projects were based on unusually large samples, utilized a variety of sources of information, and involved the collection of extensive follow-up data.

Their most carefully crafted and widely known investigation was the Unraveling Juvenile Delinquency (UJD) study that began in 1939. Five hundred adolescent males selected from the Massachusetts correctional system were matched with 500 nondelinquent males chosen from Boston public schools. The delinquents and nondelinquents were matched on a case-by-case basis by age, race/ethnicity, neighborhood, and intelligence. From 1939 to 1948, the Gluecks' research team collected information on the boys' social and psychological characteristics, family life, work experiences, and involvement in deviant behavior. Data collection included interviews with the boys as well as with their families, teachers, neighbors, employers, and social welfare officials. Interview data were supplemented by careful record checks across various social agencies. Given contemporary standards regarding the protection of human subjects, it is unlikely that any study will duplicate the detail and range of information found in this study (Sampson and Laub, 1993).

The Gluecks completed two different follow-ups of the UJD sample, the first when the men were 25 years of age and the second when they were 32 years of age. Sampson and Laub (1993), who have completed extensive reanalyses using the Gluecks' data set, calculated that an extraordinary 92 percent of the original sample was successfully interviewed at these follow-ups. The Gluecks published their findings in scores of journal articles and books, but they are best known for the two books *Unraveling Juvenile Delinquency* (1950) and *Delinquents and Non-delinquents in Perspective* (1968).

Based on their data, the Gluecks championed three findings that were later corroborated by longitudinal research completed during the late 1980s and 1990s. First, they argued that age of onset of delinquency was a key factor in understanding criminal careers. The younger the age of onset, the more persistent and serious the criminal career. Second, they concluded that antisocial behavior tends to be relatively stable across the life course. "Beyond a reasonable doubt," they asserted, "the men who as boys comprised our sample of juvenile delinquents have continued on a path markedly divergent from those who as juveniles had been included in the control group of nondelinquents" (Glueck and Glueck, 1968, 169–170).

Finally, the Gluecks argued that the most important determinant of delinquent behavior was family environment. Based on their data, they contended that three family factors were especially important: parental supervision, disciplinary practices, and child-parent attachment. Children were at high risk for delinquency when their parents failed to provide supervision and engaged in lax or erratic discipline, and when weak emotional ties existed between the parent and the child.

Unfortunately, the Gluecks' research was viewed as provocative and exerted little influence on social scientists interested in crime and deviance. There are several reasons why this was the case (see Laub and Sampson, 1991; Sampson and Laub, 1993). Chief among them, however, was the Gluecks' perspective on theory. They did not attempt to develop a theory of crime, as they viewed abstract theory as mere speculation. Rather, they used an inductive approach that involved gathering empirical facts and searching for patterns that suggested a law or principle (Sampson and Laub, 1993). The Gluecks conducted their research and published their findings at the same time criminology and the study of deviant behavior emerged as an important area of investigation within sociology. Contrary to the Gluecks' research strategy, the sociological approach entailed developing and testing general theories. Sociologists such as Edwin Sutherland, the dominant criminologist of the twentieth century, harshly criticized the Gluecks' work. Their research was attacked for being atheoretical and for ignoring factors identified as important causes of crime in sociological theories (Laub and Sampson, 1991).

During this same time period, a physician and social philosopher by the name of Richard Cabot initiated the Cambridge-Somerville study (see McCord and McCord, 1959). Cabot believed that a strong bond with a supportive adult early in life would deter high-risk youth from engaging in delinquent behavior. In 1936, he initiated the study of 650 boys from disadvantaged neighborhoods in Cambridge, Massachusetts. Half of the boys were placed in a treatment group. These boys received treatment in the form of a close, intimate relationship with a counselor. Information on the boys in the treatment and control groups was first collected in 1936–1937. Follow-up data was collected from 1939 to 1945. Analysis of this longitudinal data indicated that the counseling did little to reduce the chances that a child would become delinquent (McCord and McCord, 1959). Sociologists viewed this finding as consonant with their contention that delinquency was a function of cultural and social structural influences. It suggested that a simple counseling relationship could do little to counter these powerful societal factors. Most sociologists and criminologists largely ignored the study's finding that level of support, supervision, and discipline provided by parents was a strong predictor of delinquent behavior (McCord and McCord, 1959).

The sociological theories of the time focused on gangs, blocked economic opportunity, and community disorganization. The Gluecks' and the McCords' emphasis on the family was seen as narrow and socially conservative. As a consequence, their findings regarding a link between parenting and delinquency were largely ignored by sociologists until Travis Hirschi published his social control theory of crime in 1969. This theory was solidly sociological, as it was based on the writings of the famous French sociologist Emile Durkheim. Yet it included the parent-child relationship as one of its elements. As a result, Hirschi's social control theory made investigation of family processes a legitimate aspect of the sociological study of delinquent behavior.

Social Control Theory

Most theories of deviant behavior are concerned with identifying the factors that cause an individual to engage in behavior that others view as unacceptable. Social control theorists argue for a different focus. Rather than trying to determine why some people are deviant, they suggest that we should ask why most people conform. They note that everyone begins life with an antisocial orientation. Infants and toddlers cry when they don't get their way, take things from others, destroy property, and push, shove, and hit in order to get what they want. Gradually, however, they begin to delay gratification and to take the needs and concerns of others into account. They strive to cooperate and to follow social norms, while eschewing socially disapproved lines of conduct. Thus, while we all enter the world as self-centered, antisocial creatures, most of us become conforming members of society. Control theorists contend that in order to understand deviance, we must identify the mechanisms whereby this transformation takes place. It must be a breakdown in these mechanisms that explains why a few individuals fail to become conforming members of society.

During the 1950s and 1960s, Albert Reiss (1951), Ivan Nye (1958), and Walter Reckless (1961, 1967) formulated control theories that emphasized the manner in which parental control (e.g., supervision, discipline) and personal control (e.g., positive self-concept, conscience) restrained youth from engaging in delinquent behavior. These theoretical perspectives, however, were never very widely accepted by sociologists and criminologists. Social control explanations for crime and delinquency were not embraced by the social scientific community until the advent of Travis Hirschi's book *Causes of Delinquency* (1969). Hirschi's ideas superceded all previous social control theorizing, and it is his theoretical perspective that criminologists have in mind when they refer to "social control theory." The theory has come to occupy a central place within the field of criminology, and it has been the most frequently discussed and tested of all theoretical frameworks within the discipline (Stitt and Giacopassi, 1992).

So what was Hirschi's answer to the question "Why do people conform?" He argued it was because people establish a bond to society. (His theory is sometimes referred to as "social bonding theory.") Conversely, he contended that "delinquent acts result when an individual's bond to society is weak or broken" (Hirschi, 1969, 16). According to his theory, the bond to society has four elements. The first is *attachment*. Attachment is the extent to which an individual feels close to, cares about, and identifies with other persons such as parents, teachers, or peers. People are concerned with meeting the expectations of those they care about and strive to avoid deviant actions that will anger or alienate them. The less individuals are attached to others, the less they are concerned about their opinions, and the freer they are to flout social norms and expectations. Although Hirschi considered all relationships within a child's social network as sources of social control, he viewed the child's attachment to the parent as exerting the most powerful influence.[1]

The second element of the bond to society is *commitment*. Commitment is the extent to which an individual is invested in conventional goals (e.g., earning good grades, making the football team, going to college, getting a good job). Such investments provide a "stake in conformity" (Toby, 1957) as conduct problems and delinquent behavior reduce the probability of achieving these goals. Individuals who lack conventional goal commitments, or a stake in conformity, experience fewer constraints against engaging in delinquent behavior.

Involvement is the third element of the bond to society. Involvement is the extent to which a person actively participates in conventional activities. Hirschi argues that adolescents who are involved in family events, religious organizations, school clubs, athletic teams, after-school employment, and the like are too busy to engage in delinquent behavior. The idea here is in keeping with the old saying, "Idle hands are the devil's workshop." Children and adolescents who have a lot of leisure time to kill are more likely to experiment with deviant behavior than those who are busy participating in conventional activities.

The final bond is *belief*. Individuals eschew deviant behavior to the extent that they believe in the legitimacy of conventional norms and values. Especially important is the extent to which they believe that society's laws are morally correct and should be followed. Conversely, "the less a person believes he should obey the rules, the more likely he is to violate them" (Hirschi, 1969, 26).

Summarizing, social control theory suggests that people conform to the social norms of society because they form attachments to others, develop goal aspirations, become involved in conventional activities, and acquire a respect for the law. Delinquents and criminals are persons who lack these bonds to society. They do not care about others, have no long-term goals, do not participate in conventional activities, and do not believe in the legitimacy of law and traditional morality.

At the time that *Causes of Delinquency* was published, the extant theories of deviant behavior posited that delinquent and criminal behavior was either learned (e.g., differential association) or adopted in order to cope with strain (e.g., anomie and opportunity theory). In contrast, Hirschi's social control theory asserted that people's innate antisocial tendencies were controlled as they became bonded to society. Hirschi noted that if his perspective was correct, it implied three predictions that were contrary to the implications of the extant theories of the time.

First, his theory implied that deviants are versatile in their antisocial behavior. Individuals who lack social controls will engage in a wide variety of deviant actions rather than specializing in any particular type of deviance. Lacking the social constraints of attachment, commitment, involvement, and belief, they are free to engage in virtually any opportunity for deviant behavior that presents itself. In contrast, the competing theories of the day assumed specialization, as deviants either learned to engage in a particular type of delinquent behavior or adopted a particular delinquent act because it resolved a strain or frustration. Deviants were thought to specialize in drug use, property offenses, criminal violence, or some other type of deviant activity. A number of studies have investigated this issue and most point to the versatility or generality of deviance (Gottfredson and Hirschi, 1990; Hirschi and Gottfredson, 1994). Consistent with Hirschi's contention, delinquent acts tend to be correlated. This means that although deviants may show a small degree of specialization, there is a strong tendency for persons who engage in one type of delinquent behavior to engage in other types as well. An individual who sells drugs, for example, is also likely to get into fights, skip school, steal, engage in risky sex, and so forth.

A second implication of his theory, argued Hirschi (1969), was that involvement in a deviant peer group is not an important cause of delinquency. One of the strongest and most widely accepted correlations in criminology is the association between having deviant friends and engaging in delinquent behavior. This is often assumed to be evidence that involvement with deviant peers leads to delinquency. Hirschi argued that the causal ordering was actually the reverse. Individuals who are low in social control are attracted to peers who are also low in social control. It is a matter of social selection. Recall the old adage "Birds of a feather flock together." People develop friendships with persons who are similar to themselves. Having deviant friends does not lead to delinquency; rather, being a delinquent leads one to select deviant friends.

Identifying the causal priorities underlying the delinquency-deviant peers correlation requires longitudinal research. During the late 1980s and 1990s, a number of such studies were completed (Elliott and Menard, 1996; Kandel and Davies, 1991; Warr, 1993). These studies found a reciprocal relationship between the two variables, with the predominant causal flow being from affiliation with deviant peers to involvement in delinquent behavior. For example, Del Elliott and Scott Menard summarized the results obtained in their national study of several hundred youths as follows:

> We found that exposure to delinquent peers preceded minor delinquent behavior in a majority of cases, and serious delinquency in nearly all cases where some order could be determined. . . . Having delinquent friends and being involved in delinquent behavior may influence one another, but the influence is not symmetric; the influence of exposure [to delinquent peers] on delinquency begins earlier in the sequence, and remains stronger throughout the sequence, than the influence of delinquency on exposure [to delinquent peers]. (1996, 61–62)

Although Hirschi may be correct that delinquents are attracted to each other, his theory fails to recognize that the delinquents' affiliation tends to amplify each other's deviant tendencies. Indeed, the research on this topic indicates that this amplification effect is stronger than the selection effect posited by Hirschi.

Finally, Hirschi argued that his theory indicated deviants do not have strong attachments or close relationships with their peers. His theory describes delinquents as having "cold and brittle" relationships with everyone (1969, 141). They are socially isolated, lacking social ties to either conventional or delinquent peers. He maintains that attachment to anyone, whether the person be conventional or deviant, reduces the probability of delinquent behavior. Thus, it is a lack of attachment to others that characterizes the delinquent, not his attachment to deviant friends. And becoming attached to another, regardless of that person's attitudes and values, is seen as having a conventionalizing influence.

Several studies have shown that these predictions are simply not correct. Relationships between delinquents appear to be as close and strong as those between nondelinquents (Giordano, Cernkovich, and Pugh, 1986; Kandel and Davies, 1991). Further, the evidence suggests that attachment to peers leads to conformity only when the friends are themselves conventional. Contrary to Hirschi's contentions, youth who are strongly attached to delinquent peers are more likely to be delinquent (Conger, 1976; Elliott, Huizinga, and Ageton, 1985; Linden and Hackler, 1973).

Although these predictions were not confirmed, research findings were more supportive of other elements of the theory. Several studies investigated the extent to which delinquents were less bonded to society than their conventional peers. With only a few exceptions, most of this research has reported that deviant adolescents, when compared with nondeviants, have less positive relationships with their parents, lack long-term goals, are uninvolved in conventional activities, and question the legitimacy of the law and police (see Akers, 2000; Shoemaker, 2000).

Although these findings support the theory, it is not clear that they add very much to our understanding of the processes that lead to delinquency and crime. The typical person on the street would not find it big news to learn that delinquents do not get along with their parents, lack goal commitments, are not involved in conventional activities, and do not respect the criminal justice system. Everyone knows that this is what delinquents are like. The important question would seem to be: Why do delinquents lack these social bonds?

One hypothesis is that parents exert a lot of influence over whether their children develop long-term goals, become involved in conventional activities, and acquire a commitment to traditional morality, including a respect for authority. This suggests that the elements of Hirschi's social bond may differ in importance and causal priority. Perhaps attachment to parents occurs prior to, and has a causal impact on, the other elements of the societal bond. The idea that parental attachment might be the most fundamental element in Hirschi's social control theory encouraged research by sociologists and criminologists on the relationship between parental behavior and delinquency.

The Elements of Effective Parenting

During the 1970s and 1980s, sociologists and criminologists completed scores of studies that examined the relationship between parental behavior and delinquency. In conducting this research, there was a good bit of confusion over how the concept of attachment should be operationalized. Some measures of attachment focused on how children feel about their parents, some examined the extent to which parents are warm and supportive, and still others assessed parental supervision and control. Although studies differed regarding the aspects of parenting that were measured, virtually all of them showed an association between parenting and delinquency.

Importantly, this research established that it was not merely attachment between the parent and child that was important, as was posited by social control theory. Rather, various dimensions of parenting, including parental warmth, monitoring, and consistent discipline, were all inversely related to the chances that a child would become delinquent (Loeber and Stouthamer-Loeber, 1986; Patterson et al., 1992; Sampson and Laub, 1993; Simons, Johnson, et al., 1998; Wright and Cullen, 2001).

These findings were consistent with research being conducted during the same time period by psychologists. For decades, developmental psychologists had been investigating how parenting influences various dimensions of child social competence, including conduct problems and delinquency. A guiding framework for much of this work was the parenting typology developed by Diana Baumrind (1966, 1991, 1996).

Baumrind's typology is organized around two dimensions of parenting: responsiveness and demandingness. *Responsiveness* involves the extent to which parents are approachable, warm, supportive, and attuned to the needs of the child. *Demandingness* refers to the extent to which parents exercise control over the child through supervision, disciplinary efforts, and willingness to confront the child when he or she disobeys. As shown in Table 2.1, these two dimensions of parenting can be used to generate a typology of four parenting styles (Maccoby and Martin, 1983). Permissive parents are high on responsiveness but low on demandingness, whereas authoritarian parents are low on responsiveness but high on demandingness. Neglectful/rejecting parents are low on both responsiveness and demandingness. Finally, authoritative parents are high on both responsiveness and demandingness.

Table 2.1
Baumrind's Typology of Parenting Styles

	HIGH CONTROL	LOW CONTROL
HIGH RESPONSIVENESS	authoritative parenting	permissive parenting
LOW RESPONSIVENESS	authoritarian parenting	neglecting/rejecting parenting

Baumrind asserts that the best approach to parenting is the style displayed by authoritative parents. She argues that the most effective child-rearing environment provides a high level of both responsiveness and demandingness. In other words, children need support and nurturance combined with structure and control. Consistent with this contention, three decades of research has shown that authoritative parenting is positively related to school achievement, psychological well-being, and social adjustment and negatively related to conduct problems and delinquency (Baumrind, 1999; Dornbusch et al., 1987; Gray and Steinberg, 1999; Lamborn et al., 1991; Steinberg, Elmen, and Mounts, 1989; Steinberg et al., 1991; Steinberg et al., 1992).

Thus research by sociologists, criminologists, and developmental psychologists underscored the importance of parental behavior in explaining child conduct problems and delinquency. These studies indicated, however, that it was more than the parent-child bond that was important. Further evidence regarding the importance of parenting was provided by longitudinal studies showing that aggression and conduct problems during childhood predicted adolescent delinquency and adult crime (see Moffitt, 1993, 1997; Patterson, Reid, and Dishion, 1992; Sampson and Laub, 1993). This suggested that the exposure to inept parenting during childhood may set the stage for a deviant life course trajectory.

Self-Control Theory

Travis Hirschi has always strived to be an empiricist. He has steadfastly maintained that data, rather than debate, should settle theoretical arguments. Consequently, based on the research findings just described, he began to change his mind about the factors that caused crime. In collaboration with Michael Gottfredson, he published a book entitled *A General Theory of Crime* (1990). Although many sociologists and criminologists remained committed to social control theory, this book suggested that Hirschi had recanted his earlier position and was shifting to a rather different theory of crime. This new explanation, more so than social control theory, placed parenting at center stage.

A General Theory of Crime begins by distinguishing between crime and criminality. *Crime* involves the use of illegal shortcuts to get what one wants. It entails using force or fraud to achieve immediate gratification. Rather than delaying gratification until rewards can be obtained through legitimate efforts, the criminal uses unlawful strategies that involve ignoring the consequences for both oneself and others. *Criminality,* on the other hand, refers to the personal characteristics that attract a person to crime. Gottfredson and Hirschi argue that it is individuals low in *self-control* who are attracted to crime. They describe individuals low in self-control as impulsive, uncompromising, self-centered, insensitive, risk-taking, and unconcerned about long-term consequences. Such persons are attracted to crime, which provides immediate gratification, whereas they avoid activities that involve a lot of time, energy, and delayed gratification.

For Gottfredson and Hirschi, the portrait of a master thief who hones his craft and outsmarts his victims at every turn is simply not accurate in the vast majority of cases. Rather, adolescent delinquents and adult criminals are lazy, lacking in self-discipline, and looking for the easy way to get what they want. They are attracted to crime because it promises immediate gratification with little investment of time and energy. Thus, offenders are likely to capitalize on criminal opportunities as they present themselves, with most crimes therefore being poorly planned and organized.

In a manner reminiscent of social control theory, Gottfredson and Hirschi argued that we all enter the world low in self-control. Infants and toddlers, for example, are impulsive, self-centered, and want immediate gratification. With time, however, most individuals learn to delay gratification. Rather than giving in to their desire for immediate reward, they exercise self-control and act in a manner that takes into account the consequences of their actions for themselves and others.

This being the case, from where does this self-control come? How does it develop? Gottfredson and Hirschi asserted that the answer involves parenting. In addition to being caring and supportive, the child's primary caregiver must set behavior standards, monitor the child's behavior, and be willing to discipline the child when the standards are not met. When caretakers do this in a consistent fashion, the child learns self-control. On the other hand, children fail to develop self-control if they are raised by caretakers who are lax in nurturance, monitoring, and discipline. Gottfredson and Hirschi contended that there is a critical period, a window of opportunity, during which self-control must be taught. Based on their reading of developmental psychology, they suggested that this window closes around 10 years of age. A child must acquire self-control by this time, or he or she will never acquire it. Although this is most unfortunate for those who fail to acquire it, they noted that the good news is that children who acquire self-control never lose it. Once socialized, an individual cannot become unsocialized and therefore is at low risk for adult criminal behavior. Those who have learned self-control by age 10 will go on to live conventional lives, whereas those who have not are expected to manifest a life course trajectory involving adolescent delinquency and adult crime.

According to Gottfredson and Hirschi, individuals low in self-control are not only at risk for crime and delinquency. They are also likely to engage in behaviors that are analogous to crime, in that they provide high levels of immediate gratification or a "rush" while also involving unpleasant risks and consequences. Gottfredson and Hirschi referred to these as "analogue activities." Smoking, drug use, driving fast cars, gambling, and engaging in sexual promiscuity are examples of such analogue activities.

Earlier we saw that social control theory asserted that delinquent and criminal acts are correlated, and that specialization is rare. Self-control theory goes beyond this assumption to posit that criminal and delinquent acts will also be correlated with analogue behaviors. Rather than specializing in a particular form of deviance, self-control theory contends that criminals are likely to display a lifestyle that involves a wide assortment of illegal and analogue activities. A few studies have found support for this contention (Arneklev et al., 1993; Evans et al., 1997).

Investigations of other aspects of the theory, however, have produced mixed results. First, a handful of studies have investigated the extent to which the relationship between exposure to inept parenting during childhood and later antisocial behavior is explained by low self-control (Cochran et al., 1998; Gibbs, Giever, and Martin, 1998; Hays, 2001; Polakowski, 1994). Overall, the evidence from these studies suggests that self-control explains only a portion of the relationship between parenting and antisocial behavior. Hays (2001), for example, found that differences in self-control explained only about one quarter of the relationship between parental monitoring/discipline and adolescent delinquency. These findings suggest that self-control theory has identified only part of the story. Apparently, parental behavior influences a child's risk for deviance in more ways than simply through its impact on self-control. Some of those avenues will be addressed in Chapter Three. Other studies have examined the extent to which low self-control predicts crime and delinquency. Recently, Pratt and Cullen (2000) performed a meta-analysis of this research. Across 21 studies, they found an effect size of .27. They note that this qualifies as "one of the strongest known correlates of crime" (952). They also observe, however, that a coefficient of .27 is far from unity, contrary to Gottfredson and Hirschi's claim that low self-control is the sole cause of crime and delinquency. Although self-control may be an important predictor of deviance, other factors are clearly important as well. Further, a recent study by Hays (2001) found that only part of the relationship between parental behavior and delinquency is explained by the child's level of self-control. This indicates that parents influence their child's behavior in more ways than those identified by self-control theory.

Self-control theory is also contradicted by studies showing that many antisocial children go on to lead conventional lives. Although it is true that most adult criminals were antisocial children, this does not mean that all antisocial children will grow up to be criminals (see Patterson, Reid, and Dishion, 1992; Sampson and Laub, 1993). Only about half of all conduct-disordered children go on to engage in serious delinquency during adolescence, and only about half of all seriously delinquent adolescents engage in criminal behavior as adults. The finding that many antisocial individuals adopt a conventional lifestyle with the passage of time is contrary to self-control theory's contention that at age 10 the window of opportunity for socialization is slammed shut, with those who have not acquired self-control being doomed to a life of delinquency and crime.

Finally, the evidence indicates that the theory is incorrect regarding its view of peer influences. Like social control theory, self-control theory maintains that peer group affiliations do not influence a person's involvement in antisocial behavior. Gottfredson and Hirschi grant that delinquents tend to form friendships with each other. They assert that this is because individuals who are low in self-control are attracted to peers who are also low in self-control. It is a matter of social selection. People develop friendships with persons who are similar to themselves. Conventional kids choose to hang out with peers who share their interests in sports, academics, and the like, whereas delinquents choose to spend their time with peers who like to skip school, take drugs, get into fights, and so forth. Gottfredson and Hirschi argue, however, that having deviant friends does not amplify involvement in delinquent behavior. Rather, inept parenting, because it fails to teach self-control, is the primary cause of delinquency.

As we have noted earlier in the chapter, longitudinal studies of peer influence contradict this view. These studies report a reciprocal relationship between affiliation with deviant friends and involvement in delinquent behavior, with the predominant causal flow being from deviant friends to delinquent behavior (Elliott and Menard, 1996; Kandel and Davies, 1991; Warr, 1993). Further, there is evidence that both delinquents (Simons, Johnson, et al., 1998) and adult criminals (Simons, Gordon, Stewart, and Conger, 2002) who switch to a more conventional friendship network tend to reduce their involvement in antisocial behavior. Delinquent youth reduce their involvement in antisocial behavior when they exchange their deviant peer group for a more conventional set of friends, and adult criminals engage in fewer illegal activities after trading their deviant friends for a more conventional set of companions. All of this suggests that a comprehensive explanation of delinquent and criminal behavior must include peer influences.

Although social control theory may contain an element of truth, the available evidence suggests that the story of crime is more complicated than that suggested by Gottfredson and Hirschi. The next chapter broadens the discussion by introducing concepts and arguments from social learning theory. We will identify additional avenues whereby parenting influences child behavior, identify reciprocal influences between parents and children, and show how parental behavior affects children's peer affiliations.

Endnote

1. Keeping in mind that the audience for this book includes family scholars, it is important to note that social control theory's use of the term "attachment" is quite different from the way the concept is de-

fined in the attachment theory of child development formulated by Bowlby, Ainsworth, and others. We will have occasion throughout this book to refer to children's attachment to their parents. In all cases we mean attachment as defined by social control, rather than attachment theory. ✦

Chapter Three

Family Interaction and Peer Influences: Social Learning Explanations

The present chapter examines the association between family processes and the deviant behavior of children, using concepts and principles from social learning theory. In the last chapter, we saw that control theories are built on the assumption that children are inherently antisocial but that effective parents are able to teach them to control these impulses. Social learning theories, on the other hand, assume that children are not inherently good or bad. Rather, they gradually acquire either prosocial or antisocial tendencies based on the nature of their interaction with the environment (Akers, 1998; Conger and Simons, 1997; Patterson, Reid, and Dishion, 1992).

As will become evident, social learning perspectives on the relationship between families and delinquency emphasize a broader set of factors than control frameworks. Whereas social control theories emphasized the impact of parental behavior on children, social learning explanations focus on the reciprocal or mutual influences that exist between parents and children. And whereas control theories exclude peer affiliations from their explanations for delinquency, social learning models stress the importance of peer effects and the manner in which parents influence their children's friendship choices.

In order to show how this is the case, the chapter is organized as follows. First, we will provide definitions of the core concepts and principles that compose social learning theory. We will then present Ron Akers' use of these ideas to construct a social learning explanation for criminal behavior. Last, we will show how Gerald Patterson and his colleagues at the Oregon Social Learning Center have developed a detailed description of the link between family interaction and delinquent behavior, which they have labeled the coercion model.

Respondent Learning

From the 1920s through the 1960s, behavioral psychologists such as John Watson, Edward Thorndike, Hobart Mowrer, Neal Miller, Nathan Azrin, and B. F. Skinner conducted research designed to elucidate the basic principles whereby the behavior of organisms is influenced by the environmental stimuli they encounter. This research focused on both respondent and operant learning (Ferster and Perrott, 1968). These two processes are sometimes referred to as classical and instrumental conditioning, respectively. Most research has concentrated on operant learning, and certainly this process is more consequential in social learning explanations for deviant behavior. It is important, however, that we briefly consider the nature of respondent learning before turning to a more detailed discussion of operant learning. This is because operant learning is concerned with the way the consequences following a particular behavior influence the probability of its recurrence. And respondent learning focuses on the avenue whereby a particular consequence comes to be evaluated as desirable or undesirable.

Respondent learning is mediated by the autonomic nervous system. According to the theory, it is the process whereby organisms acquire either an attraction or an aversion to various stimuli in their environment. Pavlov first described this method of learning in his classic study of conditioning in dogs (Ferster and Perrott, 1968). While investigating the physiological mechanisms of digestion, he observed that the dogs in his experiment tended to salivate when they heard the custodian of the kennel open the door and begin to walk down the hall. Pavlov noted that animals are innately predisposed to salivate in response to the sight or smell of food. The custodian had the regular responsibility of feeding the dogs. Pavlov concluded that, through the repeated pairing of the custodian with food, the dogs had learned to respond to the sound of the custodian's approach as if they were being presented with food.

Using his terminology, food was an *unconditioned stimulus* that produced the *unconditioned response* of salivation. He noted that this stimulus-response connection is as unconditioned as it is innate. He posited that whenever a neutral stimulus, such as the custodian, is paired over and over with an unconditioned stimulus, it begins to elicit the same response, in this case salivation, as the unconditioned stimulus. When this happens, the neutral stimulus has become, using Pavlov's terminology, a *conditioned stimulus* that produces the *conditioned response.* In order to corroborate the phenomenon, he conducted an experiment in which he banged a tuning fork and then presented the dogs with food. After a few trials, the dogs began to salivate at the sound of the tuning fork. The tuning fork had become a conditioned stimulus, which produced the conditioned response of salivation.

Individuals such as the psychologist John Watson at Johns Hopkins University began to apply this paradigm to the study of human behavior. In a classic piece of research labeled "the little Albert study" (Watson and Rayner, 1920), Watson investigated the manner in which a child might learn to fear a furry, white rat. Today, this study would never be approved by the university human subjects review committee, but these oversight organizations did not exist back in the 1920s.

The study consisted of sitting a toddler, little Albert, on the floor and then introducing the rat. As soon as Albert began to orient to the animal, a lab assistant located behind Albert banged a hammer on a piece of steel. Small children are innately predisposed to respond to such loud noises with a startled response and crying. In other words, a loud noise is an unconditioned stimulus that produces an unconditioned response involving shock and fear. After several trials, Albert began to cry at the mere sight of the rat. By pairing the rat with the frightening noise, the rat became a conditioned stimulus that produced the conditioned response of fear and crying. Learning theory assumes that we develop either pleasant or aversive emotional responses to the various elements that constitute our environment based on such paired associations.

Much of the respondent learning that takes place early in life involves the pairing of neutral stimuli with primary reinforcers. *Primary reinforcers* consist of stimuli that are innately reinforcing, such as food, sleep, and contact comfort. Moms, for example, are a source of primary reinforcement for their infants, and over time the mere sight of the mother will cause an infant to manifest a positive emotional response. As another example, parents may give their child a candy treat and hug him affectionately when they are pleased with him. After repeated occurrences, the child will learn to value parental approval. A neutral stimulus that acquires value because of its association with a primary reinforcer is labeled a *secondary reinforcer.* In the two examples just cited, mother's presence and parental approval have become secondary reinforcers.

Neutral stimuli that are associated with secondary reinforcers will also become reinforcing. Respondent learning that involves the pairing of neutral stimuli with secondary reinforcers is called *higher-order conditioning* (Ferster and Perrott, 1968). As the child grows older, most respondent learning is of this type. Parental approval, for instance, may be paired with academic success, so that the child comes to value getting good grades.

As was evident in the little Albert experiment, respondent learning does not always result in pleasant associations. It is also the mechanism whereby we acquire our fears and anxieties. In some cases, neutral stimuli may be paired with innately aversive events. A child may choke and cough on water while playing in the swimming pool and thereby develop a fear of putting her head underwater. In other cases, neutral stimuli may be paired with events that the child has learned to dislike, such as disapproval from others (i.e., higher order conditioning). Thus derisive laughter from peers during a class presentation may cause a child to develop an aversion to public speaking.

Obviously, individuals differ greatly in terms of what they value and what they find fearful or unpleasant. According to classical learning theory, this is a function of the fact that people have their own, unique history of respondent conditioning. It is through respondent learning that we learn to value some events and circumstances and dislike or fear others. Because people differ in their conditioning history, they differ in their likes and dislikes, the things that they desire and the things that they fear.

As Albert Bandura (1969, 1977, 1986) and the more cognitively oriented learning theorists have argued, however, this is only part of the story. Although respondent learning is important, individuals also develop preferences and aversions for different events because of conscious connections that they make between various incidents and circumstances. For example, a young woman who decides to become a doctor is apt to value good grades, as she will recognize that there is a connection between grades and getting accepted to medical school. A teenager concerned with obtaining a car may strongly value his after-school job, as it is a step toward earning the money to buy a car. Or a person uncomfortable with her physical appearance may develop an aversion to going swimming or water-related sports because they require wearing a swimsuit. Thus, while many of our likes and dislikes are acquired via respondent conditioning, we also develop preferences and aversions based on the conscious associations that we make between various events and circumstances.

Operant or Instrumental Learning

Whereas respondent learning focuses on the autonomic nervous system, operant, or instrumental, learning involves the voluntary nervous system. It is concerned with the manner in which behavior is influenced by its consequences. These consequences can be desirable or aversive. Desirable consequences increase the probability that under similar circumstances, the behavior will be displayed again. When this takes place, *reinforcement* of the behavior is said to occur. The desired consequence serves to "reinforce" the behavior so that it is likely to be repeated.

As shown in Table 3.1, there are two types of reinforcement corresponding to two different types of desired outcomes. The first, *positive reinforcement*, occurs when a valued outcome accrues fol-

Table 3.1
Types of Reinforcement and Punishment

	REINFORCEMENT (probability of response >)	PUNISHMENT (probability of response <)
POSITIVE (something is introduced)	Something of value is added	Something aversive is added
NEGATIVE (something is taken away)	Something aversive is removed	Something valued is removed

lowing an action. The term *positive* refers to the fact that something was added to the situation following the behavior in question. This increases the chance that the behavior will recur when the individual encounters similar circumstances in the future. For example, parents increase the probability that their daughter will say "please" when asking for something if they praise her for asking in this fashion. A college student is more likely to form a study group with his classmates if he used that strategy in a previous class and received an A. Or it increases the chances that a person will wear a particular outfit if work colleagues or friends are effusive about its attractiveness.

Although these examples involve conventional behaviors, positive reinforcement may also increase the probability of a deviant behavior. For instance, a boy is apt to increase his bullying of a classmate on the playground if his friends laugh and provide encouragement when he engages in this behavior. Of particular interest are occasions when parents inadvertently positively reinforce deviant behavior. As an example, a mother may be talking on the phone in the kitchen when her son interrupts and demands a popsicle. The mother tells the child that he has already had one and that he should stop interrupting and go outside and play. The mother then tries to continue talking with her friend, but the son begins crying and pulling on his mother's dress while begging for a popsicle. Out of exasperation, the mother opens the freezer, pulls out a popsicle, hands it to her son, and says, "OK, but this is the last one you get today; now go outside and play."

Although the mother may have thought she was being a good parent, she positively reinforced the child for nagging and for not taking "no" for an answer. The son's nagging was followed by the desired consequence of receiving the popsicle. The mother has inadvertently taught the child that the way to get what he wants is to be persistent when Mom says "no." He has learned that she will eventually give in and he will get what he wants. Parents often give in to crying, begging, nagging, tantrums, and so forth. Doing so reinforces the behavior, thereby increasing the probability that their children will display this deviant behavior again the next time they do not get their way.

Negative reinforcement is the second type of reinforcement. As shown in Table 3.1, this occurs when a behavior is followed by the removal or termination of something aversive. The term *negative* refers to the fact that something is being removed or terminated. It is a desirable outcome if something unpleasant ceases or is avoided. Therefore, just as we are likely to repeat actions that result in the introduction of something we value, so we are likely to repeat behaviors that result in the termination of unwanted circumstances or events. If a child's mother, for example, becomes less angry and adopts a more conciliatory demeanor after her son apologizes profusely for breaking a table lamp, it increases the probability that the child will display such apologetic behavior the next time he gets into trouble. The mother's anger was threatening to the child. This threat ceased once the child apologized, thereby reinforcing the child's display of an apologetic and contrite demeanor.

As a second example, imagine that James forgets his girlfriend's birthday and she responds by pouting and giving him the silent treatment. He finds this very disturbing and sends her flowers along with a note stating, "I love you." If this results in an end to her pouting, James' action will have been negatively reinforced. As a consequence, he is more likely to send flowers and profess love the next time his girlfriend gets upset.

Negative reinforcement, like positive reinforcement, can sometimes increase antisocial behavior. Suppose that Joe pushes his little 2-year-old sister out of the way to climb up the ladder of the slide. She falls to the ground, crying, and their mother comes outside looking very upset and angrily asks Joe, "What did you do to her?" Joe says, "I didn't do anything; she just fell off the ladder." Assume that Mother then replaces her angry look with one of concern, and switches her attention from Joe to his sister. In this sequence of events, Joe's lie terminated the threat posed by his mother. This experience increases the probability that Joe will lie the next time he is in trouble.

Or consider the case of Sara, who is upset because her older brother is teasing her. Imagine that Sara responds to this obnoxious behavior by punching her brother on the shoulder, with the result being that the brother stops the teasing and leaves the room in a huff. The punch terminated an aversive behavior, which increases the probability that Sara will resort to physical violence the next time her brother engages in an unwanted behavior.

Thus far, we have considered consequences that a person finds desirable (the introduction of something positive or the removal of a negative). It is oftentimes the case, however, that an action results in an undesirable outcome. This is referred to as punishment. Unlike reinforcement, punishment decreases the probability that a particular action will be repeated. Table 3.1 shows that there are two types of punishment. *Positive punishment* takes place when an aversive stimulus follows the behavior. Again, the term positive is used to indicate that something was added to the situation. In the case of positive reinforcement it is a reinforcing or desired event that is introduced, whereas positive punishment involves the introduction of an aversive or undesired event.

A child who misbehaves might be grounded or receive a timeout. In some cases, he might even be spanked. These are instances of positive punishment that should reduce the chances that the misbehavior will be repeated. But punishment is not just limited to unpleasant outcomes administered by authority figures. If, for example, singing elicits derisive laughter from peers and at-bats consistently result in strikeouts, a child is apt to reduce or terminate public singing or playing baseball, respectively. Of course, punishment doesn't just happen to children. A young man might attempt to "do a donut" in the fresh snow with his car and slide into the ditch. Or a young woman may behave in an angry and hostile fashion toward her boyfriend for much of the evening after he showed up an hour late for their date. These aversive consequences are likely to reduce the probability of trying to do donuts in the snow or of being late when picking up the girlfriend.

Whereas positive punishment involved the introduction of something aversive, *negative punishment* entails the removal of something that is valued. Again, the term *negative* refers to the fact that something is being terminated or taken away following a behavior. A child who violates curfew might be told, for instance, that next week she will receive no allowance or that she cannot go to the party planned for the following weekend. Or a young woman with a chronically late boyfriend may refuse to go out with him when he once again shows up late for their date. In these examples, the person is being punished by having something positive taken away. Sometimes this form of punishment is called *response cost,* as the punished person incurs the cost of forfeiting something of value.

Punishment, like reinforcement, can sometimes result in unanticipated deviant behavior. This usually happens when the punished person perceives the aversive consequence as unfair because it is viewed as arbitrary, inconsistent, or too harsh. These perceptions may cause the punished individual to engage in hostile and vengeful behavior. The mother of one of the authors of this book once placed him in the closet of her bedroom for a 10-minute time-out. While in the closet, he proceeded to spitefully chew holes in his mother's dresses. Consonant with this incident, the employees of child treatment centers often report that angry residents often try to destroy the time-out room. As a further example of this phenomenon, children angry over punishments received at school sometimes vandalize the property of the teachers who meted out the aversive consequences. For example, a teacher who is an acquaintance of one of the authors had her car keyed by an irate student to whom she had given detention.

There are steps that can be taken to increase the chances that a particular punishment will be perceived as fair, so that angry and vengeful deviant behavior is averted. First, individuals need to be warned of the aversive consequences that will occur if they violate some rule. They then know what to expect when violations occur, thereby reducing the likelihood that the punishment will be perceived as arbitrary and unfair. Second, punishment needs to be consistent if it is to be perceived as just. People are apt to regard a punishment as capricious if they are sometimes allowed to engage in the behavior without punishment whereas other times they are punished, or if they are punished for the behavior while others are not.

Further, the severity of punishment should be proportional to the infraction. Both children and adults feel inequitably treated, angry, and vengeful when they believe that they were punished too harshly (Walster, Walster, and Bersheid, 1978). Finally, punishments are more likely to be perceived as fair if the punishment is logically related to the infraction. Although this is not always possible, a child who slams the door might be asked to go back and walk through it properly 10 times, a teen with a chronically messy room might be required to pick things up and then wash the windows in the room, and an adolescent caught with cigarettes might be asked to research and write a report on the health dangers of using tobacco.

A particular behavior rarely produces the same consequence every time it is displayed. Rather, sometimes it results in a rewarding consequence, at other times the consequence may be neutral, and on still other occasions it may be aversive. A particular study strategy, for example, may result in a high test score most of the time, but not every time. Or cracking a joke may elicit laughter on some occasions and awkward silence at other times. How often the individual chooses to engage in a particular action is a function of the balance of rewards and punishments that have followed it in the past. The behavior is likely to be repeated if the balance has been largely positive, whereas it is less likely to occur again if the balance has been largely negative.

Mutual Training

For the most part, our discussion of how consequences influence behavior has focused on the mechanisms whereby the actions of children are shaped by the reinforcing contingencies provided by their parents. It is certainly the case, however, that the behavior of adults, and not just that of children, is also affected by the consequences that it elicits. Thus, just as parents provide consequences for their children's behavior, so children provide consequences for their parents' behavior. Parent-child interaction often consists of mutual influences exercised through a process of reciprocal reinforcement. Although the parties may be largely unaware of what is taking place, parents are often being trained by their children at the same time that they are training their children. In many cases this *mutual training* involves deviant behavior.

To see how this is the case, recall the example cited earlier in the chapter where the mother gave in to her son who persisted in nagging for another popsicle. We noted that the mother's action served to positively reinforce the child's disruptive, nagging behavior. By giving in after first saying "no," the mother was inadvertently training her son to be difficult and obnoxious. If one shifts the focus from the son to the mother, however, there is yet another undesirable lesson being learned in this situation. The mother relents and the son discontinues his disruptive behavior. He happily leaves the situation, allowing the mother to continue the conversation with her friend. The mother's acquiescence resulted in the termination of an aversive condition. Thus, through negative reinforcement, the mother is being taught to give in to her son's nagging. The interaction sequence involves the child being reinforced for antisocial behavior while the mother is being reinforced for ineffective parenting.

Unfortunately, such dysfunctional, mutual training is often evident in parent-child interaction. For example, at night a mother may rock and breastfeed her infant until the baby falls asleep. The baby is then placed in the crib and the mother tiptoes out of the room. A few minutes later the baby may wake up and start crying. The mother then picks up the baby and rocks her until she again falls asleep. The baby is returned to the crib but wakes again after a short time and begins to cry. In this interaction sequence, the baby's crying is reinforced by the contact comfort and rocking provided by the mother. The mother is negatively reinforced for picking up her baby because it terminates the crying. (In some instances, the infant may cry every time the mother tries to put the baby down so that she is being punished for putting the child in the crib.) Thus the child is being trained to cry when alone in the crib, and the mother is being trained to pick up the child whenever she cries. Over time this pattern can escalate to the point that it takes several frustrating hours every night to put the baby to bed.

As another example, consider the child who throws a tantrum in order to get his way. He throws himself on the floor, kicks, and cries. The parent may either tell the child to stop or strive to ignore the behavior. Eventually, as the behavior becomes more disruptive, the parent may relent and tell the child he can have his way but must stop the obnoxious behavior. The parent acquiesces, and the child's behavior immediately improves. The child is positively reinforced for his emotional outburst and for refusing to take "no" for an answer, whereas the parent is negatively reinforced for acquiescing to such behavior.

These ugly interaction sequences may take place several times every day. As a result, both the deviant behavior of the child and the ineffective practices of the parent will tend to escalate over time. It is this mutual training that explains, at least in part, why seemingly smart people are sometimes very ineffective parents. Perhaps the reader has visited acquaintances and been shocked at the inept manner in which they responded to the disruptive behavior displayed by their child. The parents are smart and capable people and yet their attempts to control their child appear misguided and feckless. What needs to be done seems so obvious that you can hardly restrain yourself from offering them a little commonsense parenting advice.

What you fail to appreciate, however, is the countless times that the parents' inept approach has been reinforced by the child. The parents were not always so ineffective, just as the child was not always so ill behaved. Rather, the parents' ineptitude and the child's misconduct have gradually developed over time through a process of mutual training. Later in the chapter, we will see that this idea is the starting point for the coercion model of delinquent behavior.

Modeling as Vicarious Learning

Classical learning theory was concerned with the mechanisms whereby behavior is influenced by its consequences. Albert Bandura (1969, 1977) contended that this perspective needed to be expanded to include cognitive processes and modeling. He noted that most behavior is not learned by directly experiencing its consequences. Indeed, this would be a very inefficient and potentially dangerous way to learn. Most of us would not survive very long, for example, if we had to learn through direct experience that we should look both ways before crossing the street. Rather than through direct experience, Bandura argued that most behavior is acquired vicariously by observing the actions of others. Hundreds of studies have documented the validity of this contention (see Bandura, 1977, 1986).

Vicarious learning involves taking note of the consequences that follow when people engage in various actions. We learn about the consequences of some behaviors by observing the people around us. More often, however, we learn from models that are presented symbolically. We learn of the positive and negative results of various behaviors by watching movies and television, by reading magazines and newspapers, and by listening to stories related by parents, teachers, and peers.

Research has shown that we are especially attentive to the actions of individuals similar to ourselves with regard to age and gender (Bandura, 1977, 1986). This is because we are likely to reap similar consequences if we engage in the behavior. The same action, if displayed by someone of a dissimilar age or gender, may result in a very different set of outcomes. In addition to persons who are similar to us, we tend to pay special attention to persons that we emulate and respect. Presumably this is because we want to achieve the positive outcomes that are being gleaned by these high-prestige models.

Vicarious learning, or learning from models, should not be confused with simple imitation. Rather, we observe the consequences of the actions displayed by others and then emulate those actions that lead to desired consequences and eschew those that lead to unwanted results. Parents sometimes criticize their children's attachment to their peer group with the proverbial statement, "If your friends jumped off a bridge, I suppose you would also." According to social learning theory, this statement would only be true if the friends appeared to have great fun when they jumped off the bridge. If jumping off the bridge resulted in pain or injury, the child most likely would not follow suit.

Bandura (1977, 1986) argues that vicarious learning does not just involve learning about the consequences of various discrete actions. Rather, we induce the underlying rules regarding the types of behaviors that are rewarded versus those that are punished. Bandura refers to this process as "abstract modeling." Based on watching a variety of people acting in various situations, we extract general rules that summarize the contingencies that appear to be operating. We then use these rules, some of which we label moral principles, to formulate our own plans of action.

Finally, Bandura (1977, 1986) notes that models also provide us with a comparison level. As a result of direct observation or symbolic modeling, we acquire information about the typical outcome associated with a particular action. This colors our expectation about how we should be treated. We are pleased and fairly treated when we receive rewards at a level consonant with what others usually receive, whereas we feel unfairly treated and angry when we receive something less. Whether it be in interactions with a parent, spouse, child, employer, or retail clerk, we tend to use knowledge we have acquired through vicarious learning to evaluate the extent to which we are being treated fairly.

Expanding classical learning theory to include cognitive processes, reciprocal influences, and vicarious learning makes the theory much more social. Back in the 1970s, researchers such as Bandura coined the term *social learning theory* to describe this broader, more comprehensive perspective. In the sections that follow, we first show how Ron Akers has used social learning principles to sharpen and elaborate differential association theory and then describe the coercion model as developed by Patterson and his colleagues at the Oregon Social Learning Center.

Ron Akers' View of Social Learning and Crime

As we noted in the previous chapter, Edwin Sutherland was one of the most influential criminologists of the twentieth century. Although he is widely recognized for his work on white-collar crime, he is best known for his differential association theory of criminal and deviant behavior (Sutherland, 1949). In what was a provocative idea at the time, Sutherland asserted that criminal behavior is learned in the same manner as conventional behavior. He argued that most of our beliefs and attitudes, whether they be favorable or unfavorable to engaging in deviant behavior, are learned within intimate or personal groups (e.g., family, friends). In describing this learning process, he emphasized the importance of *differential association*. People differ in their associations, and, according to Sutherland, we are most influenced by relationships that are of high intensity, priority, frequency, and duration of interaction (Sutherland, 1947). People engage in criminal behavior, he contended, because through differential association they have acquired more definitions of behavior favorable to violation of the law than those unfavorable to violation of the law.

Sutherland's theory was quite popular during the 1950s and 1960s. Sociologists and criminologists were attracted to the notion that deviant behavior was learned like any other behavior, and it seemed eminently reasonable that this learning took place through interaction with friends and family. Unfortunately, the theory was difficult to test. It was not clear, for example, how one should define and assess factors such as the intensity and priority of relationships. Further, how should the various components of differential association be combined? Is a relationship high in intensity but involving infrequent interaction more or less important than one lower in intensity but involving frequent interaction? Problems such as these were an impediment to research on differential association theory.

During the mid-1960s, the sociologists Ron Akers and Robert Burgess recognized that differential association theory might be given a sharper, more precise focus by translating and recasting it into the terminology of social learning theory. They labeled their perspective "differential association-reinforcement theory." They first presented their views in a paper at the 1966 meeting of the Pacific Sociological Association. Donald Cressey, who had worked closely with Sutherland, was in the audience. He stated that he believed if Sutherland were alive he would be very supportive of the direction in which Akers and Burgess were taking his theory. Following the publication of this paper in *Social Problems* (Burgess and Akers, 1966), Burgess lost interest in criminology and turned to other fields of inquiry. Ron Akers, however, has devoted his career to the investigation of deviant behavior using a social learning theory perspective.

Akers has presented his theoretical perspective in three editions of *Deviant Behavior: A Social Learning Approach* (1973, 1977, 1985) and, more recently, in *Social Learning and Social Structure: A General Theory of Crime and Deviance* (1998). Using the concepts and principles of social learning theory, he argues that people differ in their associations, which results in differences in learning. The groups with whom a person interacts serve as the social contexts in which social learning takes place. Through operant reinforcement and modeling, some individuals learn beliefs, attitudes, and behaviors favorable to engaging in deviant behavior.

Akers and his colleagues (e.g., Marvin Krohn, Lonn Lanza-Kaduce) have tested this perspective in studies of smoking, substance use, cheating on exams, and sexual violence (see Akers, 1998). This research generally supports the theory. It shows that individuals are more likely to engage in these deviant actions when such behavior is modeled, cued, and reinforced by others in their social network. Further, the findings indicate that much of what individuals learn involves definitions either favorable or unfavorable to the commission of a particular deviant act. This includes neutralizing definitions that encourage the deviant act by justifying or excusing it (e.g., "It's not a big deal as everybody does it," "Bad guys deserve whatever happens to them," or "What does it matter as long as it doesn't hurt anybody?").

While this approach has contributed to our understanding of the etiology of deviant behavior, it implies that individuals learn deviant acts one at a time. Stated differently, it suggests a specialization view of deviant behavior whereby an individual may learn to engage in a particular deviant behavior while remaining conventional in most respects. As we noted in the previous chapter, past research has established that this is usually not the case. Rather, delinquent acts tend to be correlated. Individuals who engage in one type of delinquent act tend to engage in a wide variety of others as well. It is not clear how Akers' social learning perspective accounts for this generality of deviant and criminal behavior.

Although parenting variables were sometimes included in the studies conducted by Akers and his colleagues, the main focus was on operant and vicarious reinforcement provided by peers. Thus, although this research has added to our understanding of the link between peer affiliations and the commission of deviant acts, it has not been very informative regarding the manner in which family processes contribute to delinquency and crime. As noted in Chapter Two, there is strong evidence from longitudinal studies indicating that persons who engage in serious delinquency during adolescence tend to have a history of oppositional and defiant behavior during elementary school (Moffitt, 1997). This suggests that antisocial tendencies tend to emerge prior to early adolescence, when deviant peer groups begin to appear. Although joining a deviant peer group during the junior high school years may amplify antisocial tendencies, these predispositions are usually evident much earlier in the person's life. It seems likely that parental behavior contributes to the child's early misbehavior, but what are the avenues whereby this is accomplished?

Whereas parental modeling may be a part of the explanation, there are also apt to be circular family processes at work in which parents are training their children to be deviant at the same time that their children are training them to engage in inept parenting. A comprehensive social learning theory of delinquent and criminal behavior needs to incorporate these reciprocal processes, as well as specify the manner in which family socialization influences the child's subsequent school and peer-group experiences. The coercion model, developed by Gerald Patterson and his colleagues at the Oregon Social Learning Center (OSLC), addresses these issues. In addition, this theory provides an explanation for the generality of delinquent behavior.

Patterson's Coercion Model

Over the past several years, Patterson and his OSLC colleagues (e.g., John Reid, Thomas Dishion, Marion Forgatch, Debra Capaldi) have pursued longitudinal studies concerned with the manner in which family and peer processes combine to produce child and adolescent conduct problems (Patterson, 1982; Patterson, Debaryshe, and Ramsey, 1989; Patterson, Reid, and Dishion, 1992; Capaldi, Chamberlain, and Patterson, 1997). This research has been distinctive in its rigorous approach to measurement. Data from family members, teachers, peers, trained observers, and criminal justice system records are used to develop measures of constructs. Findings from this program of research provide support for the coercion model of antisocial behavior. The theory posits that delinquency and crime develop in the following fashion.

The process begins with an irritable, explosive parent. The parent may be depressed, under a lot of stress, or simply bad tempered. Regardless of the explanation, such individuals tend to engage in negative scanning of their child's behavior so that even neutral actions evoke criticism and denigration. These verbal assaults often produce an angry, defiant response from the child, who feels unfairly attacked and mistreated. The result is an escalating spiral of aversive exchanges that operate to reinforce the child's antisocial behavior and the parent's inept parenting. A typical exchange might be as follows:

Mom arrives home from work and finds her son sitting in front of the TV instead of mowing the lawn as he was instructed. The mom responds by berating the child for not having completed the assigned task. For example, she might bellow: "What the hell are you doing? Get off your lazy butt and mow the yard!" Since people tend to reciprocate aversive verbal attacks, the child is likely to react to this barb by yelling back at the parent. He might forcefully declare, for instance, that Mom should "chill out," as he will mow the yard when the TV program is finished. The parent is likely to escalate her verbal attack in an attempt to coerce the child into complying with her request. She might threaten the child by loudly asserting, "I've told you repeatedly to do your chores before watching TV, so I'm grounding you and you're not going to the game tonight!" The child, in turn, may show anger and defiance by throwing down the sandwich he was eating and shouting, "You're crazy; I've already made plans and my friends are counting on me!"

Importantly, in families with antisocial children, at least half of the time these escalating aversive exchanges terminate with the parent capitulating. In the above scenario, for example, the interaction might end with the mother exclaiming, "Fine, you can go tonight, but next time I tell you to mow the lawn you better do it, and you better be home by midnight tonight!" Rather than engaging in effective discipline, the parent merely engages in what Patterson and his colleagues (Patterson et al., 1992) label *nattering*. Nattering is characterized by verbal remonstrations and threats, but little or no actual follow-through. The child responds defiantly, and the parent eventually backs down. Using the principles of social learning theory, the parent gives in to the child, thereby positively reinforcing his oppositional and defiant behavior. The child learns that if he is nasty enough, he will get his way. Also, negative reinforcement is operating as the child's aggressive behavior neutralizes or deflects the unpleasant intrusions of the parent. The child behaves aggressively, and the parent discontinues her criticism and threats.

Concomitantly, the parent is negatively reinforced for giving in to the child. Usually, the child's behavior improves and his aggressive posturing gives way to a more pleasant demeanor, once the parent backs down. In addition, the parent experiences punishment when she tries to discipline the child. Any attempt to correct the child elicits a very unpleasant response from the child. Therefore, the interaction taking place within such families trains parents to be inconsistent and to back down, while training children to use aggressive actions to coerce others into giving them their way.

These aversive exchanges between the parent and child often take place several times a day. The parent and the child direct aversive behavior toward each other in an attempt to get their ways. Although the parent sometimes wins, at least half the time the exchange ends with the child having the final say. Children subject to these contingencies fail to learn prosocial, problem-solving behaviors involving sharing, compromising, and the like. Instead, they learn to use anger and defiance as a way of solving problems and getting what they want from others.

Patterson and his colleagues note that this interpersonal style tends to be generalized to interactions with peers. The child insists on having his way, refuses to compromise, and uses angry, aggressive behavior to bully others into complying with his wishes. Much of the time, this behavior is rewarded, as conventional children often give in to this display of belligerence and hostility. Thus, interaction with peers tends to reinforce the aversive interpersonal style that the child learned at home. Although the behavior of the antisocial child often leads to immediate or short-term rewards, the long-term effect is usually quite different. Conventional youth do not want to play with someone who uses aggression and defiance to get his way. Thus the long-term consequence of the antisocial child's aversive behavior is rejection by conventional peers. The coercive child might argue his way out of being called out of bounds during a touch football game, but next time the more cooperative kids will not include him when they form teams.

These antisocial youngsters also tend to fail academically. Just as they defy the directives of their parents, so they refuse to comply with classroom rules and requests from teachers. Further, they fail to listen to the teacher and invest little time in schoolwork. As a result, they tend to experience academic failure and rejection by their teachers. Thus, in many respects, the antisocial child leads a rather unhappy life. He has a stormy relationship with parents, peers, and teachers, and is an academic failure. As a consequence, these children are often *co-morbid* (Patterson, Debaryshe, and Ramsey 1989; Patterson, Reid, and Dishion 1992). They display two kinds of emotional problems. In addition to their conduct problems, they are also frequently psychologically depressed. What they fail to recognize, however, is the manner in which their coercive style of interaction contributes to their interpersonal and academic difficulties.

By default, these socially rejected youths establish friendships with each other, forming a deviant peer group. Whereas conventional peers will not tolerate their aggressive demeanor, antisocial youngsters are tolerant of each other's selfish, coercive interpersonal style. Importantly, affiliation with deviant peers is the primary avenue whereby a child's coercive interpersonal style escalates to delinquent and criminal behavior. The deviant peer group provides a context for experimenting with various deviant behaviors. It serves as a training ground for shoplifting, drug use, fighting, and the like. Association with other deviant youngsters provides antisocial youths with attitudes, motivations, and rationalizations that support involvement in a wide variety of illegal activities (Dishion, McCord, and Poulin, 1999; Patterson, Debaryshe, and Ramsey, 1989; Patterson, Reid, and Dishion, 1992).

Patterson and his colleagues distinguish the delinquent behavior displayed by these antisocial youths from that displayed by their more conventional peers. They refer to the first group as *early starters* and the latter group as *late starters.* Early starters are the coercive youngsters we have been describing. They manifest antisocial behavior at an early age. Inept parenting has caused them to develop serious social-skill deficits. They are aggressive and defiant in their interactions with others, and are rejected by teachers and conventional peers. By default, these socially rejected individuals form a deviant peer group that escalates antisocial tendencies into delinquent and criminal behavior.

Late starters, on the other hand, are youths who experiment with delinquent acts during mid- to late adolescence, when such rebellious behavior tends to be quite prevalent. Indeed, dabbling in minor delinquent acts such as underage drinking or smoking, shoplifting, or skipping school is almost normative during this period. Studies show that 80 to 90 percent of all adolescents engage in a delinquent act for which they could have been adjudicated delinquent had they been caught. Late starters experiment with such activities in an attempt to establish their independence from adults and because of encouragement and support provided by their peers. In contrast to early starters, they possess ample social skills, have performed adequately in school, and are accepted by conventional peers. In all probability, many of the readers of this book were late starter delinquents during their adolescent years. Early starters, however, are unlikely to read this book or to be in college.

Distinguishing between these two types of delinquents is important, according to Patterson and his colleagues, because they have very different prognoses. Whereas late starters tend to discontinue their delinquency within a short period, early starters are at risk for chronic offending during adolescence and criminal careers as adults (Patterson et al., 1989; Patterson, Reid, and Dishion, 1992; Patterson and Yoerger, 1993). Indeed, the coercion model theory posits that these individuals will follow a very dismal life course trajectory. Lacking essential skills at one stage of life, they are unprepared for the next one. They tend to inflict pain, misery, and sorrow on the people close to them, such as romantic partners, children, and coworkers. They are at risk for a constant stream of crises, marital problems, marginal employment, arrest, and substance abuse problems.

Terrie Moffitt (1993a, 1993b, 1997) distinguishes the same two groups of delinquents but uses different labels. She identifies *life course persistent delinquents* as doomed to a dismal, antisocial life course trajectory. They manifest oppositional/defiant behavior as children, conduct problems as adolescents, and criminal and other antisocial behavior as adults. *Adolescent limited delinquents,* on the other hand, are conventional as children, experiment with delinquent behavior during adolescence, and then return to a conventional lifestyle as adults. In other words, their delinquent behavior is limited to the rebellious experimentation with deviant behavior that most adolescents display to some degree. Although Moffitt's typology of delinquents directly corresponds to Patterson's distinction between early and late starters, she has gone into greater detail regarding the theoretical, interventional, and research-related implications of differentiating these two groups of deviants.

Several studies have attempted to test the extent to which these two groups can be clearly distinguished. Most studies find at least some support for the idea. Although the line between the two groups is sometimes blurred, there does appear to be a small group of socially unskilled, hard-core deviants who persist in antisocial behavior throughout the life course. Conversely, most delinquents have adequate social skills, limit their deviant behavior to the adolescent years, and live conventional adult lives (Moffitt et al., 1996; Nagin, Farrington, and Moffitt, 1995; Paternoster and Brame, 1997; Simons, Wu, et al., 1994).

The coercion model of Patterson and his colleagues is built upon carefully crafted, methodologically sophisticated research. The theory is impressive in its precise description of the reciprocal family processes that give rise to inept parenting and child conduct problems. And it provides a clear theoretical link between family functioning, problems with peers, academic failure, and entrance into a deviant peer group. The theory also describes the manner in which the deviant peer group amplifies the antisocial tendencies learned in the family into delinquent and criminal behavior. Although the theory demonstrates these strengths, it also has some limitations.

First, it fails to identify the factors that account for the large number of antisocial children who do not go on to engage in adolescent delinquency or adult crime. We will see in Chapter Nine that researchers such as Sampson and Laub (1993), Warr (1998), and Simons and his colleagues (Simons, Johnson, et al., 1998; Simons, Stewart, et al., 2002) provide at least a partial answer to this question.

Second, Patterson's coercion model ignores the way parents influence their child's selection of a peer group. This omission is also evident in Akers' social learning perspective. There is rather strong evidence that parental behavior influences a child's friendship choices (Conger and Simons, 1997; Simons, Johnson, et al., 1998). Past research indicates that parents often employ a variety of strategies to structure their children's peer affiliations: They encourage their children to join one group over another (Brown, Mounts, et al., 1993), they carefully select the schools that their children attend (Bryant, 1985; Parke and Bhavnagri, 1989), and they promote participation in various conventional activities such as organized sports and other extracurricular activities at school (Ladd, Profilet, and Hart, 1992). Such efforts reduce the probability that a child will affiliate with deviant peers (Scaramella, et al., 2002; Simons, et al., 2001). Theoretical models based solely on social learning principles (e.g., operant learning, modeling) usually fail to incorporate this important avenue whereby parents influence the chances that their child will become involved in deviant behavior.

Finally, the coercion model gives little attention to vicarious learning or modeling processes that occur within the family. This is unexpected, given the importance that social learning theory places on vicarious learning (Akers, 1998; Bandura, 1977, 1986). Patterson and his colleagues (1992) maintain that criminal and deviant behavior is widely depicted on television, in movies, and on the playground. Therefore, they argue, virtually all children have been exposed to antisocial models. What is necessary for children to adopt this behavior, however, is that it be reinforced or produce positive results in their daily interactions. Thus, it is the reinforcing contingencies provided by parents, and not the behavior that they model, that cause children to become defiant and oppositional.

Patterson grants that intergenerational transmission of antisocial behavior often occurs. There is a much higher probability that a child will become delinquent if his parents are involved in an antisocial lifestyle. He contends, however, that this is not a result of parental modeling. Rather, this intergenerational effect is a consequence of the fact that antisocial individuals are not very conscientious parents. Hirschi (1969) first posited this to be the case in the early 1980s. And Gottfredson and Hirschi (1990) made the same argument in their statement of self-control theory. Thus Patterson, a social learning theorist, agrees with control theorists who claim that it is the disruptive effect of a deviant lifestyle on parenting that accounts for the finding that antisocial behavior often runs in families. Adults caught up in a deviant lifestyle (e.g., crime, substance abuse, fighting, etc.) are rarely responsible, conscientious parents. It is this ineffective parenting, and not the behavior modeled by the parents, that places the child at risk for delinquency. Stated differently, the coercion model, like self-control theory, asserts that the effect of parental antisocial behavior is indirect through quality of parenting.

Several studies have reported support for this hypothesis. Patterson et al. (1992) and Sampson and Laub (1993), for example, found that the association between parental and child antisocial behavior is no longer significant once the effect of parenting is taken into account. Other studies report, however, that only part of the relationship between parental antisocial behavior and child delinquency is explained by ineffective parenting. This research finds that there continues to be a relationship between parental deviant behavior and child conduct problems after the effect of parenting is taken into account (Chassin, et al., 1993; Conger and Rueter, 1995; Conger, Rueter, and Conger, 1994; Loeber et al., 1998; McCord, 1991a; Simons and Associates, 1996). These results suggest that it is not simply the reinforcing contingencies provided by antisocial parents that shapes children's behavior; children are also influenced by the deviant behavior that their parents model.

These contrasting findings may be a consequence of the different measures researchers have used in assessing parental deviant behavior. Generally, measures that focus on serious criminal behavior find that the effect of adult deviance is mediated by quality of parenting. It is not surprising that these studies fail to find a modeling effect, as children usually do not witness their parents committing serious criminal acts, and when they become aware of such actions, it is often because the parents have been arrested. Thus they observe the aversive consequences associated with such behavior.

The studies that find an association between adult deviance and child conduct problems, after controlling for quality of parenting, tend to use measures of parental deviance that focus on relatively minor, everyday antisocial acts. It seems quite plausible that children learn about the advantages or rewards of various deviant actions by observing their parents engaging in these behaviors. They might, for example, witness a parent skip work because of a hangover, lie to relatives about the reason for missing a family outing, cheat a clerk over the price of merchandise, falsely assert to creditors that the check is in the mail, sneak money from their spouse's pocket, break traffic laws to get to an appointment on time, or threaten to punch a neighbor who knocks on the door to complain about a noisy party. In each of these cases, the parent's deviant behavior is likely to have resulted in either positive or negative reinforcement. The parent either obtained a valued outcome (e.g., money) or avoided an aversive consequence (e.g., disapproval, criticism). We would expect that observing such behavior increases the chances that children will engage in similar actions when they encounter comparable circumstances (Bandura, 1977, 1986).

Such modeling effects may be weakened by the fact that parent-child relationships are often turbulent in families with an antisocial parent. Antisocial parents tend to alienate their children through their inconsistent, hostile, and explosive approach to parenting. This is an important consideration, as research on modeling has shown that individuals are most responsive to behavior modeled by persons they like, identify with, and respect (see Bandura, 1977, 1986). Generally, conventional parents have a stronger emotional bond with their children than do antisocial parents. This being the case, it may be that the actions modeled by conventional parents have more of an effect on children than those modeled by antisocial parents. Although this may be true, even children subject to abuse and neglect often continue to display a modicum of attachment to their parents. Thus even children with antisocial parents are likely to be influenced, at least to some degree, by the deviant behavior modeled by their parents.

As we saw earlier, Akers' social learning perspective emphasizes the importance of modeling. However, his research has focused primarily on vicarious learning within peer groups. His studies have devoted little attention to the types of deviant behaviors acquired through parental modeling. The same is true of other researchers who have investigated delinquency from a social learning perspective (Elliott and Menard, 1996; Kandel and Davies, 1991; Warr and Stafford, 1991). Although there have been several impressive investigations of vicarious learning within child and adolescent peer groups (see Bandura, 1986), there has been little consideration of the modeling processes that take place within families. It is hoped that future research will give greater attention to this issue. ✦

Chapter Four

The Corporal Punishment Controversy

As described in the two previous chapters, several contemporary theories of deviant behavior agree that effective parenting decreases the probability of delinquent behavior. These theories are also in agreement regarding the components of effective parenting. Competent parents show high levels of warmth and support, articulate standards for behavior, monitor their child's behavior, and engage in inductive reasoning and consistent discipline when infractions occur. This approach to parenting, we noted, has been labeled "authoritative parenting" (Baumrind, 1991b; Maccoby, 1992). Decades of research by psychologists, sociologists, and criminologists has established that this style of parenting promotes positive child development, whereas the absence of these parenting behaviors increases the chances that a child will engage in aggressive and delinquent behavior. This conclusion is based on findings from numerous studies, is generally accepted by the social scientific community, and has been widely used by prevention specialists concerned with designing instructional materials and classes for parents.

In recent years, some researchers have argued that there is convincing evidence for another generalization regarding the effect of parental behavior on child conduct problems. They contend that research has confirmed that children subjected to corporal punishment are at risk for delinquent and criminal behavior (Cohen and Brooks, 1994; Gershoff, 2002; McCord, 1991, 1997; Straus, 1991, 1994; Straus and Donnelly, 1994; Straus, Sugarman, and Giles-Sims, 1997). Physical discipline has this effect, they argue, because parents who engage in this behavior inadvertently teach their children that aggression and coercion are legitimate approaches to solving problems. Further, they assert that corporal punishment fosters anger and generates opposition and defiance. Thus, physical punishment is seen as having a paradoxical effect. Instead of deterring misbehavior, it operates to amplify a child's antisocial tendencies. These researchers consider exposure to corporal punishment during childhood to be a major cause of adolescent delinquency and adult crime and aggression (Cohen and Brooks, 1994; McCord, 1991, 1997; Straus, 1991, 2001; Straus and Donnelly, 1994).

Some believe that scientific support for this position is so strong that Congress should follow the example of several European countries and pass legislation prohibiting adults from utilizing corporal methods to discipline children (Hyman, 1997; Straus, 1994, 2001). Currently, parents are forbidden to use corporal punishment as a form of discipline in Austria, Cyprus, Denmark, Finland, Germany, Italy, Latvia, Norway, and Sweden (EPOCH-USA, 2000). We are sympathetic to concerns over the use of corporal punishment. We have moral reservations about parents hitting their children and believe that parents should strive to use less coercive forms of punishment. It is clear, however, that many parents take a different position.

Several studies have reported that the majority of American parents sometimes use corporal punishment to discipline their children (Straus and Gelles, 1986; Straus, Gelles, and Steinmetz, 1980). One investigation found, for example, that more than 90 percent of American parents have spanked their children by the time they are 3 or 4 years of age (Straus and Stewart, 1999). Although we take ethical exception to this approach to punishment, we do not believe that current evidence warrants viewing all parents who spank as abusive and ineffective. And it is certainly premature to suggest that their approach to parenting be criminalized. The effects of corporal punishment are an empirical question. Moral objections are a separate issue. We will focus on research findings and let readers draw their own conclusions regarding the ethics of physical forms of punishment.

Past studies have been fraught with conceptual and methodological weaknesses limiting the drawing of firm conclusions regarding the link between corporal punishment and negative child outcomes. Often, for example, there are problems in the way that corporal punishment is assessed, potentially confounding variables are not controlled, and questionable causal assumptions are imputed to the data. We begin this chapter by describing these methodological weaknesses. There is currently a vigorous debate taking place within the United States regarding the impact of spanking (American Academy of Pediatrics, 1998; Baumrind, Larzelere, and Cowan, 2002; Gershoff, 2002; Straus, 1999), and this controversy is likely to last for some time. We hope that the methodological concerns described below will make the reader a more sophisticated consumer of research on this issue.

After detailing these methodological considerations, we will briefly examine how various theories of child aggression and delinquency view physical discipline. It is generally assumed that these theories contend that corporal punishment promotes deviant behavior. Careful consideration indicates, however, that they imply a more complex view of the consequences of physical discipline. We will utilize these theories to formulate a tentative conclusion regarding the effect of physical discipline on child conduct problems. The final portion of the chapter examines the extent to which past research supports this conclusion.

Methodological Problems

The first methodological problem involves the manner in which the parental use of corporal punishment is assessed. Most studies utilize a frequency measure in which the researcher assesses the number of times per week, month, or year that the parent administers some type of physical discipline to the child (e.g., McCord, 1991; Straus, 1991). The problem with such measures is that they confound discipline with child infractions (Larzelere, 1996). Parents with difficult children engage in disciplinary acts more frequently than those with conforming children. There is no need to discipline children unless they are misbehaving. Thus, when a frequency measure is used to assess parental discipline, all types of disciplinary strategies (e.g., verbal reprimand, inductive reasoning, time-out, corporal punishment) tend to be positively associated with the frequency of conduct problems (Larzelere, 1996; Baumrind, Larzelere, and Cowan, 2002), suggesting the absurd conclusion that discipline of any sort operates to amplify antisocial behavior.

One can avoid this methodological problem by assessing the *proportion* of time that the parent employs a particular disciplinary strategy when the child misbehaves. Instead of focusing on the frequency of corporal punishment, the researcher measures how often the parent resorts to physical punishment when some type of discipline is required. Studies that employ a frequency measure usually find a positive association between physical punishment and child misbehavior, whereas those that utilize a proportional measure tend to find either a negative association between spanking and child misbehavior (Larzelere, 1996), or no relationship between the two variables (Simons, Johnson, and Conger, 1994). Other forms of punishment may involve redirection, time-out, inductive reasoning, and taking away of privileges. Spanking may be used as an occasional supplement to these other disciplinary strategies. Or some parents may use corporal punishment in response to any infraction. The first approach would be an example of the use of corporal punishment a low proportion of the time, whereas the second would be an example of the use of corporal punishment a high proportion of the time.

A second methodological limitation involves the failure to take into account the effects of other dimensions of parenting (Simons, Johnson, and Conger, 1994; Simons, Wu, Lin, Gordon, and Conger, 2000). As noted earlier, an uncaring attitude, poor supervision, inconsistent discipline, and a failure to explain moral principles all serve to increase the probability that a child will grow up to engage in delinquent and criminal behavior (Gottfredson and Hirschi, 1990; Hirschi, 1969; Patterson, Reid, and Dishion, 1992; Sampson and Laub, 1993; Simons, Johnson, et al., 1998; Wilson and Herrnstein, 1985). Importantly, such inept parenting practices tend to be correlated with the use of corporal punishment (Simons, Johnson, and Conger, 1994; Simons et al., 2000; Simons, Lin, et al., 2002). Thus, when researchers report a correlation between parental use of physical punishment and offspring involvement in antisocial behavior, it may be that the association is spurious due to the correlation of both of these variables with factors such as parental warmth, monitoring, and inductive reasoning.

Although most research has ignored this possibility, studies that include a variety of parenting behaviors usually find that the positive correlation between corporal punishment and delinquent or criminal behavior is eliminated once the effects of these other dimensions of effective parenting are taken into account (Caroll, 1997; McCord, 1991; Simons, Johnson, and Conger, 1994; Simons et al., 1999; Simons, Lin, et al., 2002). Further, these studies report that absence of parental warmth, monitoring, and inductive reasoning is a much better predictor of adolescent antisocial behavior than parental use of corporal punishment.

The few studies that continue to find an association between corporal punishment and child conduct problems after controlling for other dimensions of parenting (e.g., Cohen and Brooks, 1994; Straus, Sugarman, and Giles-Sims, 1997) usually include only a limited set of parental behaviors. Although they control for the effects of parental warmth, they fail to control for other components of effective parenting, such as monitoring and inductive reasoning.

A final methodological difficulty concerns the fact that most studies fail to recognize the reciprocal relationship that exists between parent and child behavior. Although it is true that ineffective parenting increases the chances that a child will engage in deviant behavior, it is also true that aggressive, oppositional children influence their parents to adopt ineffective parenting practices (see Lytton, 1990; Patterson, Reid, and Dishion, 1992; Simons, Johnson, et al., 1998). Given this finding, a positive correlation between corporal punishment and child antisocial behavior may simply mean that parents often resort to corporal punishment when they have a difficult child (Baumrind, Larzelere, and Cowan, 2002; Larzelere, 1996). Even longitudinal studies that assess antisocial behavior several months or years after exposure to corporal punishment cannot preclude this possibility. In order to establish that physical punishment promotes antisocial behavior, the researcher must show that corporal punishment predicts delinquent or criminal behavior after controlling for the amount of oppositional and defiant behavior that the child displays toward the parent.

Many of the conflicting findings reported in past research on corporal punishment can be attributed to the fact that studies vary widely regarding the extent to which they address these methodological issues (see Baumrind, Larzelere, and Cowan, 2002). Even when problematic studies are excluded, however, there is still much variability in the findings reported. Many studies find a positive relation, whereas some find a negative association between corporal punishment and child conduct problems. Still others fail to find any relationship between the two variables. In the next section, we attempt to articulate a theoretical principle that would allow us to make sense of these seemingly contradictory findings.

Theoretical Considerations

At first glance, it appears that the theories we discussed in Chapters Two and Three would view corporal punishment as fostering, rather than deterring, child conduct problems. Patterson's coercion model contends that harsh discipline elicits an aggressive, oppositional response from the child, and corporal punishment might be considered a harsh discipline. Social control theory stresses the importance of the parent-child bond, and physical discipline might be seen as undermining the child's attachment to the parent. Both self-control theory and Baumrind's concept of authoritative parenting suggest that effective parents combine warmth with control. Physical punishment might be seen as an approach to control that is contrary to warmth. Finally, social learning theory emphasizes lessons taught to children via behavior modeled by parents, and corporal punishment may teach the child that violence is a legitimate avenue for settling interpersonal disputes.

Chapters Two and Three only included theories that identify parental behavior as a major cause of child conduct problems and delinquency. Some of the more general theories of deviant behavior that were not included are also often interpreted as predicting that corporal punishment promotes delinquency. General strain theory (Agnew, 1985, 2001; Agnew and White, 1992), for example, argues that aversive or stressful situations often produce anger and frustration, which lead to delinquency. According to the theory, anger is most likely to occur when the person perceives that the stressful event entailed gratuitous or unjust treatment. This irritation, in turn, increases the chances that the individual will engage in aggressive and vengeful actions in an attempt to vent frustration. Agnew (1985) cites harsh, unfair, or inconsistent discipline as an example of aversive circumstances that might be expected to foster anger and delinquent behavior.

Similarly, differential coercion theory (Colvin, 2000) posits that chronic exposure to coercion promotes a complex of emotions and personality traits (e.g., anger, belligerence, aggressiveness) that increase the chances a person will engage in delinquent or criminal behavior. Coercion occurs when "one is compelled to act in a certain way through direct force or intimidation" (Colvin, 2000, 36). Coercive interactions may take place in any number of settings, including the family. Harsh disciplinary practices involving corporal punishment are among the family-centered coercive acts cited by the theory.

All of these theories seem to link physical punishment to child conduct problems, but this is actually an oversimplification or distortion of their position. Although social learning theory suggests that corporal punishment may teach a child that violence is a legitimate avenue for handling interpersonal conflict, this is not necessarily the lesson taught by this approach to discipline. The lesson learned depends on the behavior displayed by the parents, including the explanations that accompany the corporal punishment.

Consider the example of a parent who uses low-impact spanking (i.e., a swat to the buttocks) as a last-resort punishment when her preschooler misbehaves, but never uses corporal punishment with her older children and frequently talks about the importance of people not being violent or aggressive with one another. Also, when she administers a swat to her preschooler, she explains the importance of the rule that her child violated and indicates that little children get spanked when they defy their parent's guidance. In this case, the child might be expected to learn that it is legitimate for parents to sometimes spank a misbehaving preschooler, whereas, in general, people should not hit each other.

Research indicates that modeling often results in discriminative learning, whereby we learn to recognize (or discriminate) between the circumstances under which an action is or is not appropriate (Bandura, 1986). Just as adults learn that violence in times of war or in self-defense are exceptions to the moral prohibition against aggressing toward others, so children may learn that low-impact spanking of preschoolers is legitimate, whereas striking a peer or sibling is not. Thus, social learning theory's emphasis on modeling does not imply that corporal punishment will necessarily cause a child to conclude that aggression is a legitimate avenue for resolving disputes.

Although they emphasize slightly different intervening processes, all of the other theories that we have discussed (e.g., Patterson's coercion model, social control theory, general strain theory, differential coercion theory) share the view that children respond with anger, aggression, and defiance when they perceive that they have been treated unjustly. Such perceptions are likely to take place when parental punishment is seen as harsh or illegitimate, given the circumstances. Corporal punishment may often foster this perception, but this is not necessarily the case. In some instances, a child may believe that physical punishment is a fair response to his misbehavior. Under these circumstances, corporal punishment should serve as a deterrent. At other times, however, children may consider corporal punishment to be unwarranted and illegitimate. When this occurs, corporal punishment might be expected to foster deviant behavior such as belligerence, aggression, and defiance.

We believe that past research shows corporal punishment is most apt to be perceived as fair and legitimate if it is mild, used with young children, and administered by a warm and caring parent, and if it occurs within a cultural context that legitimates corporal punishment. Under such circumstances, physical discipline is apt to operate as a deterrent to child conduct problems. Conversely, physical discipline is likely to elicit perceptions of injustice and mistreatment when it is severe, directed toward older children, or dispensed by a rejecting parent, or when it occurs within a cultural context that disapproves of corporal punishment. Under these circumstances, physical discipline is apt to generate belligerence, defiance, and other conduct problems. The remainder of the chapter reviews the evidence in support of these contentions.

Severity of Punishment

When attempting to evaluate the effects of corporal punishment, it is essential that one distinguish between harsh and punitive physical discipline and the more moderate application of normative spanking (Baumrind, Larzelere, and Cowan, 2002; Deater-Deckard and Dodge, 1997; Simons et al., 2000). A few years ago, a conference of developmental psychologists defined *spanking* as an approach to physical discipline that is noninjurious and administered with an opened hand to the extremities or buttocks (Friedman and Schonberg, 1996a). At most, such punishment inflicts only a minor, temporary level of physical pain (Baumrind, Larzelere, and Cowan, 2002). We expect that a spanking delivered in this fashion is much more likely to be perceived by the child as fair than more severe forms of physical discipline involving slapping, pushing, shoving, or hitting with an object. Although a child may perceive a mild spanking as proportional to her misbehavior, more extreme forms of physical discipline are apt to be experienced as too harsh a response to the infraction.

If this line of reasoning is true, there is no reason to expect that a mild spank will have the negative effect of eliciting oppositional and defiant behavior. Indeed, such punishment might be expected to deter child misbehavior. In contrast, harsh corporal punishment would be expected to produce feelings of injustice, anger, and hostility that serve to amplify the child's antisocial behavior. Social psychological studies have shown that severe punishment often produces a boomerang effect, as the victim feels mistreated and resists or retaliates against the perpetrator (Homans, 1974; Walster, Walster, and Berschied, 1978). Thus, harsh or relentless use of corporal punishment might be expected to foster the negative results found in many studies of corporal punishment.

Unfortunately, research on corporal punishment usually does not distinguish between the consequences of mild forms of physical punishment and more extreme forms that might be considered abusive (Baumrind, Larzelere, and Cowan, 2002; Deater-Deckard and Dodge, 1997). The few studies that have taken severity into account, however, have found that individuals exposed to moderate levels of physical punishment are no more likely to engage in antisocial behavior than those whose parents did not use corporal punishment. The studies also showed that persons who experience severe physical punishment show significantly higher levels of antisocial behavior than those who receive either no or moderate corporal punishment (Caesar, 1988; Deater-Deckard and Dodge, 1997; Holmes and Robins, 1988; Mahoney et al., 2000; Simons et al., 2000). This suggests that the negative effects of corporal punishment are largely confined to instances in which the caretaker is administering more than a mild spanking.

More severe forms of corporal punishment involving slapping, kicking, shoving, and hitting with an object might be considered abusive. Several studies report that physically abused children are at risk for a variety of antisocial behaviors, including delinquency and substance abuse (Dembo et al., 1990; Dembo et al., 1992; Ireland and Widom, 1994; Ireland, Smith, and Thornberry, 2002; Kakar, 1996; Lemmon, 1999; Smith and Thornberry, 1995; Widom, 1989,

1991; Zingraff et al., 1993). These longitudinal studies have found a significant relationship between child maltreatment and both self-reported and official delinquency, even after controlling for a variety of other factors.

Past research by Ken Dodge and his colleagues (Dodge, 1980, 1986, 1991; Dodge, Bates, and Pettit, 1990) suggests that, at least in part, abusive parenting increases the probability of antisocial behavior because it causes children to develop a hostile view of relationships. This biased perspective leads them to attribute malevolent motives to others and to assume that an aggressive, belligerent attitude is necessary to avoid exploitation. Past research has shown that this view of relationships is strongly held by both aggressive children and institutionalized delinquents (Dodge, Bates, and Pettit, 1990; Dodge and Newman, 1981; Nasby, Hayden, and DePaulo, 1980; Perry, Perry, and Rasmussen, 1986; Slaby and Guerra, 1988). Thus, persistent exposure to harsh corporal punishment fosters a distrusting, hostile view of other people and their motives, and this orientation leads to actions that are oppositional, defiant, and antagonistic.

Generally, the association between harsh parenting and antisocial behavior is stronger for children who have experienced more extensive abuse (Smith and Thornberry, 1995). This is further evidence that the negative effects of physical discipline escalate as the punishments become more severe. If perceptions of injustice and oppositional and defiant behavior are to be avoided, it appears that corporal punishment must be limited to temperate forms, such as a mild spanking.

Age of Child

There is good reason to expect that the consequences of corporal punishment vary by age of child (Baumrind, Larzelere, and Cowan, 2002; Larzelere, 1996). Both children and adults tend to view corporal punishment as most appropriate for preschoolers, less appropriate for elementary-school children, and inappropriate for children in middle school and high school (Day, Peterson, and McCracken, 1998; Flynn, 1998). If warned about the consequences of persisting in a particular behavior, a preschooler may accept a couple of swats on the buttocks as an unpleasant but legitimate parental response to his misconduct. Older children, on the other hand, are apt to experience a spanking as humiliating and illegitimate. Further, because swats on the buttocks are not very physically painful to an older child, there will be a tendency for the parent to resort to more extreme measures such as slapping, kicking, or the use of a belt (Straus and Stewart, 1999). The recipient is apt to view such measures as humiliating, too harsh, and a violation of society's moral injunction against people physically attacking each other. The perception that such punishment is illegitimate will be reinforced by the older child's observation that his peers are rarely, if ever, treated in this manner by their parents.

All of this suggests that the effects of physical discipline are likely to differ by age of child. Although moderate spanking may be a deterrent for preschoolers, corporal punishment might be expected to escalate the deviant behavior of older children and teens. Past research provides support for this observation. Clinical studies with preschoolers and kindergartners have found that nonabusive corporal punishment (i.e., spanking) increases compliance, as well as the effectiveness of time-out and reasoning (Bean and Roberts, 1981; Bernal et al., 1968; Larzelere and Merenda, 1994; Larzelere et al., 1995; Roberts, 1982, 1988; Roberts and Powers, 1990; Sather, 1992). Although researchers agree that spanking by itself may do little to promote moral character development, evidence suggests that spanking used as a back-up to other disciplinary tactics (e.g., reasoning, time-out) increases the efficacy of these alternative disciplinary tactics in preschoolers with behavior problems (Friedman and Schonberg, 1996b).

Whereas studies with young children usually report positive effects, those that focus on parental behavior during late childhood or early adolescence tend to find either no association between corporal punishment and deviant behavior (MacIntyre and Cantrell, 1995; McCord, 1988), or a positive relationship between the two phenomena (Gelles and Straus, 1979; Hemenway, Solnick, and Carter, 1994; Lieh-Mak, Chung, and Liv, 1983; Straus, 1991; Tennant, Detels, and Clark, 1975). Indeed, there is rather strong evidence that the more negative effects of corporal punishment tend to occur with older children (Gunnoe and Mariner, 1997; Rothbaum and Weisz, 1994). Thus, overall past research indicates that corporal punishment often enhances compliance among preschoolers, whereas it is not a deterrent and may increase the probability of antisocial behavior when administered to older children. These findings indicate that corporal punishment is certainly not an appropriate or effective form of punishment for older children, especially teenagers.

Quality of the Parent-Child Relationship

It seems likely that a child's reaction to physical punishment will depend, at least in part, on the quality of the relationship that she has with the caregiver (Deater-Deckard and Dodge, 1997; Simons et al., 2000). Children who possess a positive relationship with their parents might accept physical punishment as a legitimate expression of parental concern for their welfare, whereas those with a negative relationship may view such punishments as an expressions of parental hostility and rejection. To the extent that this is the case, warm and supportive parents may be able to use corporal punishment to obtain child compliance. On the other hand, corporal punishment may foster defiance and aggression when it is administered by cold, harsh, or uninvolved parents.

Consistent with this observation, Diane Baumrind (1972, 1991b) has reported that many authoritative parents sometimes use corporal punishment. As described in Chapter Two, authoritative parents are high on both warmth and control, and this parenting style has been shown to be a very effective approach to child socialization. Children of authoritative parents tend to be socially and academically competent while showing few behavior problems. Thus, Baumrind's research on different styles of parenting indicates that effective parents sometimes use corporal punishment.

Research by others provides additional support for the idea that the consequences of corporal punishment vary by the quality of the parent-child relationship (Deater-Deckard and Dodge, 1997; McCord,1991b; Simons et al., 2000). These studies find that corporal punishment delivered by a hostile, rejecting parent tends to increase conduct problems, whereas physical punishment administered by a warm, supportive parent rarely has this untoward result. Thus, although few studies address this issue, the evidence suggests that corporal punishment tends to escalate child behavior problems when it takes place within the context of a troubled parent-child relationship. These negative effects are much less likely to occur when physical discipline occurs within a warm and nurturing family environment.

Cultural and Community Context

The vast majority of research on corporal punishment has focused on European American (or white, non-Hispanic) families living in the United States. This is a major limitation, as the effects of corporal punishment may differ by cultural context. The dominant culture in the United States maintains that healthy child development requires an environment that encourages individuality and freedom of expression. This ethic suggests that parents should be nurturant, but not too controlling (Bronfrenbrenner, 1985; Wilson, 1983). However, other cultural traditions provide a different perspective on children and parenting. Chinese culture, for example, stresses the importance of child obedience and emphasizes the importance of strict, controlling parenting practices to achieve this goal (Chiu, 1987; Kriger and Kroes, 1972; Lin and Fu, 1990; Yee, 1983). Whereas past research has established that authoritarian parenting is associated with low school achievement for European American children, such parenting practices are related to high levels of achievement for Chinese students (Dornbusch et al., 1987; Steinberg, Dornbusch, and Brown, 1992). Chao (1994) argues that this contradictory finding is obtained because American children view high parental control as illegitimate and unfair, whereas Chinese children perceive these parenting behaviors as an indication of parental involvement and concern.

A similar cultural difference may operate for corporal punishment. It may be that European American children tend to consider physical forms of punishment indicators of parental rejection, and respond by resisting parental attempts to control their behavior. On the other hand, corporal punishment may operate as an effective deterrent in cultures such as Chinese, where such parenting practices are accepted as expressions of love and concern. Research on African American families provides some support for this idea.

Several studies have reported that physical discipline is more widely used and accepted by African American than European American parents (see Heffer and Kelley, 1987; Hill, 1999). Further, there is evidence that African American and European American families differ in their perception of the meaning of corporal punishment. Disciplinary styles can be either parent or child centered (Baumrind, 1971; Maccoby and Martin, 1983). A parent-oriented approach considers obedience to parental authority as an end in itself, whereas a child-oriented perspective views discipline as a vehicle for helping children to become self-respecting, responsible adults. Although physical discipline tends to be correlated with a parent-oriented approach among European American parents, Kelley and colleagues (Kelley, Power, and Wimbush, 1992; Kelley, Sanchez-Hucles, and Walker, 1993) found that corporal punishment was associated with both parent- and child-oriented parenting styles among African American parents.

Consistent with the finding that physical discipline is often associated with child-focused parenting in African American communities, several researchers have observed that African Americans are overrepresented in dangerous, crime-ridden areas and that corporal punishment in such neighborhoods relates to concerns about survival (Baumrind, 1972; Belsky, 1993; Kelley, Power, and Wimbush, 1992; Mason et al., 1996; Whaley, 2000). In contrast to white parents, who can afford to be tolerant of mild levels of misbehavior, the consequences of disobedience are much more serious in many African American neighborhoods. Kelley and colleagues (1992) argue that the residents of such communities often view corporal punishment as a means of teaching children respect for authority, in order to protect them from the adverse consequences of violating social norms. These negative consequences include harassment by the police (Belsky, 1993). Whaley notes that a common saying in the African American community is, "I'd rather my child get a beating from me than from the police" (2000, 8). He goes on to assert that from an African American cultural perspective, firm disciplinary practices such as spanking are often considered necessary in order to protect children from the various dangers posed by their social environment. Brody and Flor (1998) make a similar point in their observation that African American parents living in highly disadvantaged neighborhoods often engage in what they term "no-nonsense parenting," given the hazardous consequences of child noncompliance. This approach to parenting involves high warmth combined with very high control (beyond what one might ordinarily associate with authoritative parenting).

All of this suggests that African Americans are much more likely than European Americans to accept corporal punishment as a legitimate approach to discipline. Consistent with this contention, unpublished data collected by the senior author of this book shows that corporal punishment is strongly related to children's feelings of parental rejection among a sample of midwestern white adolescents but is not related in a sample of African American children living in the Midwest and Southeast. This finding indicates that European American children often view physical discipline as an expression of parental hostility and disregard, whereas African American children tend to accept such discipline as a valid expression of parental concern.

Throughout this chapter we have argued that the effects of corporal punishment vary by the extent to which it is viewed by parents and children as normative parental behavior. Children are less likely to respond to physical discipline with hostility and defiance, we have reasoned, if they consider such practices to be an appropriate approach to parenting. For such children, corporal punishment may even act as a deterrent. If these arguments are true, African American children should show less aggression and defiance in response to physical punishment than European American children. Indeed, they should tend toward increased compliance as a result of such punishment. Several studies indicate that this is the case.

A variety of cross-sectional and longitudinal studies of European American families have reported a positive association between corporal punishment and child externalizing problems (see Gershoff, 2002; Straus, 2001). These results suggest that physical discipline may promote, rather than deter, antisocial behavior. Studies of African American families, on the other hand, have reported a different pattern of results. These investigations have found either no relation or an inverse association between corporal punishment and child conduct problems (Baumrind, 1972; Deater-Deckard and Dodge, 1997; Deater-Deckard et al., 1996; Gunnoe and Mariner, 1997; Wasserman et al., 1996). This pattern of findings suggests that corporal punishment tends not to have negative consequences, and may even enhance child compliance, when the family is part of a culture that legitimates such parenting practices.

A study by Simons, Lin, Gordon, Brody, Murry, and Conger (2002) provides additional support for this idea. They investigated the extent to which the effects of corporal punishment vary by community context. The study focused on 10-year-old children. Simons and colleagues hypothesized that corporal punishment is apt to be perceived as an illegitimate approach to parenting in communities where physical discipline rarely occurs, and the use of corporal punishment would be expected to evoke defiance and antisocial behavior among children living in such neighborhoods. In contrast, children residing in communities where corporal punishment is highly prevalent and therefore normative would not be expected to demonstrate an adverse response to being physically disciplined. They predicted that there would be either no association or a negative relation between exposure to physical discipline and conduct problems for children living in such areas. Their findings supported the hypotheses.

Thus, the available evidence suggests that the consequences of physical discipline vary by cultural context. Physical discipline administered within a cultural context that opposes such punishments may serve to enhance child misconduct. This negative outcome may not be evident, however, in communities that embrace corporal punishment as a legitimate approach to discipline. Indeed, physical punishment administered within such a cultural context may enhance child compliance.

Conclusion

Although the majority of American parents sometimes spank their children, many social scientists feel strongly that corporal punishment serves to foster, rather than deter, deviant behavior. As support for their position, they cite the profusion of studies that have shown a positive relationship between exposure to physical discipline during childhood and adolescent and adult antisocial behavior. As stated in the introduction to this chapter, we have moral reservations about parents hitting their children and believe that parents should strive to use less coercive forms of punishment. We disagree, however, with those who argue for legislation that would criminalize the millions of conscientious parents who sometimes spank their children. Certainly, research to date does not justify such a strong response.

As we noted, studies of corporal punishment are plagued by methodological difficulties. These weaknesses include problems in defining and measuring corporal punishment, confusion over whether corporal punishment is a cause or a consequence of child misconduct, and failure to control for important variables such as the parent's level of warmth and support. When these weaknesses are taken into account, it appears to be an overstatement that corporal punishment leads to increased deviant behavior. Rather, the consequences of physical discipline seem to vary by the extent to which it is accepted as a fair and legitimate form of discipline by the child. Physical discipline is apt to be perceived as legitimate when it is mild (e.g., a spank to the buttocks with an open hand); when it is administered by a caring, supportive parent; and when the child is between 2 and 6 years of age. In contrast, physical discipline is likely to foster defiance and aggression when it is severe; when it is administered by a harsh, rejecting parent; and when the child is a preadolescent or adolescent.

This chapter discussed the effects of corporal punishment. Although we summarized the results of a profusion of studies, the decision to use physical punishment to discipline children involves more than the question of efficacy. It is also an ethical matter. Whereas social scientists can address the question of effectiveness, it is beyond the scope of science to draw moral conclusions. Ultimately, each individual must determine the circumstances, if any, under which it might be appropriate to use physical discipline. ✦

Chapter Five

Family Structure and Delinquency

Family structure is often cited as an important cause of child and adolescent conduct problems. Out-of-wedlock births, divorce, and absentee fathers are some of the family forms that have faced criticism and have been linked to an increased risk for delinquency. In this chapter, we present information regarding the changing shape of American families, review the literature that shows an association between family structure and delinquency, and present evidence that, regardless of family structure, quality of parenting is still one of the most important family factors in explaining delinquent behavior.

Changing Family Forms

Traditionally, the two-biological-parent family form has been considered the cultural ideal. Although a few studies have recently investigated differences between biological offspring and adopted children in two-parent homes, those studies have revealed few significant differences in terms of family functioning. This finding holds true even for children adopted by same-sex couples (Stacey and Biblarz, 2001). For this chapter, we will use the term *intact nuclear family* to refer to a married couple and their shared biological or adopted children. This family form is often cited as the norm, but today less than 25 percent of U.S. families fit this model. This represents a dramatic change from 1960, when 44 percent of families were of the intact nuclear type (U.S. Census Bureau, 2001a).

According to the U.S. Census, births to unmarried mothers have increased from 26 percent in 1970 to 44 percent in 2000 (25 percent for whites, 70 percent for blacks, and 41 percent for Hispanics). An estimated one half of all children born during the 1980s and 1990s will experience the divorce of their parents and spend some time in a single-parent home. Until the early twentieth century, most children living with only one parent were doing so due to the death of the other parent. Approximately 15 percent of children will spend some time as part of a blended family or stepfamily following the remarriage of one or both parents, which represents a 50 percent increase within the past two decades. Increasingly, children find themselves members of multigenerational households in which a grandparent or other relative assumes a parent/caregiver role.

Clearly, to continue to use *Ozzie and Harriet* as a representation of the cultural norm when discussing the American family is to employ an image that has become, in many ways, outdated. There has been some debate as to whether the changes described above represent a decline in the American family or are simply reflective of other rapidly changing social norms in Western culture. Proponents of the first position maintain that the intact nuclear model is the "gold standard" to which all other family forms should be compared. Those on the other side of the issue argue that all family forms are equally valid, each with its own strengths. Settling this debate is beyond the scope of this chapter, but it is important to note the following: Although children of divorced- and single-parent families do experience behavior problems at two to three times the rate of children in intact nuclear families, the rates of conduct disorder are roughly 5 percent for kids in intact nuclear families and 10 to 15 percent for kids in divorced- or single-parent homes (Hetherington, 1999; McLanahan and Sandefur, 1994; Simons and Associates, 1996). This means that while there is an *increased risk* of engaging in delinquent behaviors for children who are not raised in a traditional two-parent home, at least 80 percent of those children do not manifest serious behavior problems.

That said, even though most kids from divorced- or single-parent homes do not experience behavioral or emotional problems, a two- to threefold increase in the rate is a concern. In the following section, we will present research on delinquency by family type. Further, we will offer evidence that the association between family structure and behavioral problems can be explained, in large part, by variance in quality of parenting. We will begin by discussing children living in single-mother homes. Although there has been an increase in father-only households in recent decades, of the 20 million children under the age of 18 who reside in a single-parent home, about 85 percent live with their mothers (U.S. Census Bureau, 2001b).

Single-Parent Households

Many single-parent households are headed by women who have never been married. Marriage rates have been on the decline in recent decades. This can be attributed to several factors, including increased rates of cohabitation, economic independence of women, and a relaxation of sexual mores. Because women now have better access to education and more occupational success than in previous periods in history, it is not necessary for a woman to have a husband in order to be financially stable. Also, it has been increasingly acceptable in Western cultures to engage in sex without the commitment of marriage. Correspondingly, there has been a decrease in cultural proscriptions against births outside of marriage. These changes represent the removal of three of the main functions of marriage: economic stability, access to sex, and procreation. As a result, more and more Americans delay marriage (average age at first marriage in the United States is 26.8 years for men and 25 years for women) or forego it altogether.

For some, cohabitation may be a temporary or permanent alternative to marriage. As any behavior becomes more and more common, it is increasingly seen as normative. This is certainly the case with such phenomena as premarital sex and cohabitation, both of which are now viewed by many as steps in the courtship process. For example, currently, 50 percent of couples cohabit before marriage and cohabitors account for 39 percent of nonmarital births (Bumpass and Lu, 2000). Clearly, births to unmarried women, an increasingly common occurrence, no longer carry the stigma they once did.

The dramatic growth in the number of female-headed households is not just a result of an increase in the rate of births to unmarried women. It is also a consequence of the rise in the divorce rate. It is often said that half of all marriages will end in divorce. It is important to understand, however, that this statement is a projection about the future, not a reflection of what has already occurred. This figure is often obtained by comparing all marriages in a given year to the number of divorces in the same year. When there are one half as many divorces as marriages, the divorce rate is said to be 50 percent. Obviously, most of the divorces that occur in any one year do not involve marriages that also took place during that same year. Present studies estimate that rates of ever-married married women that are now divorced are 35 percent for whites, 45 percent for blacks, and 27 percent for Latinas (Teachman, 2000). The divorce rate began a dramatic rise in the late 1960s and peaked in the late 1980s. There was little change in the divorce rate for over a decade, but there is evidence of a slight decline in recent years (U.S. Census Bureau, 2000a).

Like their never-married counterparts, divorced women experience higher rates of economic pressure, work stress, and negative life events than married women (Simons and Associates, 1996). These factors are, in turn, related to an increase in risk for depression. When parents are stressed and depressed, they tend to engage in less conscientious and effective parenting practices. The next section focuses on the association between single parenthood and quality of parenting.

Quality of Parenting in Single-Parent Households

Both control theories (Gottfredson and Hirschi, 1990; Hirschi, 1969) and social learning theories (Elliott, Huizinga, and Menard, 1989; Patterson, Reid, and Dishion, 1992), as discussed in earlier chapters, posit that quality of parenting has a significant effect on the probability of conduct problems. Although these two theoretical perspectives differ in some important respects, they both assert that inept parenting (i.e., hostility, little monitoring, inconsistent discipline) increases the probability that adolescents will be impulsive, defiant, and risk taking. Such youths find delinquent acts more alluring than youths who have been socialized to possess strong internal controls. Furthermore, poorly socialized adolescents are attracted to peers with the same rebellious characteristics. Such affiliation is apt to take place when parents exercise little supervision or control. Involvement with deviant peers, in turn, leads to amplification of the adolescent's antisocial tendencies, because the deviant peer group serves as a training ground for delinquent and other criminal behavior.

In other words, inept parenting is viewed as having both a direct and an indirect effect on adolescent delinquent behavior. It directly contributes to oppositional and defiant tendencies that make delinquent behavior attractive to the child, and it allows youths to drift into association with peers who encourage antisocial behavior. Several cross-sectional and longitudinal studies provide support for this perspective (Conger and Simons, 1997; Elliott, Huizinga, and Menard, 1989; Patterson, Reid, and Dishion, 1992; Sampson and Laub, 1993).

Unfortunately, there is compelling evidence that divorced parents are more apt to display ineffectual parental practices than those who are married. Several studies report that divorced parents tend to make fewer demands on children, engage in less monitoring, display more hostility, and use less-effective disciplinary strategies than married parents (Amato, 1987; Astone and McLanahan, 1991; Brody and Forehand, 1993; Capaldi and Patterson, 1991; Furstenberg and Nord, 1985; Hetherington, Cox, and Cox, 1982; McLanahan and Sandefur, 1994; Simons and Associates, 1996; Thomson, McLanahan, and Curtin, 1992). It should be noted, however, that the majority of mothers, regardless of marital status, are competent parents (Acock and Demo, 1994; Simons et al., 1996). Only a minority of mothers display inadequate discipline and control. Research suggests that roughly 20 to 25 percent of single mothers engage in dysfunctional parenting practices, but this is twice the percentage of married mothers who fail to provide adequate discipline and control. Thus, the relationship between family structure and adolescent delinquent behavior can be explained in large part by this difference in parenting practices (Simons and Associates, 1996; Brody and Forehand, 1988; Hetherington, Cox, and Cox, 1982).

The Stress of Being a Single Parent

This difference in quality of supervision and control appears to be a function of the high stress and impaired psychological functioning experienced by many single mothers. Many single mothers experience role overload. This means that they must play the role of sole provider and sole parent to their children. Unlike married women, they often do not have a partner with whom to share those roles. Obviously, it is not possible for anyone to be in more than one place at any one time. As a result, many single mothers spend long hours at work in order to provide economically for their family. This may mean that children come home after school to an empty house with no adult to monitor their behavior. There is, then, increased opportunity to engage in delinquent behaviors without being observed or caught by the working mother.

Further, many single mothers are struggling with the stress associated with poverty. Approximately 60 percent of all female-headed households have income below the poverty line. This figure varies by marital status of the mother. While 45 percent of children raised by divorced, single mothers live in poverty, 70 percent of children living with a never-married mother do so. In fact, evidence suggests that the effect of family economic pressure on adolescent delinquent behavior is indirect through its disruptive effect on parenting. In large measure, family financial hardship and associated stressful life changes increase an adolescent's probability of conduct problems to the extent that they have a corrosive effect on parental involvement (Brody and Flor, 1998; Conger et al., 1992; Simons et al., 1996).

One important way in which fathers can contribute to the well-being of their children is through economic support. For nonresidential fathers, this usually comes in the form of child support. In 1996, 58 percent of custodial parents were awarded child support. In 1997, only 40 percent of custodial parents received the full amount of child support owed. On average, custodial parents received less than 60 percent of the child support they had been awarded. One third of families received none of the awarded support (Grall, 2000).

The positive and significant relationship between father's payment of child support and child outcomes is well documented. Payment of child support has been shown to influence school success (Graham, Beller, and Hernandez, 1994; King 1994; Knox and Bane, 1994; McLanahan et al., 1994) and is associated with fewer behavior problems for children (Amato and Gilbreth, 1999; McLanahan et al., 1994). Of course, fathers are important in the lives of their children far more than the economic contribution they make. The next section focuses on father involvement and child outcomes.

Nonresidential Fathers

There is extensive evidence that fathers who do not live with their children have limited contact with those children. In a report based on the National Survey of Children, 23 percent of divorced fathers had no contact in the previous five years with their children aged 11 to 16 years and only 26 percent of fathers averaged visitation on a bimonthly basis (Furstenberg, Morgan, and Allison, 1987; Furstenberg and Nord, 1985). Never-married fathers had even less contact with their children.

Such men are sometimes labeled "absentee fathers," and it is often the case that their involvement with children declines after the romantic relationship with the mother ends. Another factor in the reduced contact between nonresidential fathers and their children can be attributed to the gatekeeping role that a mother may play in facilitating or impeding contact between her children and their nonresidential father (Marsiglio et al., 2000). For example, if a father has plans to see his children on Saturday, their mother can ensure that the children are available at the agreed-on time by being at home and having the children ready when the father arrives. If she does not wish to facilitate the visits, she could instead not be at the designated meeting place on time, or she could even make other plans for the children without informing their father. Whereas much attention has been focused on the degree to which nonresidential fathers live up to their responsibilities and stay involved in the lives of their children, it is only recently that researchers have begun to focus on the extent to which custodial mothers attempt to make access to the children easier or more difficult for fathers. It is possible that some of the decrease in postdivorce contact can be explained by the level of gatekeeping engaged in by mothers.

Although the importance of contact between children and their nonresidential fathers is generally taken for granted, research in this area has failed to demonstrate that frequency of visitation with fathers is a good predictor of children's adjustment or development. In a meta-analysis of 38 studies on this topic published during the 1990s, Marsiglio and colleagues (2000) report that, in general, there is not strong support for the belief that visitation with nonresident fathers benefits children. Both Furstenberg and colleagues (1987) and Seltzer (2000) report, however, that visitation is associated with regular payment of child support.

The fact that frequency of contact is unrelated to child adjustment does not mean that nonresidential fathers have little impact on their child's development. Rather than frequency of contact, the important factor appears to be the extent to which the fathers engage in authoritative parenting. Simons and his colleagues, for example, have reported that quality of nonresidential fathers' parenting (measured by assessing levels of emotional support, giving reasons for decisions, providing consistent discipline, and praising children's accomplishments) is negatively related to externalizing problems for adolescent girls and boys (Simons and Associates, 1996; Simons et al., 1999; Simons, Whitbeck, et al., 1994). A meta-analysis of studies by Amato and Gilbreth (1999) supports the notion that authoritative parenting by nonresidential fathers is associated with positive child outcomes.

In general, these studies suggest that the key to involvement by nonresidential fathers is how they interact with their children, rather than simply the amount of time they spend with them. Too often, the time that nonresidential fathers and their children spend together is recreational, rather than instrumental. Nonresidential fathers are more likely to take their child on an outing (e.g., go to a movie or the zoo) than to spend time helping the child with his homework. It is certainly understandable that nonresidential fathers would want to spend their precious hours with their child doing something the child enjoys rather than playing the role of taskmaster. By setting the interactions up in this fashion, the child is more likely to view time spent with Dad as fun and to look forward to his visits. Unfortunately, such interaction appears to have little impact on the child's adjustment.

Compared with fathers in two-parent households, nonresidential fathers provide less assistance with homework, are less likely to set and enforce rules, and provide less monitoring and supervision of their children (Furstenberg and Cherlin, 1991). If nonresidential fathers plan a day at the amusement park every time they have an opportunity to spend time with their child and rarely engage in behaviors consistent with authoritative parenting, the contact is apt to have little impact on the child's development, even if it does involve having fun together. Nonresidential fathers must play the role of parent, and not simply that of entertainer or friend, if they are to influence their child's adjustment. Research shows that when nonresidential fathers engage in authoritative parenting, their children are less likely to engage in delinquent behavior (Simons, Whitbeck, and Beaman, 1994; Simons et al., 1999).

The preceding sections of this chapter have addressed challenges faced by single-parent families. As mentioned above, children in two-parent households are more likely to have fathers who engage in authoritative parenting and also have lower rates of conduct problems. This raises the issue of whether any available adult can successfully fulfill the role of secondary caregiver. Next we will turn to family forms, other than the intact nuclear model, that involve two adults in a household both engaging in the caregiver role.

Blended or Stepfamilies

Despite the high rates of divorce, remarriages became increasingly frequent during the last half of the twentieth century. Seventy-five percent of divorced women remarry within 10 years, and 83 percent do so within 15 years (Bramlett and Mosher, 2001). In 1988, 46 percent of all marriages involved a remarriage for at least one partner. A slight decline in the remarriage rate in recent years may be due to the rise of cohabitation as an alternative to marriage.

One of the significant consequences of this high rate of remarriage is that more Americans are parenting other people's children and more children are living with people other than their biological parents (Lamanna and Riedmann, 2003). When children become part of a blended family, they reside with one biological parent and one stepparent. Often, there is the addition of new stepsiblings (offspring of the new stepparent from a previous relationship) or half-siblings (offspring between the biological parent and the stepparent). The most common form of stepfamily involves a child (or children) living with a biological mother and a stepfather. In 1990, this family form accounted for about 15 percent of all U.S. households (13 percent of white families, 31 percent of black families, and 15 percent of Hispanic families). Approximately 1 percent of households are composed of children living with their biological father and a stepmother. This figure does not vary significantly by race or ethnicity (U.S. Census Bureau, 2000b).

Difficulties associated with being part of a blended or stepfamily may be rooted in what Cherlin (1978) labeled an "incomplete institution." Despite the fact that remarriage has become a common occurrence in our culture, it is, in many ways, a normless state. This means that there is no cultural script, or socially prescribed and understood guidelines, for relating to each other or for defining responsibilities and obligations (Ganong and Coleman, 2000; Grizzle, 1998). For example, there is no rule to guide what a child is to call a stepparent. "Mom" or "Dad" may seem inappropriate if the biological parent is still living or if the child doesn't have a particularly close relationship with the new stepparent. Additionally, there is role ambiguity regarding stepparent involvement in parenting and disciplining the children of one's new spouse. For example, it may be the case that a new stepfather has expectations about the behavior of his new wife's children that are not consistent with the way Mom has been parenting during the preceding few years. An attempt to introduce his new rules may be met with resistance or hostility by both the children and their mother. Such situations can lead to stress in the new marriage as well as in the parent-child relationship.

Challenges in stepfamilies can arise from a variety of sources. For example, children may have a difficult time adjusting to a new living situation in which the stepparent is now living in the home; conflict may arise between new stepsiblings who must suddenly share space, possessions, or attention from a parent (Bernstein, 1997); family rule differences may produce tension; or biological parents may feel divided loyalties between their child and their new spouse (Bray, 1999). For these reasons and others, it is not surprising that remarriages are less stable than first marriages, and the presence of children from previous relationships makes them even less so.

Another consequence of the normative ambiguity associated with stepfamilies is the lack of legitimacy a stepparent may have in the eyes of the new stepchildren. Resistance by children to the influence of a new stepparent is influenced by the age of the child at the time of the marriage (Hetherington, 1993, 1999), with older children being more resistant. There is evidence that both stepmothers and stepfathers play their roles with more distance, relate to their stepchildren more as friends than parents, and engage in less monitoring than biological parents (Coleman and Ganong, 1997; Coleman, Ganong, and Fine, 2000). Clinicians have suggested that this detached style of parenting may be necessary in order to improve relations with new stepchildren, and research has demonstrated that stepfathers with such a parenting style do have better relationships with their stepchildren (Hetherington, 1987). Further, stepchildren have less positive views of stepfathers who attempt to carry out the role of disciplinarian (Claxton-Oldfield, 1992).

Because the parenting role of stepparents is often constrained in the ways described above, the benefit of having two adults to share the responsibilities of parenting may not be fully realized. It may be the case that the two newly married adults do not agree on parenting strategies. Another possibility is that the noncustodial parent is still active in the life of his children, and this may cause stepparents to have feelings of divided loyalty. Finally, because children in single-parent homes often have a more egalitarian relationship with their parent than do children in a two-parent home, the introduction of the new stepparent may mean a role change for the child. It may not be a change that the child is ready or willing to make (Lamanna and Riedmann, 2003). Because of obstacles such as these, a stepparent may adopt the previously described detached parenting style. This leaves the biological parent in the position of performing most of the behaviors associated with authoritative parenting without much backup from the stepparent. They are, in many ways, operating with fewer parenting resources than single parents, and they have the additional strains described above.

In light of these challenges, it is not surprising that children in stepfamilies do less well in school (Jeynes, 2000; Zill, 1994), experience more family conflict (Hanson, McLanahan, and Thomson, 1996), are less well adjusted (Coleman and Ganong, 1997; Coleman, Ganong, and Fine, 2000), and have more behavior problems (Hetherington, 1993, 1999) than children in first-marriage families. McLanahan and Sandefur (1994) note that children in stepfamilies do no better than children of mothers who never marry. Like children living in single-parent households, children in stepfamilies are two to three times as likely to manifest conduct problems and delinquency as are to those living in a nuclear intact family.

Again, the degree to which a new stepparent is able to engage in authoritative parenting influences the extent to which children in blended families experience increased adjustment problems (Amato, 1994; Arendell, 1997). We have noted, however, that there is evidence indicating this is easier said than done. Research shows that children are more receptive to discipline administered by a stepparent after a period of family adjustment. Also, clear communication between the biological parent, the children, and the new stepparent regarding role expectations for the stepparent is likely to lead to more positive feelings for all involved (Coleman and Ganong, 1997; Coleman, Ganong, and Fine, 2000), and a positive relationship with a stepparent is associated with better child outcomes (White and Gilbreth, 2001). Until this is established and the stepparent is able to carry out the parenting role in a way that carries legitimacy with the children, it may be enough that the new stepparent serve as a backup for the biological parent by reinforcing that parent's decisions.

Multigenerational and Extended-Kin Households

A study design that compares intact nuclear families with all other family forms ignores the importance of other caregivers in children's lives. Past research has rarely investigated the nature and structure of families containing a nonparental secondary caregiver. For instance, does it matter what the relationship of the second caregiver is to the child or children? How do families with two biologically related caregivers (such as a parent and grandparent) compare with stepfamilies? What about families with other nonfamilial caregivers (such as friends or romantic partners)? Present research has largely ignored these issues.

The living arrangements of single mothers are diverse and variable, with a majority living with a parent at some point in their children's upbringing (Deleire and Kalil, 2002). More than one in 10 white children live in an extended family, and one in five black children live in this type of family (Glick et al., 1997). Multigenerational households headed by grandparents are more common in African American families (9.2 percent) than in white families (2.3 percent) (Smith and Drew, 2002). One in 10 grandparents will raise a grandchild for at least six months (Roe and Minkler, 1998). Goodman and Silverstein (2001) found that the majority of single parents living with grandparents are doing so for financial help needed due to divorce or adolescent parenthood. The most common types of multigenerational families are those in which mother and children reside with at least one grandparent and those in which grandparents care for grandchildren without any parent in the home. Small numbers of families include both parents, children, and grandparents or father, children, and grandparent(s) (Roe and Minkler, 1998; Targ and Brintnall-Peterson, 2001).

Only a small number of studies have examined outcomes for children in multigenerational families. What research has been completed suggests that children residing in multigenerational or extended biological families have better outcomes than those raised in single-parent families. For instance, Deleire and Kalil (2002) found children from multigenerational families no more likely to drink or smoke and just as likely to go to college as children from intact nuclear families. Black children in multigenerational families have been shown to have better conduct at school than black children in single-mother homes (Entwisle and Alexander, 1996). Adolescent children of single mothers living with the mother and other relatives exhibit fewer behavior problems than children of single mothers living alone. Single mothers living in extended families benefit as well, reporting less depression and better physical health than mothers living alone (Amato, 2000).

Clearly, there are advantages for children and mothers living in multigenerational families compared with single-parent homes. This may be because residing with kin provides benefits in the form of enhanced financial stability (Furstenberg, Morgan, and Allison, 1987), emotional support and socialization, and monitoring and supervision. Additionally, the presence of a second caregiver may reinforce the authority and influence of the mother (Dornbusch et al., 1985; Thomson, McLanahan, and Curtin, 1992). However, the relationship of the secondary caregiver to the child appears to be consequential. As previously noted, children in intact nuclear families have the most positive outcomes, children in single-mother families or stepfamilies have the poorest, and children in extended-kin households fall somewhere in between.

Conclusion

The research findings discussed above indicate that children of divorced- or single-parent households are two to three times more likely than those from intact nuclear families to display conduct problems and delinquency. Indeed, although gender is considered a powerful predictor of a child's risk for conduct problems (Gottfredson and Hirschi, 1990), the effects of family structure are as large or larger than that of gender (Simons and Associates, 1996). Clearly, family structure is an important risk factor for child adjustment problems. Further, research provides strong support for the idea that disruptions in quality of parenting largely mediate the association between family structure and child behavior problems. The stresses associated with single-parent families and stepfamilies often result in less parental monitoring and control than is evident in intact two-parent families.

There has been a substantial increase in many types of adolescent problems since the mid-1960s. The rates of adolescent crime, substance abuse, suicide, school dropout, and teen pregnancy, for example, all have shown dramatic growth during this period. The prevalence of several of these behaviors has continued to climb during the 1990s, especially among African American youth. Between 1985 and 1992, the homicide rate for young, white males went up approximately 50 percent; for young, African American males, it tripled (Wilson, 1995). Some have noted that the rise in child and adolescent problems parallels the increase in divorce, cohabitation, and births to never-married mothers that has occurred in recent decades. Indeed, several studies have reported strong associations between the proportion of female-headed households and adolescent and adult antisocial behavior (Messner and Tardiff, 1986; Roncek, 1981; Sampson, 1985, 1986; Schuerman and Korbin, 1986; Smith and Jarjourna, 1988). In most of these studies, the effects of family structure are as strong or stronger than those of variables such as poverty or race. Sampson (1985, 1986), for example, found that rates of violent victimization are two to three times higher among residents of neighborhoods with high levels of family disruption.

Although family structure is a risk factor for child behavior problems, it is also true that there is great variability in outcomes among children from single-parent and stepfamilies. The evidence indicates that the majority of these children do not manifest behavior problems. Indeed, a teacher or counselor would be ill advised to expect that a child is going to develop emotional or behavioral difficulties simply because of his or her family structure. Most children from a single-parent family or stepfamily do not develop conduct problems, hence such an expectation would turn out to be erroneous more often than not. Accurate prediction of which individuals are most vulnerable to a particular risk factor usually requires knowledge of the mechanisms by which the condition produces its deleterious effects. Thus, if we are to identify children from single-parent and stepparent families most at risk for adjustment problems, we need information regarding the manner in which family structure increases a child's odds for developmental difficulties. Our review indicates that, in large measure, family stress and disrupted parenting explains which children are likely to manifest conduct problems.

Finally, given that diverse family forms are an inevitable feature of American society, there is some controversy associated with doing research on the consequences of variations in family structure. Findings of such research are often used by political groups opposed to diversity and gender equality. Also, most parents who divorce undoubtedly do so as a last resort, and the welfare of their children is of great concern to them. Some have suggested that to do research on these families highlighting their problems may seem cruel in light of the other difficulties they face. Although these issues are important, social science is concerned with describing and explaining empirical reality. Hence, it is essential that we, as scientists, do our best to avoid denying or distorting facts because of personal values or ideology. Such a commitment is not only in the best interest of science; it is also the approach that is most likely to benefit society. Research has clearly established a link between family structure and an elevated risk for developmental problems. This effect is modest, however, and appears to be largely explained by the fact that the stresses associated with single-parent, divorced-parent, and stepfamilies tend to compromise the quality of parenting that children receive. ✦

Chapter Six

The Effects of Parental Work and Neighborhood Conditions on Family Processes

Theory and research presented in the previous chapters suggest that the family is the primary agent of socialization for children. We reviewed evidence indicating that child misconduct and adolescent delinquency are less likely to occur when parents display a parenting style that combines warmth and support with monitoring and consistent discipline, whereas parenting styles that are permissive, rejecting, harsh, or inconsistent increase a youth's risk for antisocial behavior. We also discussed various factors internal to the family that influence quality of parenting. We noted, for example, that children's temperament, the number of parents or caregivers in the home, and changes in family structure such as divorce or remarriage often impact parental behavior. The present chapter expands our focus by considering factors external to the family that influence the extent to which parents are able to effectively socialize their children.

Although the family may be the primary agent of socialization for children, it does not exist in a vacuum. Families are embedded in a broader social environment that can operate to either enhance or undermine parental effectiveness. A family's ability to effectively perform its socialization function is strongly affected by the social context in which it is embedded. This context consists of social institutions such as the economy, the polity, the church, and the neighborhood or community (Bronfrenbrenner, 1979). The values, policies, and integrity of these social systems necessarily influence the functioning and efficacy of families.

A consideration of the manner in which all these contexts affect family processes is beyond the scope of this book. Hence, in the interest of parsimony, we have chosen to limit our focus to only two of them—the economy and the neighborhood. Past research has linked both of these factors to the parenting practices discussed in the earlier chapters.

We will describe two avenues whereby the economy influences parental behavior. First, we will review research showing that economic hardship disrupts parenting and increases the chances of delinquent behavior. Second, we will discuss the manner in which the type of paid work that parents perform can influence their approach to parenting. Building on this idea, Colvin and Pauly (1983; Colvin, 2000) formulated an "integrated structural Marxist theory" of delinquency, and John Hagan (1989; Hagan, Gillis, and Simpson, 1987) developed a power control theory to explain gender differences in adolescent behavior problems. We will briefly present both of these theoretical perspectives.

The remainder of the chapter is concerned with the effect of community factors on families and children. First, we will present evidence suggesting that the consequences of parental discipline may vary by neighborhood context. Second, research will be presented regarding the importance of "collective socialization," or the manner in which the adults residing in a community often deter misbehavior among children who are not their own (Sampson, 1992). Finally, we review recent studies that indicate that contact with the police or juvenile court has a disruptive effect on families and often leads to an escalation in delinquent behavior.

Economic Hardship and Parenting

During the past 20 years, the U.S. economy has been plagued by a major contradiction (White and Rogers, 2000). On the one hand, compared with the economies of other advanced industrialized countries, the U.S. economy has been robust with steady growth, minimal inflation, and low unemployment. Below this surface of prosperity and stability, however, a large proportion of the population has experienced increasing economic hardship. To a large degree, their plight has been the result of structural transformations in the U.S. economy (Wilson, 1996).

In the past, parents of low education were able to support their families working at well-paying factory jobs. Often these jobs were union positions that provided security and opportunities for advancement. Unfortunately, there has been a steady erosion of these positions in recent decades as manufacturers have downsized, automated, or relocated their plants overseas in an attempt to reduce labor costs (Devine and Wright, 1993; Wilson, 1996). The economy has continued to generate jobs at a high rate, but most of the growth has been in service-sector positions such as sales clerk, cashier, fast-food worker, or nursing-home attendant. These jobs tend to pay minimum wage and usually do not provide benefits such as health insurance or sick leave. Minimum wage in the United States has failed to keep pace with inflation and has been set at a little more than $5 an hour for the past several years. A full-time worker employed at minimum wage has an annual income of roughly $11,000, which is well below the poverty line of $17,000 for a family of four. Yet 40 percent of persons making minimum wage are the sole breadwinners for their families (Seccombe, 2000).

In addition to service-sector jobs, there has been a dramatic increase in the number of part-time, subcontracted, and temporary positions (Hipple, 1998; Presser and Cox, 1997). In most cases, these jobs are characterized by irregular work schedules, high rates of layoff, and low pay with no benefits. Part-time workers made up approximately 25 percent of the labor force in 1988 but nearly one half by 2000 (Castro, 1993; Morrow, 1993). Thus, the problem faced by most poor parents is not one of finding work. Low-paying jobs are readily available. The challenge, given their limited education, is finding a position that pays enough to support a family (Seccombe, 2000).

These structural changes in the economy have produced a growing inequality in income between those at the top and those at the bottom of the income distribution. Those in the upper quintile have continued to experience gains, whereas those in the lower quintile have experienced losses (White and Rogers, 2000). As a consequence, approximately 19 percent of children under the age of 18 reside in a family that lives in poverty (White and Rogers, 2000).

The everyday lives of poor families tend to be characterized by high levels of financial strain, worry, and hardship. One study found that, during a one-year period, more than half of poor families experienced eviction, housing disrepair, disconnected utilities, or lack of a refrigerator, stove, or telephone (Federman et al., 1996). Poverty tends to engulf a person's total existence. It is stressful and humiliating, and requires that one struggle to achieve some sense of respectability in a society that emphasizes the importance of material success and denigrates the poor as lazy or incompetent.

Unfortunately, there is strong evidence that children who grow up in poor families are at increased risk for a variety of negative developmental outcomes, including conduct problems and delinquency (Chafel, 1993; Duncan, Brooks-Gunn, and Klebanov, 1994; Duncan et al., 1998; Lichter, 1997; Seccombe, 2000). Past research indicates that poverty tends to have a disruptive effect on quality of parenting, and this is one of the major reasons that poverty increases a child's chances of deviant behavior (McLoyd, 1998; Seccombe, 2000; White and Rogers, 2000). Several studies have reported that economically stressed parents provide less support and monitoring and higher levels of inconsistent and harsh discipline than parents who are more affluent (Conger et al., 1992; Conger et al., 2002; Elder, 1974; McLeod and Shanahan, 1993; McLoyd, 1990; Simons et al., 1992; Simons, Lorenz, et al., 1993; Simons, Whitbeck, Conger, and Wu, 1994). There appear to be several reasons why financial hardship has a deleterious effect on parental behavior.

At least in part, the less effective parenting demonstrated by poor parents is a consequence of their being preoccupied and consumed with the challenges and stresses of everyday life. They face the daily strain of not being able to pay bills or purchase basic necessities, and with making financial adjustments such as borrowing money, taking an additional job, or terminating medical insurance. Given these concerns, they are often minimally involved in the parenting role until serious or flagrant child misbehavior jars them into action. Such transgressions are likely to demand a harsh response, so that the pattern of parenting displayed is inconsistent and explosive (Conger et al., 1992; Elder and Caspi, 1988; Simons et al., 1994).

The psychological distress associated with economic hardship also increases the chances of ineffective parenting. Evidence from both laboratory and survey research indicates that aversive events promote feelings of hostility, negative thoughts and memories, psychomotor tension, and a tendency to behave aggressively toward others (Berkowitz, 1989). These findings suggest several avenues whereby economic hardship is likely to influence parental behavior. First, economic strain is apt to foster an irritable, aggressive psychological state that operates to decrease warmth and increase hostility toward others, including one's children (Conger et al., 1992; Conger et al., 2002; Elder and Caspi, 1988; Simons et al., 1992; 1994). Second, this irritability and explosiveness increases the chances of marital conflict. Marital conflict is psychologically draining, exacerbates hostility, and reduces the amount of psychological energy available for parenting (Conger et al., 1992; Conger et al., 2002).

Finally, depressed and irritable persons tend to engage in negatively biased scanning of their environment (Abramson, Seligman, and Teasdale, 1978; Berkowitz, 1989). They tend to be glass-half-empty people who focus on what is wrong rather than what is right. They are inclined to notice failures more than successes. Thus, depressed parents are more likely than nondepressed parents to be dissatisfied with social relationships, including the relationships with their children. Several studies have reported, for example, that depressed mothers tend to perceive their children as difficult (Brody and Forehand, 1988; Simons, Beaman, et al., 1993a). Parents are more likely to engage in harsh or punitive parenting when they perceive their child as difficult.

Thus, past research suggests several ways in which economic strain disrupts the quality of parenting. The preoccupation and psychological distress that accompanies financial hardship tends to decrease warmth and monitoring while increasing inconsistency and hostility. As we saw in previous chapters, this approach to parenting places a child at risk for conduct problems and delinquent behavior. For several years, Rand Conger and his colleagues have been conducting studies of the negative effects that economic hardship has on families. Many of the research findings presented in this section were produced by Conger and his associates. Conger and colleagues have formulated the *family stress model* to summarize research findings regarding the links that exist between economic strain, family processes, and child outcomes (Conger et al., 1992; Conger et al., 2002; Conger, Ge, et al., 1994). The family stress model posits that economic strain encourages parental hostility, irritability, and depression. This emotional state disrupts parenting both directly and indirectly by fostering marital conflict. As the family stress model makes clear, parenting does not take place in a vacuum. Family interaction is influenced by external factors and events. One powerful, outside force is economic pressure. Family conflict and hostility tend to occur when families are struggling with financial problems. Unfortunately, this style of family interaction increases the chances that children will engage in deviant behavior.

Given extant patterns of income inequality in the United States, families of color are more likely to experience this family stress process than white families. The poverty rate for white families during the late 1990s was 8.4 percent, for example, whereas the percentage of African American and Hispanic families living in poverty during this period was 24 percent and 25 percent, respectively (U.S. Census Bureau, 1999). Past research has shown that nonwhite children have a higher rate of involvement in delinquent behavior than have white children (Elliott, Huizinga, and Menard, 1989). Economic hardship and disrupted parenting, at least in part, probably explain this ethnic difference.

Linking Parental Employment to Family Processes

Over a period of several years, Melvin Kohn and his colleagues (Kohn, 1977; Kohn and Schooler, 1982, 1983; Kohn et al., 1986) have documented a relationship between parents' working conditions and the approach they adopt in socializing their children. Their research suggests that parents strive to foster styles of behavior in their children that are conducive to success in their own paid work. Blue-collar occupations usually entail the manipulation of things, routinized activities, and close supervision. Thus, parents with these types of jobs will tend to use child-rearing strategies stressing obedience and conformity to externally imposed standards. White-collar occupations, on the other hand, involve manipulation of complex tasks and ideas, usually with little direct supervision. These jobs permit a good deal of autonomy, flexibility, and self-direction in the performance of work responsibilities. Parents with these more complex white-collar jobs will adopt child-rearing strategies that emphasize self-direction and internalization of values and norms. In recent years, two theories of delinquent behavior have been developed using these findings: Colvin and Pauly's integrated structural-Marxist theory of adolescent deviance and Hagan's power-control theory of gender differences in rates of delinquent behavior.

Colvin and Pauly (1983; Colvin, 2000) have developed a class-based explanation for delinquency. Their theory combines a Marxist emphasis on working conditions in a capitalist economy with elements of social control theory. Hence, they label their theoretical perspective an *integrated structural-Marxist theory of delinquency*. The theory asserts that workplace experiences are class differentiated and exert important influences on family interaction. Building on the work of Kohn and his colleagues, they contend that degree of workplace supervision is the key to understanding how parents choose to control and discipline their children in the home. Lower-class parents who are subject to close supervision and control at work will adopt a harsh, coercive approach to parenting. Children subject to this parenting style tend to develop weak social bonds to their parents. These weak bonds reduce parental influence and increase the chances of child conduct problems. Further, according to the theory, the child's experiences at home tend to be reinforced at school. Lacking a strong bond to parents, the initial authority figures in a person's life, the child also resists school authorities. Often these lower-class children are placed in "non-college" tracks that emphasize obedience over initiative and self-direction. Thus, the alienation that the child experiences at home is buttressed by events at school. In response, the child is apt to affiliate with similarly alienated youths and engage in delinquent and criminal behavior.

Colvin and Pauly present an intriguing explanation for the fact that chronic delinquency and street crime tend to be more common among lower-class youths. Essentially, their argument is that the working conditions experienced by lower-class parents foster a harsh, coercive approach to parenting. This parenting style, in turn, triggers a sequence of weak social bonds and oppositional behavior that leads to involvement in serious crime. Although Colvin and Pauly's ideas seem compelling, empirical research has failed to corroborate the main tenets of their perspective.

Studies that have investigated the causal sequence suggested by Colvin and Pauly generally find that coercive parenting is related to weak social bonds and delinquency (Messner and Krohn, 1990;

Simpson and Ellis, 1994). This relationship, however, would also be predicted by both control and social learning theories (see Chapters Two and Three). The more critical predictions are that parents' work conditions are related to adolescent delinquency, and that coercive parenting and weak social bonds mediate this association. Past research has failed to support these hypotheses. Adolescent delinquency shows no significant association with assessments of parental work in terms of either complexity (Parcel and Menaghan, 1994) or authority and skills (Messner and Krohn, 1990; Simpson and Ellis, 1994). Further, parents' working conditions are not related to the use of coercive parenting (Messner and Krohn, 1990; Paternoster and Tittle, 1990). Finally, Paternoster and Tittle (1990) found that coercive parenting strategies, such as the use of corporal punishment, did not predict weak social bonds to parents. (The latter finding is consistent with research discussed in Chapter Three showing that corporal punishment does not necessarily lead to defiance and other negative results). Together, these various studies cast doubt on the validity of Colvin and Pauly's class-based theory of delinquency.

It should be noted, however, that some studies have found that the negative relationship between social class and serious delinquency is mediated by quality of parenting. Larzelere and Patterson (1990), for example, found that weak monitoring and coercive discipline accounted for class differences in early antisocial behavior. Socioeconomic status measured in the fourth grade was a strong predictor of parental disciplinary style in the sixth grade, which, in turn, was a powerful predictor of delinquency assessed in the seventh grade. Similarly, Simons, Wu, and colleagues (1994) found that quality of parenting mediated the association between family socioeconomic status and early adolescent conduct problems. The disconfirming results obtained in tests of Colvin and Pauly's theory suggest, however, that it is not parental work conditions that explain these findings regarding an association between social class, parenting, and delinquency. One hypothesis is that they are a reflection of the processes discussed in the previous section regarding economic hardship. Family social class might be considered a crude surrogate measure of family economic pressure. Thus, the finding that parental behavior mediates the association between social class and delinquency may simply be further corroboration of the well-established finding that economic hardship disrupts parenting, which in turn places a child at risk for conduct problems.

John Hagan's *power-control theory* represents another theoretical perspective that builds on the idea that work conditions influence family relationships and risk for delinquency. Hagan is concerned with explaining gender differences in delinquency. His theory assumes that boys generally display higher rates of delinquency than girls, but that this difference will expand or contract depending on family structure variations in parental control over boys relative to girls.

Past research has shown that gender differences in antisocial behavior and crime appear in all societies. Males are always and everywhere more likely than females to engage in delinquent and criminal behavior (Gottfredson and Hirschi, 1990; Hirschi and Gottfredson, 1983). And gender differences in behavior analogous to crime (i.e., risky and dangerous behaviors; see Chapter Two) are similar to those found for crime. These differences emerge early in life and are relatively stable across the life course. It is interesting to note, however, that whereas males show much higher rates of antisocial behavior than females, females demonstrate much higher rates of depression than males. Indeed, following puberty, girls are three times more likely than boys to experience depression (Ebata, Petersen, and Conger, 1990; Graham, 1979). Thus, it appears that adolescent females tend to respond to stress with internalization or emotional problems, whereas males tend to react with externalization or conduct problems (Aneshensel, Rutter, and Lachenbruch, 1991). When boys do exhibit symptoms of depression, they are often preceded by hostile antisocial behavior and are not usually associated with the self-castigation that accompanies the dysphoria of girls (Block and Gjerde, 1990). These gender differences in internalizing and externalizing problems have led many developmental psychologists to assume that biological factors (e.g., temperament, hormones) account for much of the gender difference in antisocial behavior and crime.

Sociological studies have shown, however, that the parental behaviors that have been linked to male antisocial behavior are also associated with antisocial behavior displayed by females. Parenting variables such as warmth, supervision, and consistent discipline predict delinquent behavior for both genders (Akers and Sellers, 2004; Gottfredson and Hirschi, 1990). Further, there is evidence that parents exercise more control over daughters than sons (Felson and Gottfredson, 1984). These findings suggest that gender differences in delinquency may be, at least in part, a function of disparities in the way boys and girls are parented. Hagan's power-control theory builds on this idea.

Hagan posits that work conditions affect parental behavior, which in turn influences gender differences in delinquency. Husbands wield more power than wives in patriarchal families. Building on the work of Kohn, Hagan argues that families are likely to have a patriarchal structure when the husband is employed but the wife does not work outside the home. This is particularly true when the husband's job involves supervising and directing other workers. In contrast, Hagan contends that the family will have a more egalitarian structure when husbands and wives work at similar positions, especially if both are managers of other employees.

Hagan goes on to argue that parents try to reproduce themselves when parenting their children. Hence, child-rearing tends to be significantly different in patriarchal versus egalitarian families. In patriarchal families, daughters are carefully supervised and develop close relationships with their mothers. They are reared in a "cult of domesticity" in which the goal is to prepare them to be housewives like their mothers. Sons, on the other hand, are reared to have traits seen as necessary in the demanding world of work. They are encouraged to be tough, risk taking, and independent.

In contrast to patriarchal families, Hagan suggests that egalitarian families strive to prepare both daughters and sons for participation in the labor force. Parents encourage their daughters as well as their sons to be assertive, adventurous, and independent. Boys and girls are supervised in a similar fashion and receive the same freedoms in such families.

According to Hagan, these dissimilarities in the way sons and daughters are parented in these two types of families account for variations in gender differences in delinquency. In patriarchal families, boys are much more likely to be delinquent than girls as they are encouraged to take risks and be independent, while their sisters are tightly controlled and taught to be feminine. Boys and girls in egalitarian families, however, are raised in a similar fashion and are therefore likely to manifest more comparable levels of conduct problems. In egalitarian families, girls become more like boys with regard to their participation in adventurous, risk-taking activities such as delinquency.

Studies designed to test power-control theory have produced mixed results. Hagan's Canadian data tend to support the theory (Hagan, Gillis, and Simpson, 1985, 1987, 1990, 1993; Hagan and Kay, 1990; McCarthy, Hagan, and Woodward, 1999). Several other researchers, however, have reported disconfirming findings. Most damaging is their failure to find a relationship between family structure and gender differences in either parental control or adolescent delinquency. These studies find that gender differences in delinquency are about the same for patriarchal and egalitarian families (Jensen and Thompson, 1990; Morash and Chesney-Lind, 1991; Singer and Levine, 1988). It may be that variability in the measurement of patriarchal and egalitarian family structures explains why some studies have failed to replicate Hagan's findings (Akers and Sellers, 2004). Some studies, for example, use social class or indirect assessments of occupational types rather than actual measures of the occupational authority of husbands relative to that of wives. Nevertheless, most studies that use measures comparable to those employed by Hagan have also failed to identify family structure differences in delinquency. Although it is too early to pass a verdict on the validity of power-control theory, the findings to date do not appear very promising.

Community Differences in the Consequences of Parental Control

As noted in the previous chapters, past research has established that parents significantly reduce their child's chances of involvement in antisocial behavior to the extent that they monitor their child's behavior and engage in consistent discipline (Loeber and Stouthamer-Loeber, 1986; Patterson, Reid, and Dishion, 1992; Simons, Johnson, et al., 1998). We also saw that corporal punishment is often not a very effective disciplinary strategy beyond the preschool years. Although these generalizations are based on an impressive body of literature, a few recent studies have reported that the impact of various parenting practices may vary by neighborhood context. This research indicates that the effect of parental monitoring and discipline, as well as the consequences of corporal punishment, depend on the prevalence of crime and deviance within the community.

Using a sample of African American families living in Georgia and Iowa, Simons, Lin, et al. (2002) investigated community variations in the impact of parental control. Parental control involved conscientious monitoring combined with consistent discipline. They tested two competing hypotheses regarding the manner in which high levels of community deviance affect the association between parental control and delinquency. The first hypothesis was that the effect of such parenting is greater in communities where deviant behavior is widely prevalent. Children who reside in conventional neighborhoods may be at low risk for conduct problems regardless of how they are parented. In contrast, parental control may be necessary if a child is to eschew delinquent behavior while living in an area where antisocial behavior is often modeled and encouraged. Simons and colleagues labeled this argument the *parental buffering hypothesis* (Simons, Lin, et al., 2002). It suggests that parental control becomes more critical when children live in a high-risk neighborhood, as such control reduces the chances that they will be influenced by environmental pressures to engage in antisocial behavior. If this is true, the association between parental control and child conduct problems should be stronger in high-crime neighborhoods than in more conventional areas.

It is also possible that the converse is true. It may be that parental control deters a child from engaging in delinquent behavior so long as antisocial influences in the broader community are modest. These parenting practices may become less effective, however, when crime and other forms of deviant behavior are widely prevalent within the community. In such neighborhoods, delinquent opportunities and pressures from deviant peers may overwhelm a parent's ability to prevent his or her child from participating in antisocial behavior. Simons, Lin, and colleagues (2002) labeled this point of view the *evaporation hypothesis*. It suggests that the deterrent effect of caretaker control decreases (i.e., evaporates) as the prevalence of antisocial behavior within the community increases.

In their analyses, Simons, Lin, and colleagues (2002) found support for the evaporation hypothesis over the parental buffering hypothesis. Their analyses indicated that the deterrent effect of caretaker control decreases as the prevalence of crime and delinquency within the community increases. Caretaker control was negatively related to conduct problems regardless of the prevalence of community deviance, but the effect was significantly stronger in those areas where the prevalence of deviance was low. This finding suggests that parental supervisory and disciplinary strategies that are effective in conventional neighborhoods may not be sufficient to prevent child antisocial behavior in high-risk areas.

Past research has reported that parents in high-crime neighborhoods often confine young children to the household (Burton, 1991; Reese et al., 1995), restrict adolescents' out-of-home activities (Clark, 1983; Furstenberg et al., 1998), chaperone children and adolescents' daily rounds in the neighborhood (Cook and Fine, 1995; Puntenney, 1997; Volk, 1994), and, in some instances, send adolescents to live in safer communities (Davidson, 1996), as was the case for Will Smith's character in the television program *Fresh Prince of Bel Air.* These more extreme approaches to monitoring and discipline may be necessary if caretakers living in high-crime areas are to protect their children from destructive neighborhood influences (Burton and Jarrett, 2000). This view is supported by previous research showing that parental restrictive control is associated with positive cognitive and achievement outcomes in high-risk neighborhoods, whereas this is not the case in safe areas (Baldwin, Baldwin, and Cole, 1990; Gonzales et al., 1996). Research findings regarding the effects of corporal punishment are also consistent with this idea.

Studies using school-age European American children usually find a positive association between corporal punishment and conduct problems (Cohen and Brooks, 1994; Dodge, Bates, and Pettit, 1990; Dodge et al., 1995; Goodman et al., 1998; Simons et al., 2000; Straus, 1994; Straus, Sugarman, and Giles-Sims, 1997). These results suggest that physical discipline may promote, rather than deter, antisocial behavior. Studies of African American families, however, have reported a different pattern of results. These investigations have found either no relation or an inverse association between corporal punishment and child conduct problems (Baumrind, 1972; Deater-Deckard and Dodge, 1997; Deater-Deckard et al., 1996; Gunnoe and Mariner, 1997; Wasserman et al., 1996).

These differences in findings for African American families compared with European American families have led to the hypothesis that the meaning of corporal punishment varies by culture (Barbarin, 1993; Deater-Deckard et al., 1996; Deater-Deckard and

Dodge, 1997; Gutierrez and Sameroff, 1990; Kelley, Power, and Wimbush, 1992; Whaley, 2000). These cultural differences are seen as rooted in the community by the fact that African Americans are much more likely than European Americans to live in highly disadvantaged neighborhoods, where more extreme parenting measures are necessary to protect children from the dangers posed by their everyday environment.

As discussed in Chapter Four, disciplinary styles can be either parent or child centered (Baumrind, 1971; Maccoby and Martin, 1983). A parent-oriented approach considers obedience to parental authority as an end in itself, whereas a child-oriented perspective views discipline as a vehicle for helping children to become self-respecting, responsible adults. Although physical discipline tends to be correlated with a parent-oriented approach among European American parents, Kelley and colleagues (1992, 1993) found that corporal punishment was associated with both parent- and child-oriented parenting styles among African American parents.

Consistent with the finding that physical discipline is often associated with child-focused parenting in African American communities, several researchers have observed that corporal punishment in black communities includes concerns about survival (Baumrind, 1972; Belsky, 1993; Kelley, Power, and Wimbush, 1992; Mason et al., 1996; Whaley, 2000). In contrast to white communities, where parents can afford to be tolerant of mild levels of misbehavior, the consequences of disobedience are much more serious in many African American neighborhoods.

Kelley and colleagues (1992) argue that the residents of such communities often view corporal punishment as a means of teaching children respect for authority, in order to protect them from the adverse consequences of violating social norms. Noncompliance with parental directives can lead to physical harm, perhaps even death. Thus, from an African American cultural perspective, harsh disciplinary practices such as spanking are often considered necessary in order to protect children from the dangers posed by their social environment (Whaley, 2000). Both parents and children view physical discipline as a component of nurturant, involved parenting and consider it to be a legitimate form of discipline.

This neighborhood-based explanation for racial differences in the effect of corporal punishment suggests that the consequences of physical discipline vary by prevalence of crime and delinquency within the community. The residents of communities where social deviance is rare are apt to consider physical discipline to be an extreme and illegitimate approach to parenting. The children in such neighborhoods might be expected to respond to corporal punishment with anger, defiance, and oppositional behavior. The residents of high-crime areas, on the other hand, are more likely to view physical discipline as a necessary and legitimate component of child-oriented parenting. Corporal punishment would be expected to operate as a deterrent to conduct problems for children living in such neighborhoods.

Previous chapters reviewed a wealth of studies in order to draw inferences regarding the manner in which parental behavior influences child conduct problems and adolescent delinquency. Among our many observations, we concluded that parental monitoring and consistent discipline serve to deter antisocial behavior, whereas corporal punishment, at least when used with school-aged children, may amplify antisocial behavior. The findings reported in this section suggest a qualification of these two propositions. When families live in high-crime neighborhoods, typical approaches to monitoring and consistent discipline may not be sufficient to prevent children's involvement in delinquent behavior. Parents may need to adopt more stringent measures in order to exercise control and protect their children from dangerous situations and toxic peer influences. And, although we do not wish to promote this parenting strategy, there is evidence to suggest that corporal punishment may be among the disciplinary tactics that are effective in these high-risk areas.

Collective Socialization: Adults Influencing Other People's Children

Social disorganization theorists contend that collective socialization is a fundamental mechanism whereby community context influences child antisocial behavior (Bursik, 1988; Sampson, 1992, 1997). Traditionally, behavioral scientists have viewed child-rearing as an activity that takes place mainly within families as parents interact with their children. The previous chapters of this book have reviewed this literature. *Collective socialization,* on the other hand, refers to the influence that adults in a neighborhood have on young people who are not their children (Bursik, 1988; Coleman, 1990; Sampson, 1997).

Collective socialization occurs in communities where the residents know one another and are committed to enhancing and maintaining the welfare of their community. The parents in such communities know the other children and parents living in the area. They know their child's friends and they are acquainted with the parents of these friends. The parents also know their child's teachers. These acquaintanceships develop as parents interact with each other either while attending their child's school and social activities (e.g., plays, concerts, dance class, Little League baseball, organized soccer or basketball), or in the course of pursuing their own adult activities (e.g., aerobics class, church activities, social clubs). These interactions enable adults to observe the behavior of each other's children in different circumstances, to talk to each other about their children, and to establish common expectations and disciplinary strategies (Coleman, 1990; Bursik, 1988).

The children in such communities are aware that the adult residents of the area know and talk to each other. The children recognize that they must be very wary if they are tempted to engage in deviant behavior. An adult who witnesses a child engaging in misbehavior may issue a public reprimand (e.g., "Jack, I don't think your dad would want you doing that!"), call the child's parents, or mention the event the next time she sees the parents at a school, church, or social event. Or, if the adult does not know the parents very well, she may call the authorities, such as the school or the police. Thus, socially cohesive communities are able to engage in collective socialization whereby they assist each other in controlling and socializing the children living in the area.

Social disorganization theorists contend that collective socialization is rare when communities are extremely poor, there is much residential turnover, crime is high, or a large proportion of the population consists of single-parent families (Bursik, 1988; Sampson, 1997; Wilson, 1987, 1996). These demographic characteristics impede collective socialization because they decrease involvement in school, church, and community activities. Consequently, the residents don't know each other and have little investment or commitment to the community. As a result, adults are limited in their motivation and ability to help each other with the task of controlling and socializing the neighborhood children. The single mother living in an apartment complex, for example, may be concerned about the rough and intimidating behavior being displayed by a group of adolescent males in front of her building. Not only may she not know the names or parents of these young men, however; she may not even know if they live in her building. And she may fear retaliation against herself or her property if she reports them to the authorities. Under such circumstances, parents may focus on the behavior of their own children while adopting the attitude that other people's children are not their concern.

Aggregate level studies have provided support for these ideas. This research finds that level of community involvement and supervision of youth is negatively related to crime (Sampson and Groves, 1989; Simcha-Fagan and Schwartz, 1986; Taylor, Gottfredson, and Brower, 1984). And, recently, two multilevel analyses (Elliott et al., 1996; Sampson, Raudenbush, and Earls, 1997) have reported that informal social control by community residents is negatively related to delinquency after controlling for individual-level variables such as family socioeconomic status. All of these studies, however, have focused on large metropolitan areas.

One might expect collective socialization to be an important process in small towns and cities where residents often know each other well and are committed to their communities. Recent analyses using multilevel data from the Family and Community Health Study (FACHS) provide support for this view. FACHS is a longitudinal study of more than 850 African American families living in small towns in Georgia and Iowa. Using FACHS data, Brody and his colleagues (Brody et al., 2001; Brody et al., in press) have reported that adolescents are less likely to belong to a deviant peer group if they live in a community characterized by high levels of collective socialization. And, Simons, Simons, Brody, and Conger (2004) found that collective socialization is inversely related to adolescent delinquency. This association remained after controlling for individual-level variables such as quality of parenting, school commitment, and affiliation with deviant peers, as well as for community-level factors such as poverty and level of crime.

These findings, regarding the importance of collective socialization, provide support for the African aphorism, "It takes a village to raise a child." Traditionally, behavioral scientists have treated childrearing as an activity that takes place mainly within families as parents interact with their children. The results reviewed in this section suggest that successful child-rearing is a community enterprise. It appears that communities may significantly reduce their risk for child conduct problems to the extent that adults know the children, parents, teachers, and recreational leaders in their area, and are inclined to act on these social ties by reprimanding children who are misbehaving or by notifying the child's parents or the proper authorities. It seems likely that these social control processes, at least in part, explain the fact that delinquency tends to be much more common in large cities than in more rural areas.

The Consequences of Labeling: The Juvenile Justice System and Family Processes

Societies establish institutions and organizations to deal with individuals who engage in deviant behavior. These agencies of social control include the police, the court system, jails and detention centers, mental hospitals, and drug-treatment facilities. Although these organizations are designed to control and reduce crime and delinquency, *labeling theory* contends that they often serve to amplify an individual's involvement in deviant behavior. The early labeling theorists, such as Howard S. Becker and Erving Goffman, were committed to the symbolic interactionist perspective of Charles Horton Cooley (1902) and George Herbert Mead (1934). Symbolic interactionist theory asserts that a person's self-concept or identity develops through interaction with others. It reflects the feedback received from others about one's character, skills, and abilities. Labeling theory is concerned with the way stigmatizing labels acquired through contact with social control agencies (e.g., delinquent, addict, crazy) influence the way the deviant is perceived and treated by others.

According to the theory, conventional people tend to treat the stigmatized person with suspicion, disdain, and rejection, and over time this causes the individual to develop a negative, deviant self-view. Thus, while social control agencies label in an effort to reduce deviance, they may produce the unintended consequence of spoiling the individual's identity and increasing his commitment to deviant behavior. Past research has provided very little support for this symbolic interactionist view of labeling (see Akers, 2000). There is little evidence that being labeled produces a deviant identity, with the result being an amplification of deviant behavior.

Recently, however, Sampson and Laub (1993, 1997) have recast labeling theory within their life course theory of crime. They observe that, contrary to classic labeling theory, there is little evidence to support the claim that official sanctions lead directly to an increase in crime. They note, however, that this does not rule out the possibility that such sanctions might elevate an individual's involvement in deviant behavior through various *indirect* avenues. Using a social control theory perspective, they contend that legal sanctions such as arrest, official labeling, and incarceration have a deleterious "snowball effect," as they undermine the delinquent's life chances with regard to schooling, employment, and marriage. Educational success, a rewarding job, and a committed marriage, they maintain, are major sources of social control for adults, and official sanctions are stigmatizing events that reduce one's opportunities in these areas (Sampson and Laub, 1993, 1997). By diminishing an individual's chances of developing roles and relationships that provide a stake in conformity, official sanctions such as arrest and incarceration thereby indirectly increase the probability of involvement in deviant behavior.

Consistent with these arguments, several longitudinal studies (Freeman, 1991; Laub and Sampson, 1994; Nagin and Waldfogel, 1992; Sampson and Laub, 1993) have shown that jail time and length of incarceration are strong predictors of unemployment and job instability, even after controlling for prior differences in criminal propensity and various factors that have been shown to influence unemployment (e.g., education, ethnic group status, age, drug and alcohol use). Unemployment and job instability, in turn, have been linked to an increased risk for crime (Sampson and Laub, 1993, 1997). Similarly, past research has shown that a committed romantic relationship reduces the chances of criminal behavior, but antisocial behavior and incarceration diminish the chances of involvement in such a relationship (Sampson and Laub, 1993; Simons, Gordon, et al., 2002; Warr, 1993). In discussing these findings, Sampson and Laub note that they "do not assume that personal identities change as a result of the labeling process. Rather . . . labels work cumulatively through the structural transformation of one's stake in conformity to conventional society" (1997, 151–152).

Sampson and Laub's social control version of labeling theory asserts that official labels indirectly increase the probability of subsequent deviant behavior because they undermine roles and relationships that provide a stake in conformity. As we have seen, their work has focused on the extent to which incarceration attenuates adult social controls involving work and marriage. Recently, Eric Stewart and his colleagues (Stewart, Simons, and Conger, 2000, 2002) have applied Sampson and Laub's labeling perspective to adolescents. Whereas work and marriage are important social controls for adults, family relationships operate as the most basic social control for children. Stewart and associates contend that a child's arrest and involvement with the juvenile justice system often has a very deleterious effect on family relationships.

As we saw in Chapter Three, child misbehavior tends to have a disruptive effect on quality of parenting. Stewart and company cite these findings but then argue that child deviant behavior is most apt to have a negative impact on family processes, such as quality of parenting, when it results in legal sanctions. They present several reasons for believing that this is apt to be the case (Stewart, Simons, and Conger, 2000, 2002).

First, a child's brushes with the law force the parents to recognize the unpleasant truth about their child's behavior. Adolescence is a time of increased freedom for children. They begin to spend much of their leisure time away from home with their peers. This increased freedom from parental supervision allows the child to experiment with delinquent acts. Parents may suspect that their child is engaging in deviant behaviors of various sorts, but it is often difficult to prove that this is the case. Once an adolescent becomes involved with the legal system, however, parents typically become fully aware of their child's delinquent actions. Furthermore, legal system involvement usually results from a serious illegal act. Therefore, the adolescent's encounter with the legal system corroborates parents' worst fears regarding their offspring.

Parents are apt to worry about what this event might portend for their child's future. In addition, they are likely to experience encounters with legal authorities as embarrassing. This emotional response is a consequence, at least in part, of the perception by the legal system as well as by others in the community that the parents have some responsibility for the misdeeds of their children. Finally, juvenile involvement in the justice system may be expensive for parents, in terms of both time and money, as they seek professional assistance to deal with such problems.

For all of these reasons, Stewart and colleagues contend that the experience of having a child involved with the legal system is very stressful for parents. And, they argue, this stress is apt to have a disruptive effect on the parent-child relationship and quality of parenting. Parents are likely to experience feelings of disappointment, anger, and mistrust as a result of their child's legal problems. These emotions strain the parent-child relationship and increase the chances of parental rejection of the child. Further, according to Stewart and colleagues, there is often increased parent-child conflict as parents attempt to assert high levels of monitoring and control, whereas the child responds with reactance and defiance. In other cases, parents may give up on the problem child and concentrate their parenting efforts on their more conventional children.

Stewart and colleagues (2000, 2002) found support for these ideas in analyses based on several years of data from a sample of 400 Iowa families. The study assessed parenting practices using parent self-report data as well as observational ratings of videotaped family interaction. These parenting measures focused on harsh parenting, hostility, physical attack, inconsistent discipline, corporal punishment, and poor supervision. The results showed that legal system involvement had a disruptive effect on the parenting practices of both mothers and fathers, and that this disrupted parenting, in turn, was related to an increase in delinquent behavior.

Ambert (1997, 1999) conducted a qualitative investigation of a sample of Canadian families that generated a similar pattern of findings. She found that parents of delinquents felt ashamed and suffered reductions in overall health and happiness. The parent-child relationship tended to deteriorate following the delinquent's release from custody. Parents no longer trusted their youngster who had engaged in lies and deceit, and they became more controlling and monitored their child more closely. As a consequence, many of the adolescents rebelled against their parents. This sequence of events led to many hostile parent-child confrontations, and an increase in the child's antisocial behavior.

Sampson and Laub (1997) recast labeling theory by emphasizing the manner in which arrest and incarceration undermine a person's educational and occupational chances, thereby increasing the probability of future criminal behavior. The quantitative work of

Stewart and his colleagues, as well as the qualitative research of Ambert, extend this social control version of labeling theory by identifying another avenue whereby legal sanctions inadvertently amplify an adolescent's antisocial tendencies. Encounters with the legal system tend to disrupt parenting and the quality of the parent-child relationship. These disturbances in family processes often amplify involvement in delinquent behavior. ✦

Part II

Adult Deviance as an Expression of Childhood Socialization

Chapter Seven

Linking Childhood Delinquency and Adult Crime: Life Course Perspectives on Antisocial Behavior

The previous chapters have focused on the various ways in which parental behavior fosters child conduct problems and delinquency. Having established that there is a strong connection between parenting practices and child antisocial behavior, the reader might ask, "So what is the long-term significance of this finding?" Perhaps most antisocial children desist from their problem behavior as they mature. Although delinquent children are undoubtedly a burden for parents and teachers, their behavior may portend little in the way of adult behavior problems. Indeed, prior to the 1990s, this was the assumption of sociological criminology, which largely ignored child antisocial behavior. The results of several longitudinal studies provide convincing evidence, however, that such a view is incorrect.

This research indicates that antisocial behavior in children is one of the best predictors of antisocial behavior in adults. Children who are aggressive and noncompliant during elementary school are at risk for adolescent delinquency and adult crime (Caspi and Moffitt, 1995; Loeber, 1982; Patterson, Reid, and Dishion, 1992; Sampson and Laub, 1993). This continuity of deviant behavior has been found in several countries, including Canada, England, Finland, New Zealand, Sweden, and the United States (Caspi and Moffitt, 1995). As the medical sociologist Lee Robins has noted, "Adult antisocial behavior virtually requires childhood antisocial behavior" (1978, 611). This finding indicates that the roots of an adult antisocial lifestyle appear to be planted during a person's formative years. It is extremely rare that a person who was a model child and adolescent suddenly begins to engage in criminal behavior as an adult. Of course, the relationship between childhood conduct problems and adult antisocial behavior is far from perfect. Many delinquent children grow up to be conventional adults, a point that we will elaborate later in the chapter. The fact remains, however, that antisocial behavior in childhood is one of the best predictors of adult antisocial behavior. So what accounts for this link between past and future offending?

Daniel Nagin and his colleagues (Nagin and Paternoster, 1991; Nagin and Farrington, 1992) have suggested that there are basically two theoretical approaches to explaining the continuity of antisocial behavior across the life course. The first is what they label *population heterogeneity.* Such theories assert that there are differences between people regarding the extent to which they possess the characteristics that cause crime. Regardless of whether this criminal propensity is viewed as a function of constitution (Rowe, 1994), personality (Wilson and Herrnstein, 1985), or inadequate socialization (Gottfredson and Hirschi, 1990), these theories assert that society includes a few "bad apples" who are created by forces that operate early in life (Paternoster and Brame, 1997; Paternoster et al., 1997). These individuals begin offending as children, engage in a wide variety of deviant acts, and tend to offend throughout life. Their persistent antisocial behavior is simply an expression of an underlying criminal propensity that became evident during childhood. The positive correlation between past and future deviant behavior is explained by continuity in this criminogenic trait. Early antisocial behavior does not cause later antisocial behavior. Rather, the two are associated because they have a common cause—the individual's enduring criminal propensity. It is this deviant characteristic that accounts for the correlation between past and future deviant behavior.

In contrast, the second approach to explaining the observed correlation between past and future offending asserts that there is a causal link between the two phenomena (Nagin and Paternoster, 1991). These *state dependent* theories assume that the commission of an antisocial act increases the probability of engaging in future criminal behavior. There are a variety of social consequences that might produce this state dependent effect. The act might, for example, weaken perceptions of certainty of arrest, weaken social ties to conventional others, increase affiliation with deviant peers, or result in negative labeling, ridicule, and exclusion (Paternoster et al., 1997). Regardless of the theoretical mechanisms that are emphasized, state dependent theories share the view that past deviance has a causal effect on the probability of future deviance. Contrary to the contention of population heterogeneity perspectives, state dependent theories assume that life events (e.g., committing a criminal act, getting married, changing friendship groups) influence future behavior.

In earlier chapters, we discussed various theories that link parental behavior and child conduct problems. Although these theories focus on child socialization, they make either population heterogeneity or state dependent assumptions regarding a child's future involvement in antisocial behavior. Indeed, two of these theories have been developed into explicit theoretical statements of the nature of antisocial behavior across the life span. Both perspectives have received wide acclaim within the field of criminology and have been subject to extensive empirical evaluation. The first is Gottfredson and Hirschi's (1990) self-control theory, which adopts the population heterogeneity position. The second is Sampson and Laub's (1993) life course version of social control theory, which takes the state dependent point of view. In the sections that follow, we will describe these two contrasting perspectives and then evaluate each in light of recent research findings.

Self-Control Theory: A Latent Trait Approach

As noted in Chapter Two, Michael Gottfredson and Travis Hirschi (1990; Hirschi and Gottfredson, 1994) have formulated a general theory of crime that asserts that antisocial acts are committed by persons who have failed to learn self-control. Their theory describes people who are low in self-control as impulsive, insensitive, risk-taking, and shortsighted. Caregiver parenting practices and, to a lesser extent, child temperament are seen as the primary determinants of a child's level of self-control (Gottfredson and

Hirschi, 1990). Differences in self-control are seen as emerging early in life and remaining reasonably stable throughout the life course. The theory views variations in level of self-control as a latent trait, which serves as the primary explanation for individual differences in involvement in antisocial behavior throughout the life course (Hirschi and Gottfredson, 1994).

Figure 7.1 is a rough approximation of a graph that Gottfredson sometimes uses in describing self-control theory. The horizontal axis represents age. It begins at age 10 because the theory posits that level of self-control is largely established by this point in a person's life. The vertical axis assesses frequency and severity of deviant behavior. Each of the curved lines on the graph represents a hypothetical individual's vacillating level of involvement in deviant behavior as he grows older. The graph shows dramatic differences between these individuals regarding their commission of deviant acts at age 10. Level of deviance at age 10 is considered to be a crude indicator of self-control during this period. Thus those who are highly deviant at 10 years of age lack self-control, and this characteristic places them at risk for high levels of antisocial behavior throughout the life

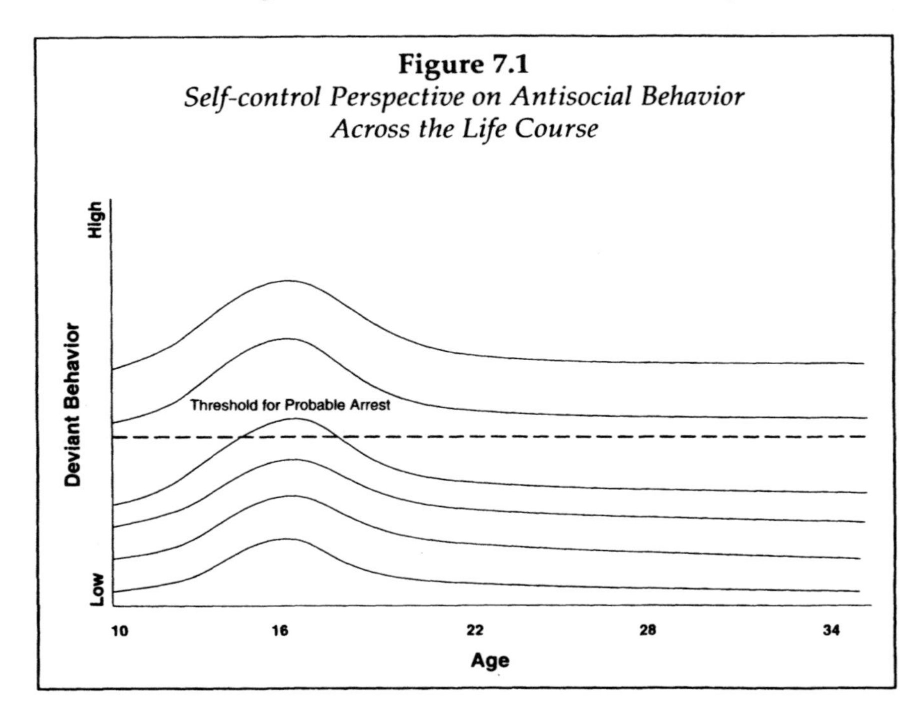

Figure 7.1
Self-control Perspective on Antisocial Behavior Across the Life Course

course. The graph also contains a dashed horizontal line that depicts probability of arrest. When frequency and severity of offending reach this threshold, the person is likely to be arrested.

Data from the United States, as well as from other industrialized countries, has consistently shown that criminal and delinquent behavior rises dramatically during adolescence, peaks at about age 16 or 17, and then declines over the remainder of the life span (Flanagan and Maguire, 1990; Hirschi and Gottfredson, 1983). Consistent with this age-curve finding, all of the hypothetical individuals show increases in deviant behavior during adolescence and then a decline throughout the adult years. Thus, the theory does not assert that a person's level of offending is consistent across the life course. Everyone's trajectory of deviant behavior is expected to conform to the age curve. However, antisocial behavior is posited to be stable in that the rank order between individuals is maintained across the life course. Those with the lowest levels of deviance in their cohort at age 10 are expected to also manifest the least amount of deviance during adolescence and throughout adulthood. Conversely, those with the highest levels of offending at age 10 are expected to show the most deviance during adolescence and adulthood. Offending is a function of an underlying trait that is established during childhood and varies little over the life course. Those who are most prone to crime during late childhood continue to be the most prone to crime during adolescence and adulthood as well. They may commit few crimes as they age, but this does not indicate an increase in self-control. Rather, it is a consequence of the "inexorable aging of the organism" (Gottfredson and Hirschi, 1990, 41).

The graph shows that persons who are serious offenders at age 10 are at risk for arrest throughout their lives. They might, for example, skip school, get into fights, drink alcohol, and shoplift at age 10; drop out of school, sell illegal substances, and commit robbery with a weapon during adolescence; and forge checks, engage in fraudulent business practices, and abuse illegal substances as an adult. Individuals with somewhat lower involvement in deviance at age 10 are at risk for arrest during adolescence, but less so during adulthood. Their deviance trajectory might involve fighting and poor school performance during childhood, skipping school and selling illegal drugs during adolescence, and unstable employment and occasional illicit drug use as an adult. Finally, those with very low rates of antisocial behavior at age 10 are unlikely to be arrested at any point during their lives. They show a small increase in deviance during adolescence, but this behavior is so minor and infrequent that it rarely attracts the attention of law enforcement. Their adolescent deviance consists of the expressions of independence and rebellion typical at this age (e.g., underage drinking, throwing parties when parents are out of town, reckless driving). Indeed, their deviant behavior is so common during adolescence that it might be considered normative or expected. The majority of people display this life course trajectory.

Gottfredson and Hirschi view their theory as encompassing Patterson's (Patterson, Reid, and Dishion, 1992) distinction between early and late starters and Moffitt's (1993a, 1993b) similar distinction between life course persistent and adolescent limited delinquents. As we noted in Chapter Three, early starters or life course persistent delinquents manifest antisocial behavior at an early age. Late starters or adolescent limited delinquents, on the other hand, manifest conventional childhoods but experiment with delinquent behavior during adolescence. Distinguishing between these two types of delinquents is important, according to Patterson and Moffitt, because the two groups have very different prognoses. Although late starters or adolescent limited delinquents tend to discontinue their delinquency within a short period, early starters or life course persistent delinquents are at risk for chronic offending during adolescence and criminal careers as adults.

Using the graph in Figure 7.1, individuals high on deviance at age 10 are early starters or life course persistent delinquents, whereas those low on deviance at age 10 are late starters or adolescent limited delinquents. Thus, from the point of view of Gottfredson and Hirschi's general theory of crime, early starters are life course persistent delinquents because they lack self-control and late starters limit their delinquency to adolescence because they exercise self-control.

Low self-control, according to Gottfredson and Hirschi, dooms a person to a rather bleak future. In addition to involvement in antisocial and risky behavior, such individuals tend to experience problems such as school failure, stormy romantic relationships, trouble with peers, and unstable employment. Gottfredson and Hirschi make it clear, however, that these difficulties are a result, and not a cause, of the person's antisocial behavior. Any relationship between these stressful events and subsequent criminal behavior is spurious—both share the common cause of low self-control. As we will see in the following section, the life course theory developed by Robert Sampson and John Laub (1993) rests upon a very different set of assumptions.

The Life Course Perspective: Explaining Both Continuity and Change

The life course perspective within sociology views people's life pathways or trajectories as a sequence of causal factors in which dependent variables become independent variables over time (Elder, 1992; Loeber and Le Blanc, 1990). This theoretical viewpoint is concerned with explaining discontinuity, as well as stability, in behavior across the life course. Thus, it focuses on life events and transitions that either accentuate or redirect behavioral tendencies.

This perspective offers a very different view of the continuity of antisocial behavior than that provided by the latent trait approach. First, it asserts that the correlation between child antisocial behavior and adult offending represents a causal sequence in which intervening life events cause a progression or escalation from defiant and troublesome behavior to involvement in serious crime. Second, researchers using this framework note that the correlation between past and future antisocial behavior is far from perfect. Indeed, at least half of all antisocial children are not delinquent during adolescence, and at least half of all delinquent adolescents do not go on to engage in adult crime (Loeber and LeBlanc, 1990). Therefore, in addition to investigating the causal process whereby childhood misconduct escalates into delinquency and crime, criminologists who employ a life course perspective are concerned with discovering the turning points that enable some individuals with a history of antisocial behavior to adopt a more conventional lifestyle. In other words, life course criminologists are concerned with explaining both stability and change in antisocial behavior.

The most popular and widely acclaimed life course perspective on crime is Robert Sampson and John Laub's (1993) age-graded, social control theory. Building on social control theory as we described it in Chapter Two, they argue that deviance and crime are a result of a breakdown in informal social control. The stability of antisocial behavior across the life course is considered to be a consequence of deviant behavior at early stages of development, which undermines relationships and activities that are important social controls during later stages. Individuals show persistent involvement in antisocial behavior to the extent that their deviant actions have an attenuating effect on the social and institutional bonds linking them to society (Laub and Sampson, 1993). This attenuating process is seen as a sequence of *cumulative disadvantage.*

The theory is age-graded, as Sampson and Laub (1990, 1993) contend that the relationships and activities that are a source of social control vary across the life course. Their arguments in this regard are depicted in Figure 7.2, which shows that family, school, and peer group are the dominant sources of social control during childhood and adolescence. In earlier chapters, we saw that quality of parenting and child temperament determine a child's probability of developing conduct problems (see the dashed arrows). According to Sampson and Laub, childhood conduct problems, in turn, increase the chances of delinquency during adolescence because they reduce ties to parents, conventional peers, and school. More specifically, in response to childhood opposition and defiance, parents often reduce their efforts to monitor and discipline. A noncompliant attitude also increases the chances that a child will experience academic failure and reduced interest in school. Finally, conventional peers tend to reject difficult children, increasing the probability that they will drift into a deviant peer group. Unencumbered by parental controls, disinterested in school, and under the influence of a deviant peer group, these antisocial youngsters graduate from oppositional/defiant behavior to more serious delinquent acts. As shown in Figure 7.2, childhood antisocial behavior leads to delinquency because of its disruptive effect on parents, school commitment, and peer affiliations.

However, although oppositional behavior *tends* to attenuate these important sources of social control, this is not invariably the case. For whatever reason, some antisocial children may actually experience a strengthening of ties to parents, conventional peers, or school. Parents may consult a counselor and strive to be more conscientious in their monitoring and discipline, the family may move to a new neighborhood where the child develops a strong friendship with the conventional children living next door, or the child may achieve success in some extracurricular activity (e.g., football) and develop more interest in school. Regardless of the reason, when

Figure 7.2
Life-course Model of Antisocial Behavior Across the Life Span

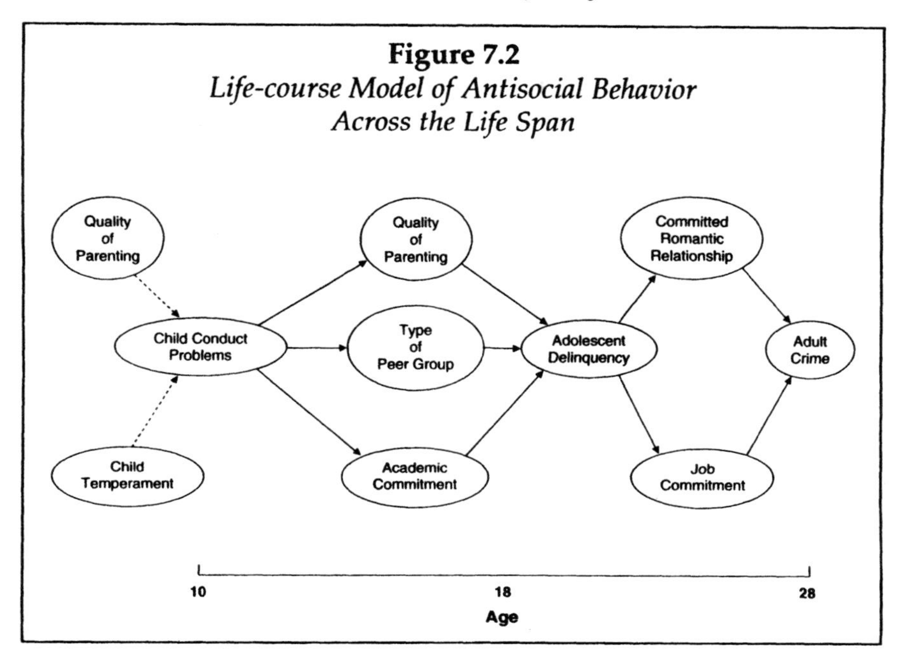

antisocial children experience a strengthening, rather than a weakening, of social controls, it operates as a turning point in their life. The theory predicts that they will reduce their involvement in antisocial behavior and adopt a more conventional lifestyle.

Sampson and Laub (1990, 1993) identify attachments to a romantic partner and to work as the fundamental informal social controls of adulthood. They contend that serious delinquency increases the chances of adult crime because it undermines the probability that these adult attachments will develop (see Figure 7.2). They also observe, however, that some seriously delinquent individuals defy the odds and develop strong marital and work commitments. Someone with a delinquent past might, for example, marry someone whom he truly cares about. Or this individual could have the good fortune of finding a well-paying job that he really enjoys. Such events provide a stake in conformity, and the theory views them as turning points that are likely to result in a reduction in criminal behavior.

It is apparent that Sampson and Laub provide a very different view of antisocial behavior across the life course than that proffered by Gottfredson and Hirschi. Gottfredson and Hirschi maintain that offending is a function of an underlying trait—low self-control—that is established during childhood and is invariant over the life course. The child who fails to develop self-control is doomed to a life of risky and antisocial behavior, troubled relationships, and occupational failure. Sampson and Laub argue that early antisocial behavior is related to future offending because it tends to undermine important social controls. This is a more optimistic perspective because these tendencies are not always realized. When they are not, people are able to escape their antisocial past and adopt a more conventional lifestyle. Next, we evaluate the evidence in support of these two contrasting points of view.

Evaluating the Evidence

We have described two very different views of the characteristics of antisocial behavior across the life course. A large number of studies have attempted to evaluate the validity of these two points of view. We will begin by discussing findings pertinent to the latent trait perspective of self-control theory. Although past research has provided some support for the theory, there is also evidence that it overstates the degree to which antisocial tendencies are stable across time.

As we noted in Chapter Two, several studies have examined the extent to which low self-control during late childhood or early adolescence predicts future crime and delinquency. Pratt and Cullen (2000) have performed a meta-analysis of this research and found an average effect size of .27. A coefficient of 1.0 indicates a perfect association between two variables, whereas a coefficient of zero indicates that there is no relation between them. Assuming perfect measurement, which is never a possibility in the social sciences, the theory predicts a very strong association between self-control during late childhood and adult deviant behavior. Those with the lowest amount of self-control during childhood should manifest the most adult deviance, whereas those with high self-control should display the least adult deviance. Even taking into account measurement error, a coefficient of .27 is far from unity and indicates that there is only a *tendency* for this pattern to take place. Although the antisocial behavior of many people may fit the predictions of the theory, numerous individuals do not follow the pattern.

Consistent with this point, longitudinal research shows that the majority of antisocial children go on to lead conventional lives. The findings from these studies are summarized in Figure 7.3. The figure depicts a hypothetical cohort of individuals as they move through the life course. The shaded area depicts the proportion of the cohort involved in antisocial behavior at ages 10, 18, and 25. To make the example more concrete, the reader might think of this cohort as consisting of all males in a particular city who were 10 years old when the study began. The figure indicates that a certain percentage of these 10-year-olds are oppositional and defiant (see shaded area). Past research suggests that somewhere between 15 and 20 percent of a cohort of boys may fall into this category. They are aggressive, impulsive, self-centered, and noncompliant; tend to be rejected by their conventional peers; and represent a challenge to their parents and teachers. By age 18, a small proportion of the cohort, roughly 10 percent, is severely delinquent. They engage in fights, truancy, robbery, drug sales, and the like. Finally, the figure indicates that a somewhat smaller proportion of the cohort, perhaps 5 percent, is involved in serious crime at age 25. Their criminal activities include a wide variety of illegal acts such as robbery, burglary, drug trafficking, gambling, and prostitution.

Figure 7.3
The Transitivity of Antisocial Behavior Across the Life Course

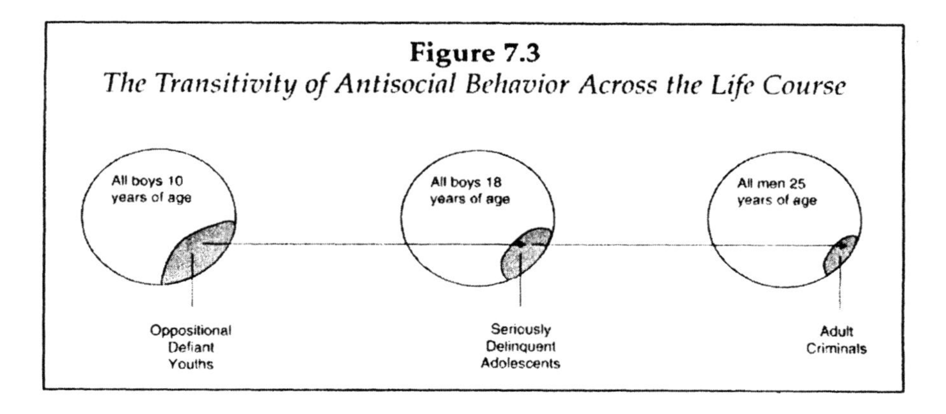

Consistent with self-control theory, the figure shows that antisocial behavior at those three points in time displays a pattern of *transitivity* (Patterson, Reid, and Dishion, 1992). Virtually all seriously delinquent adolescents were oppositional or defiant at age 10. And nearly all adult criminals were seriously delinquent during adolescence. This pattern of transitivity does not mean, however, that antisocial children necessarily grow up to become adult criminals (see Patterson, Reid, and Dishion, 1992; Sampson and Laub, 1993). As Figure 7.3 shows, only about half of all conduct-disordered children go on to engage in serious delinquency during adolescence, and only about half of all seriously delinquent adolescents engage in criminal behavior as adults. Thus, although childhood deviance increases the chances of adult antisocial behavior, many individuals "age out" or "mature out" of their antisocial tendencies and adopt a more conventional way of life.

The finding that many antisocial individuals embrace a conventional lifestyle with the passage of time is contrary to self-control theory's contention that by age 10 the window of opportunity for socialization is slammed shut, with those who have not acquired self-control being doomed to a life of delinquency and crime. Rather, the evidence suggests that antisocial behavior shows both continuity and change (Sampson and Laub, 1993). Some individuals manifest antisocial behavior throughout their lives, whereas others change and adopt a more conventional lifestyle. Gottfredson and Hirschi's self-control theory can account for stability in antisocial behavior, but it cannot explain discontinuity and change. Sampson and Laub's life course theory, on the other hand, purports to explain change as well as stability. Next, we examine research findings relevant to this theory.

As we noted earlier, Sampson and Laub (1990, 1993) argue that deviance and crime are the result of a breakdown in informal social control. The stability of antisocial behavior across the life course is considered to be a consequence of deviant behavior at early stages of development, which undermines commitment to relationships and activities that are important social controls during later stages. Sampson and Laub contend that the relationships and activities that are a source of social control vary across the life course. They assert that family, school, and peer group are the dominant sources of social control during childhood and adolescence. Thus, according to their theory, childhood oppositional behavior increases the chances of delinquency during adolescence because it often weakens ties to parents, conventional peers, and school. However, although oppositional behavior tends to attenuate these important sources of social control, this is not invariably the case. For a variety of reasons, some antisocial children actually experience a strengthening of ties to parents, conventional peers, or school. The theory predicts that these children will show little or no involvement in adolescent delinquency; that is, they will desist from antisocial behavior.

Past research has largely supported these elements of the theory. Several studies have reported that childhood problems are not related to adolescent delinquency, or exert only a small effect, once the effects of family processes, school commitment, and peer affiliation are taken into account (Elliott, 1993; Sampson and Laub, 1993, 1994; Simons et al., 2001; Simons, Johnson, et al., 1998). Further, Simons, Johnson, and colleagues (1998) found that boys who were highly oppositional during childhood, but who subsequently experienced improved parenting, increased school commitment, or reduced involvement with deviant peers, showed no more conduct problems during adolescence than did boys who displayed little oppositional behavior during childhood. Together, these findings indicate that childhood antisocial behavior increases the chances of delinquency because of its corrosive effect on important social controls, but that difficult children are at no greater risk for delinquency than are their conventional counterparts when social control does not wane, or even increases, in the face of problem behavior.

As discussed earlier, past research has also provided support for Sampson and Laub's view of the social processes that link adolescent delinquency and adult criminal behavior. Sampson and Laub (1990, 1993) identify attachments to a romantic partner and to work as the fundamental informal social controls of adulthood. They contend that serious delinquency increases the chances of adult crime because it undermines the probability that these adult attachments will develop. They also observe, however, that some seriously delinquent individuals defy the odds and develop strong marital and work commitments. The theory predicts that these persons will desist from involvement in criminal behavior. Sampson and Laub reprised the Gluecks' well-known longitudinal data set (see Chapter Two) to test this thesis. Consistent with their theory, they (Laub, Nagin, and Sampson, 1998; Sampson and Laub, 1990, 1993) found that spouse and job-support attachment mediated the association between delinquency and adult crime, and that these attachments are associated with a reduction in adult crime even among those with a history of conduct problems during childhood and adolescence.

Other longitudinal investigations have produced similar results. Simons, Stewart, et al. (2002), for example, found that job satisfaction and a committed romantic relationship mediated a significant proportion of the relationship between adolescent delinquency and adult crime. Cernkovich and Giordano (2001) recently reported that social bonding (e.g., intimate family communication, marital happiness) accounted for much of the relationship between adolescent and adult antisocial behavior. And a study by Wright and colleagues (2001) indicates that prosocial ties, such as employment and family ties, explained a good portion of the association between low self-control (assessed in childhood and adolescence) and criminal behavior during adulthood. Of particular interest in this study was the finding that prosocial ties deter crime most strongly among those individuals lacking in self-control. This result, as Wright and colleagues note, provides reason for optimism, as it indicates that "it is possible for severely crime-prone youth to be successfully deterred from crime by strong, prosocial ties" (2001, 343).

While supporting Sampson and Laub's contentions regarding the importance of romantic relationships and job commitment, findings from these studies also suggest a direction in which their theory of adult crime needs to be expanded. All three of these studies found that affiliation with deviant peers accounted for much of the association between adolescent delinquency and adult crime. Peer influences were a central part of Sampson and Laub's explanation for child and adolescent behavior problems, but peer effects are not included in their explanation of adult antisocial behavior (see Figure 7.2). This is an important omission, as peer influences continue to be salient in adulthood. Sampson and Laub argued that child conduct problems alienate conventional peers, leading to involvement with deviant peers and increased risk for delinquent behavior. Results reported by Cernkovich and Giordano (2001); Simons, Stewart, and colleagues (2002); and Wright and colleagues (2001) suggest that a similar process links adolescent delinquency to adult crime. Delinquent behavior distances conventional peers and leads to affiliation with a deviant social network that encourages future antisocial behavior, including crime.

We believe these findings demonstrate the utility of incorporating social learning concepts into Sampson and Laub's social control theory. As we saw in Chapter Two, social control frameworks fail to recognize the influence of deviant peer groups. By building their life course theory on social control principles, Sampson and Laub have difficulty accommodating peer influences. We see no inherent conflict between social learning and social control perspectives, as social control theories, like social learning theories, emphasize incentives and costs associated with various lines of action (Akers, 1998; Conger, 1976). Social control theories emphasize the costs associated with deviant behavior when a person is attached to the rewards provided by conventional people and activities, whereas social learning theories take a broader view and also consider the rewards provided by deviant associates and activities. Past research indicates that both points of view have merit (Agnew, 1991; Cernkovich and Giordano, 1992; Elliott and Menard, 1996; Patterson, Reid, and Dishion, 1992; Sampson and Laub, 1993; Simons, Johnson, et al., 1998).

Extending the life course model to include peer influences suggests additional avenues whereby a romantic partner might influence future antisocial behavior. Building on social control theory, Sampson and Laub argue that a committed romantic relationship decreases deviant behavior because it provides a stake in conformity. However, romantic partners, like friends, can either encourage or discourage criminal behavior. Conventional partners are apt to promote socially acceptable activities, whereas antisocial partners are likely to advance situations and opportunities involving deviant behavior.

Further, a social learning perspective on romantic relationships suggests that people will be attracted to persons similar to themselves. It is rewarding to be around an individual who engages in actions that one regularly enjoys, but unpleasant to spend time with a person who behaves in ways that one finds foreign and uninviting. Consequently, mate selection tends to be an assortative process in which individuals are attracted to persons similar to themselves (Collins, 1988). This suggests that antisocial individuals are likely to meet, date, and fall in love with persons who are also antisocial (Cairns and Cairns, 1994; Rowe and Farrington, 1997; Simons, Johnson, et al., 1993). Thus, deviant persons are apt to form romantic relationships with individuals who encourage continued involvement in deviant behavior.

On the other hand, through chance encounters and circumstances, some antisocial persons may fall in love with conventional partners. For example, an individual with a troubled past is invited to join an office softball team, through which he meets a nice woman from a different department. The same thing could happen at church, a party thrown by a neighbor, or a community activity. An individual with an antisocial past might strike up a relationship with a conventional person who gets to know the antisocial individual while engaging in activities that are socially valued. The new conventional partner generalizes the valued activity to her new acquaintance and decides that they have something positive in common. If the individual with the troubled past wants to maintain this new connection, he will need to modify his deviant lifestyle so as not to jeopardize the relationship.

Simons, Stewart, and colleagues (2002) found strong support for this idea. They found that antisocial romantic partners tended to encourage adult crime, whereas conventional partners discouraged such behavior. Unfortunately, delinquents tended to develop relationships with antisocial partners who amplified their deviant tendencies. These results suggest that one of the reasons delinquency often leads to adult crime is because it increases the probability of cohabitation with, or marriage to, an antisocial partner. However, delinquents who buck the odds and became involved with a conventional partner often discontinue their involvement in antisocial behavior.

Mark Warr (1998) has suggested still another avenue whereby romantic partners might influence desistance from criminal behavior. He argues that marriage discourages criminal behavior because it disrupts or dissolves relations with deviant friends. This argument is consistent with past research showing that marriage often produces dramatic changes in a person's social network (Wellman, et al., 1997). Using multiple waves of data from the National Youth Survey, Warr (1998) has reported strong support for this hypothesis. His findings indicate that marriage leads to a reduction in crime, and that this reduction is largely a consequence of decreased involvement with deviant peers. Findings reported by Simons, Stewart, et al. (2002) provide additional support for this idea. Their results indicate that a committed romantic relationship tends to decrease criminal behavior because it weakens affiliation with deviant peers. Together, these various findings suggest that a more complete explanation of the life course processes influencing adult crime is obtained when Sampson and Laub's social control perspective is expanded to include peer influences.

Summary and Conclusion

The criminological literature contains two very different views of antisocial behavior across the life span. Gottfredson and Hirschi's self-control theory argues that differences in self-control are established by age 10 and remain reasonably stable throughout life. The theory views variations in level of self-control as a latent trait that serves as the primary explanation for individual differences in involvement in antisocial behavior throughout the life course (Hirschi and Gottfredson, 1994). The life course theory of Sampson and Laub (1993), on the other hand, posits that the stability of antisocial behavior across the life course is a consequence of deviant behavior at early stages of development, which undermines relationships and activities that are important social controls during later stages. In addition to describing the causal process that accounts for the continuity of antisocial behavior, the theory identifies events and circumstances that serve as the turning points which enable individuals with a history of antisocial behavior to adopt more conventional lifestyles.

Recent longitudinal research tends to support the life course perspective over self-control theory. These studies show, for example, that some individuals manifest antisocial behavior throughout their lives, whereas others desist and adopt a more conventional lifestyle. The finding that many antisocial persons eventually embrace a more conventional way of life is contrary to self-control theory's contention that by age 10, the window of opportunity for socialization is closed, with those who have not acquired self-control being doomed to a life of delinquency and crime.

Studies generally find that low commitment to conventional social activities and relationships explains much of the relationship between childhood measures of self-control and future deviant behavior. Further, these investigations show that antisocial individuals who buck the odds and develop strong commitments to such activities and relationships tend to discontinue their deviant lifestyle. These findings are consistent with the life course perspective but contradict self-control theory. Finally, although past research provides much support for Sampson and Laub's life course theory, we reviewed findings from several studies indicating that the theory might be strengthened by expanding it to include the effects of adult peer relationships. ✦

Chapter Eight

Marital Violence: Antisocial Behavior Learned in Childhood?

All of the prior chapters in this book have been concerned with general involvement in antisocial behavior. The first several chapters explored the various avenues whereby family environment increases the chances of child conduct problems or adolescent delinquency. The previous chapter was concerned with the extent to which conduct problems and delinquency predict adult crime. The present chapter switches the focus from antisocial behavior in general to a specific type of deviant behavior—marital violence.

We will begin by discussing the nature and incidence of this behavior. Various theoretical explanations are then discussed. As part of this discussion, we will examine the extent to which the theoretical explanations presented in the earlier chapters apply to marital violence as well. We investigate, for example, the extent to which exposure to negative family interaction as a child increases the probability that a person will engage in marital violence as an adult. We will also review the evidence regarding the extent to which individuals who engage in marital violence tend to participate in other types of antisocial behavior as well. Finally, the chapter analyzes the seemingly puzzling finding that women who have been the victims of harsh and violent parenting as children are often the victims of marital violence during adulthood.

The Incidence of Marital Violence

The first national survey of family violence was conducted in 1975 by Murray Straus and his colleagues (Straus, Gelles, and Steinmetz, 1980). They completed a second national survey in 1985 (Straus, 1990). Both surveys utilized the Conflict Tactics Scale (CTS) to assess violence. This instrument asks respondents to report how often they have used various tactics during a conflict with their romantic partner. The acts of violence include pushing, grabbing, slapping, kicking, choking, hitting with fist, hitting with an object, and threatening with a knife or gun (Straus and Gelles, 1990).

The 1985 survey found that approximately 16 percent of all married couples reported that a violent incident had occurred in the previous year. When respondents were asked whether there had *ever* been an incident of violence in their marriage, the rate rose to 30 percent. A little more than 6 percent of the couples reported that there had been an incident of severe violence. To be classified as severe, the violence had to involve at least one of the following acts: kicking, biting, punching, beating up, choking, hitting with an object, threatening to use a knife or gun, or actual use of a knife or gun (Straus, 1990). Subsequent studies have reported incident rates comparable to those found by Straus and his colleagues (Dutton, 1995).

While the two national surveys by Straus and colleagues added much to our understanding of domestic violence, they also created a good bit of controversy. To the surprise of almost everyone, both studies found that wives hit their husbands slightly more often than husbands hit their wives. Other studies during the 1980s and 1990s reported similar findings. Indeed, a recent meta-analysis (Archer, 2000) found that this pattern held across hundreds of studies. Although this finding is interesting, it certainly should not be taken as an indication that husband abuse is a serious social problem comparable to that of wife abuse.

Contrary to surveys using the CTS, analysis of police records, emergency room data, and the annual National Crime Victimization Survey (NCVS), all indicate that women are much more likely to be the victim of domestic violence than men (Felson, 2002). Well over 80 percent of partner assaults reported to the NCVS, for example, involve men attacking women (Bureau of Justice Statistics, 1997). The discrepancy between these data and studies using the

CTS is primarily due to differences in the types of violence being assessed.

As Felson (2002) notes, police records, emergency room data, and criminal victimization surveys such as the NCVS are concerned with severe violence. These attacks often involve injury to the victim. The CTS, on the other hand, primarily assesses slaps, pushes, and other less serious acts that rarely result in injury. Men engage in serious violence more frequently than women, but CTS survey data fail to detect this pattern because such acts are rare. Violent acts that result in serious injury account for only a small proportion of marital violence. Given this fact, social surveys end up comparing husbands and wives on minor acts of violence.

To correct for this problem, Straus and Gelles (1986) created a subscale from the CTS designed to assess severe forms of violence. Their findings indicated that men and women continued to show roughly comparable levels of partner violence when the comparison was limited to this subscale. Their subscale included, however, behaviors such as kicking, punching, and throwing an object. The seriousness of these acts depends on the force utilized and more-minor incidents are apt to dominate this measure, just as is the case with the instrument as a whole (Felson, 2002).

Further, it is misleading to treat these acts as the same whether they are perpetrated by a male or a female. As Angela Browne (1992, 1993) has noted, men and women differ dramatically in strength, ability to deliver forceful blows, and capacity to resist and escape. Consequently, almost every act assessed by the CTS tends to be more serious and injurious when delivered by a man. Consistent with this view, studies that examine injury, rather than simply number of incidents, find that husbands are much more violent than their wives (Archer, 2000; Tjaden and Thoennes, 1999).

In recent years, several domestic-violence researchers have argued for the importance of making distinctions among types of marital or partner violence (Dutton, 1998; Holtzworth-Monroe and Stuart, 1994; Jacobson and Gottman, 1998; Johnson, 1995, 2000). Such distinctions, they argue, help to resolve the alleged gender symmetry in partner violence (Johnson and Ferraro, 2000). Johnson (1995, 2000; Johnson and Ferraro, 2000), for example, distinguishes between *common couple violence* and *intimate terrorism.* Common couple violence occurs when one or both of the partners lash out physically during the course of an argument. This type of violence has a low per-couple frequency, usually does not escalate over time, rarely involves severe violence, and is often mutual (Johnson, 1998, 2000). Johnson presents evidence indicating that virtually all of the violence assessed in general population surveys consists of common couple violence. Therefore, research based on such samples is only relevant to this type of partner violence. This being the case, the oft-reported finding that men and women are equally likely to engage in partner violence is only applicable to common couple violence.

Intimate terrorism, on the other hand, tends to be one tactic in a general pattern of control over one's partner. It involves more per-couple incidents than common couple violence, usually is accompanied by emotional abuse, tends to escalate over time, rarely is mutual, and often leads to serious injury (Johnson, 2000). One of the distinguishing features of intimate terrorism is a strong concern with controlling the partner's behavior. Importantly, intimate terrorism is usually perpetrated by men.

This distinction between common couple violence and intimate terrorism corresponds, in a very crude way, to the differences that we identified between spanking and child abuse. Although some people have moral objections to parents exercising corporal punishment with their preschoolers, there is little evidence that it produces any negative effects. The majority of parents sometimes spank and children often have warm and affectionate relationships with their parents, even though the parents sometimes use corporal punishment as a disciplinary strategy. Frequent and severe physical discipline, on the other hand, is a different matter. Such punishment is considered to be abusive, as it destroys the parent-child relationship, damages the child's self-concept, and fosters emotional and behavioral problems. Thus, society tolerates the use of moderate spanking, whereas harsh corporal punishment is criminalized and negatively sanctioned.

Similarly, many couples sometimes resort to violence in the midst of an argument. Although such actions are morally and socially undesirable, we saw that such common couple violence occurs infrequently, does not escalate over time, and rarely results in physical injury or psychological trauma. This is not the type of violence that human-service workers or policy makers have in mind when they refer to spouse abuse or battering.

As Johnson and Ferraro state, "in everyday speech and even in most social science discourse, 'domestic violence' is about men beating women" (2000, 948). In other words, it is intimate terrorism that concerns society. This type of violence is frequent, persistent, severe, and results in physical injury and emotional trauma. It is in response to this social problem that we have established shelters, strengthened restraining orders, instituted mandatory arrest policies, and implemented treatment programs.

Although there certainly are exceptions, this type of violence is usually committed by a man against a woman. Thus, just as men are much more likely than women to engage in other criminal acts, so they are also more likely to engage in serious violence toward a romantic partner (Felson, 2002). The next section examines explanations for this behavior. We will be particularly concerned with the extent to which the theories that explain crime and delinquency can also explain spouse abuse. Also, we will investigate whether men who engage in domestic violence are those who are committing other crimes as well.

Explaining Marital Violence

There are two dramatically different perspectives on the causes of marital violence. The first assumes that most perpetrators are male and that their behavior is explained by patriarchal societal norms that legitimate men's control over women. This view is associated with feminist scholars such as Dobash and Dobash (1992), Pagelow (1984), and Walker (1989). The second perspective assumes that both men and women commit marital violence and that oftentimes it is mutual (Straus and Gelles, 1990; Straus, Gelles, and Steinmetz, 1980). This group of researchers focuses on social psychological variables that influence both men and women. Much of their work utilizes a social learning framework and investigates the manner in which childhood exposure to family violence increases the chances that a person will engage in such behavior as an adult. We will examine each of these positions, and then show how the latter one might be elaborated to incorporate elements of the control and social learning theories of deviant behavior discussed in earlier chapters.

Patriarchy and Male Dominance

The patriarchy explanation for marital violence emerged from a combination of feministic scholarship, historical evidence, and interviews with women in shelters. The basic assumption of the perspective is that a cultural commitment to patriarchy and patriarchal institutions is the main cause of wife assault (Archer, 1994; Bograd, 1988; Koss et al., 1994). As Dobash and Dobash state,

> Men who assault their wives are living up to cultural prescriptions that are cherished in Western society—aggressiveness, male dominance, and female subordination—and they are using physical force as a means to enforce that dominance. (1979, 24)

Thus, husbands who direct aggression toward their wives are maintaining the extant patriarchal power structure of society.

Their behavior is not an indication of psychopathology, a troubled childhood, learned aggression, or some other personal defect. Rather, wife assault stems from the cultural assumption that men should be the head of the household and that violence is a legitimate strategy for enforcing this power arrangement (Bograd, 1988; Dobash and Dobash, 1979). Men who batter, according to this perspective, do not differ dramatically from those who do not. A commitment to patriarchy and the use of aggression is part of male sex role socialization. There is, therefore, the potential for all men to use violence as a means of subordinating and controlling women.

A cross-cultural investigation by the anthropologist Daniel Levinson (1989) provides support for this perspective. He used data from the Human Relations Area Files to examine the correlates of wife beating in 90 societies. The historical, ethnographic data from the files was coded to form several measures of patriarchy. The measures focused on male control over wealth, inheritance, divorce, household decisions, and so forth. These various indicators of patriarchy correlated between .20 and .45 with a measure of the society's rate of wife abuse.

This finding indicates that differences in level of patriarchy may explain part of the variation between societies in wife battering. Extremely patriarchal countries tend to have high rates of violence toward wives, whereas such behavior is much less prevalent in more equalitarian societies. This pattern suggests that patriarchal institutions and values contribute to wife battering in highly male-dominant societies, but it is not clear that this is the cause of such violence in cultures that have progressed toward gender equality. The United States might be seen as falling into the latter group. Although the vestiges of patriarchy certainly remain, social norms and values in the United States have become much more equalitarian in recent decades. And recent research in the United States suggests that the remnants of patriarchy evident in this country are not a major cause of either common couple violence or intimate terrorism. Several types of evidence support this position.

First, the vast majority of men do not engage in marital violence. Research using the CTS indicates that roughly 25 to 30 percent engage in common couple violence at some point during the course of their marriage (Dutton, 1998; Straus, 1990). This proportion is slightly higher for women (Archer, 2000). If one focuses only on clear cases of spouse abuse (i.e., intimate terrorism), researchers estimate that approximately 2 percent of all males engage in this behavior. These data indicate that men who are socialized in the same cultural milieu show considerable differences in their intimate behaviors, with the vast majority eschewing violent behavior.

It is likely to be the case, however, that some men are more strongly socialized into a patriarchal belief system than others. Perhaps it is these men, rather than men in general, who are at high risk for using aggression to control their wives. Recently, Felson (2000) reviewed several studies regarding whether men who hold traditional attitudes about gender roles are more likely to engage in marital violence. He found two studies that supported this idea, six that reported no association between gender role beliefs and partner violence, and three in which traditional men were *less* violent toward their partners. Thus, about half of the studies failed to find an association between gender role beliefs and marital violence. And of those that found a relationship, the majority reported results contrary to the idea that patriarchy leads to violence. Rather than elevating risk for violence, traditional gender role beliefs were associated with lower rates of wife assault.

Felson (2000) suggests that traditional gender beliefs may discourage the use of violence toward women because this belief system tends to include the norm of chivalry. In support of this contention, he reviews research showing that participants in laboratory experiments are much more likely to deliver shocks to men than women, women are more likely to receive help than men, participants generally evaluate violence against wives more negatively than violence against husbands, and men are much *less* likely than women to say that husband violence is justified in response to partner provocations.

Research on the criminal justice system provides further support for the idea of chivalry. A meta-analysis of 50 studies showed that women generally receive more lenient treatment than men (Daly and Bordt, 1995). This is especially true for capital punishment. Although 10.5 percent of murder defendants in 1998 were women, only 1.5 percent of prisoners under sentence of death in 2000 were women (Bureau of Justice Statistics, 2001; Fox, 2001). Based on all of this evidence, Felson (2000) concludes that our culture encourages men to protect women while branding those who hit women as deviant and cowardly. This finding, he notes, challenges the contention that patriarchy is the primary explanation for marital violence.

The patriarchy explanation is also contradicted by research on homosexual couples. Tjaden and Thoennes (1999) compared rates of violence for heterosexual and gay relationships. They found that heterosexual men were no more violent toward their partners than homosexual men. The fact that the victim's gender did not affect incidence of violence is contrary to the idea that men's aggression toward intimate partners is a function of male dominance or special attitudes toward females (Felson, 2000).

Even more telling evidence comes from research on lesbian relationships. These studies report relatively high rates of partner violence (Renzetti, 1992). Indeed, Turrel (2000) found that lesbians were more likely than gay men to be physically attacked by their partners. Similarly, a study of 136 women who had had prior relationships with both men and women found that the respondents had been abused more frequently by lesbian than male partners (Lie et al., 1991). Forty-two percent reported having been victimized by men, whereas 57 percent reported having been victimized by women. These results are clearly contrary to the thesis that intimate violence is propagated by male domination.

In summary, although patriarchy may explain why some societies have very high rates of wife abuse, it does not appear to be the primary cause of marital violence in more equalitarian societies such as the United States. Men raised in these cultures exhibit dramatic differences in the way they treat women. Most do not hit their intimate partners and disapprove of those who do. A small percentage of men, however, do use violence to control and dominate their wives. If gender beliefs do not explain this behavior, what does? As we will see in the next section, many family-violence researchers contend that such violence is rooted in childhood exposure to family violence.

Childhood Exposure to Family Violence

The most popular and widely accepted view of marital violence among social scientists is that it represents a behavior pattern learned in childhood. Childhood exposure to family violence is seen as increasing the chances that a person will engage in violence toward his or her spouse as an adult. The concept of modeling from social learning theory is used to link childhood experiences to adult behavior. Originally, it was posited that having witnessed violent parental interaction as a child is the primary explanation for marital violence. It was assumed that children acquire information regarding the role of a marital partner by observing their parents interact with each other. Thus, children exposed to violent parental interaction learn that aggression is a normal part of marital interaction and, as adults, are apt to engage in such behavior when they have a conflict with their spouse. Early studies supported this idea, as adult marital violence was found to be related to a childhood history of having witnessed violence between parents (Pagelow, 1981; Rosenbaum and O'Leary, 1981; Straus, Gelles, and Steinmetz, 1980).

The pioneering national study of family violence by Straus and colleagues (1980) suggested that it was not simply exposure to between-parent violence that placed a person at risk for adult marital violence. Straus and colleagues found that having been subjected to harsh corporal punishment as a child was also associated with adult marital violence. This finding indicated that what was being learned in violent families consisted of more than marital scripts based on observing parental interaction. Straus and company (Straus and Smith, 1990; Straus, Gelles, and Steinmetz, 1980) posited that childhood exposure to family violence, whether marital violence or harsh parenting, teaches children that it is legitimate, indeed, often necessary, to hit those you love. As we saw in Chapter Three, modeling is not merely a matter of imitation. Rather, modeling often results in the induction of abstract rules or principles that are used to guide behavior in future situations (Bandura, 1977).

Based on this idea, Straus and his colleagues argue that exposure to either harsh parenting or interparental violence trains children to believe that it is normal and acceptable to hit family members. And, they assert, individuals who grow up with this belief are likely to hit their romantic partners when they become adults.

Several studies have investigated the potential link between growing up in a violent family and engaging in marital violence as an adult. Although the results are somewhat mixed, most studies find an association between the two phenomena. Stith, Rosen, and Middleton (2000), for example, completed a meta-analysis of 39 studies published between 1978 and 1997. They found that reports of having witnessed interparental violence or of having been subjected to harsh parenting were both associated with adult marital violence. These results provide support for Straus' contention that childhood exposure to family violence, regardless of whether it involves abusive parenting or between-parent aggression, increases the probability of adult marital violence.

Recently, however, Simons, Lin, and Gordon (1998) have suggested that exposure to harsh parenting may be a more important cause of marital violence than witnessing interparental violence. They note that most applications of modeling to the learning of marital violence fail to incorporate an important principle of social learning theory. Social learning theory maintains that individuals observe the contingencies that follow people's actions in a particular situation and then use this information to design a plan of behavior when they encounter a similar situation (Bandura, 1977). According to the theory, individuals do not simply copy or imitate the behavior of others. Rather, they emulate actions that lead to positive consequences and eschew behaviors that produce undesirable results. Even if a behavior is viewed as legitimate, it is unlikely that a person will engage in the action unless he perceives that it will have a positive effect.

Simons and colleagues go on to argue that children usually observe few, if any, positive consequences when their parents engage in violence toward each other. Persons who are slapped or shoved by their spouse are apt to respond with an emotional outburst, a threat, or violence. It is unlikely, assert Simons and colleagues, that a child who witnesses such exchanges would conclude that physical violence is an effective strategy for getting your way. On the other hand, Simons and company observe, children often modify their behavior when faced with the threat of corporal punishment. Harsh punishment may produce residual feelings of anger or rejection, but it often produces at least a temporary change in behavior. Given this fact, children who experience harsh punishment may conclude that physical violence is sometimes a necessary and effective strategy for achieving behavior change in family and intimate relationships.

Most research on marital violence has focused on *either* exposure to harsh parenting *or* interparental violence. When studies include both factors, they usually report the effect of each without controlling for the other. Earlier, for example, we described the meta-analysis by Stith and colleagues (2000). They noted that many of the respondents in their study had experienced both harsh parenting and interparental violence, but their analytic procedure only examined the effect of each event, without taking into account the effect of the other. This approach does not rule out the possibility that witnessing interparental violence during childhood is correlated with adult marital violence because of its association with exposure to harsh parenting.

Simons and colleagues (1998) examined the impact of interparental violence after controlling for harsh parenting. Virtually all research on the intergenerational transmission of family violence has used retrospective reports of childhood experiences (Stith, Rosen, and Middleton, 2000). In contrast, Simons and colleagues used prospective data where persistent exposure to interparental aggression and harsh parenting during adolescence was used to predict violence toward romantic partners during early adulthood. Their results showed that harsh parenting predicted violence toward romantic partners even after controlling for interparental violence. The converse, however, was not the case. Interparental violence was not related to violence toward a romantic partner once the effect of exposure to harsh parenting was taken into account. A prospective study of adult behavior showed similar results (Simons and Johnson, 1998). Multivariate analysis showed that harsh corporal punishment predicted family violence, whereas witnessing marital violence did not. Although these findings suggest that exposure to harsh parenting is more consequential than witnessing interparental violence, it is not possible to draw definitive conclusions based on the results of two studies.

Given the retrospective data and statistical weaknesses that have characterized prior research, it is still not clear whether interparental violence, harsh parenting, or both are important risk factors for marital violence. Resolution of this question will require longitudinal studies and the use of statistical procedures that isolate the *unique* effects of interparental violence and harsh parenting on adult marital behavior. Another limitation of past research on this topic is that it has focused almost exclusively on common couple violence. Hence, these studies provide little information regarding the extent to which childhood exposure to family violence increases the probability of serious and persistent spouse abuse.

This section has described the emphasis that family violence researchers have placed on the link between childhood family experiences and adult marital interaction. Virtually all of this research has assumed that modeling is the theoretical mechanism, whereby growing up in a violent family increases the probability of assaulting one's marital partner. The early chapters of this book presented various control and social learning arguments regarding the manner in which childhood exposure to dysfunctional parental behavior gives rise to a general antisocial orientation that includes involvement in a wide assortment of deviant behaviors. The next section examines the extent to which this perspective can be applied to marital violence. Our discussion will be more concerned with severe and persistent spouse abuse—intimate terrorism—than with common couple violence.

The Criminological Perspective

Thus far we have discussed two explanations for marital violence: patriarchy and parental modeling of family violence. Both of these theoretical perspectives have assumed that marital violence is a distinct form of antisocial behavior that requires its own special theory or explanation. Indeed, most partner-violence researchers assume that batterers are specialists who tend to be ordinary citizens in all respects except for their abusive behavior (Pagelow, 1984; Moffitt et al., 2000). Given this assumption, marital violence theorizing has focused on cultural or family experiences that might give rise to this particular deviant behavior. The criminological theory and research discussed in earlier chapters, however, would suggest an alternative perspective.

This literature notes that deviant acts tend to be correlated—individuals who engage in one type of deviant behavior tend to participate in other types as well (Donovan and Jessor, 1985; Farrington, 1991; Osgood et al., 1988). There is also evidence that antisocial behavior is relatively stable across the life course (Caspi and Moffitt, 1995; Loeber and Le Blanc, 1990; Sampson and Laub, 1993). Those who manifest high levels of antisocial behavior at an early age are at risk for chronic delinquency during adolescence and continued reckless and irresponsible behavior during adulthood (Farrington, 1991; Loeber and Le Blanc, 1990; Patterson and Yoerger, 1993). In other words, antisocial behavior shows the characteristics of a behavior trait, a pattern of behavior that is expressed across time and situations (Allport, 1937). This body of research suggests that partner violence is likely to be an expression of a more general antisocial pattern of behavior. It indicates that persons who engage in persistent aggression toward romantic partners are likely to have a history of involvement in a variety of other antisocial behaviors as well.

If partner violence is an expression of a general antisocial orientation, how does such an orientation develop? Theory and research reviewed in prior chapters suggests that antisocial tendencies tend to emerge in childhood as a result of ineffective parenting practices such as low supervision, rejection, and inconsistent discipline (Gottfredson and Hirschi, 1990; Patterson, Reid, and Dishion, 1992; Sampson and Laub, 1993). Further, this research indicates that there is an increased probability that parents will engage in ineffective parenting if they have antisocial tendencies like excessive drinking, erratic work performance, and altercations with peers (Patterson, Reid, and Dishion, 1992; Sampson and Laub, 1993; Simons et al., 1996). These antisocial tendencies often include domestic violence (Fagan, Stewart, and Hansen, 1983; Hotaling, Straus, and Lincoln, 1990; Simons et al., 1995; Walker, 1979). Thus, antisocial parents are likely to hit each other and their children, and to engage in ineffective parenting. This ineffective parenting, in turn, increases the probability that their children will grow up to engage in antisocial behavior of all sorts, including violence toward romantic partners. In other words, it is a general pattern of antisocial behavior, not specific lessons regarding male dominance or marital violence, that is transmitted across generations in violent families.

Only recently have investigators begun to test this criminological perspective on marital violence. In the past, family researchers conducted investigations based on the specialization premise, whereas criminologists have largely ignored the phenomenon of domestic violence (Moffitt et al., 2000). In the last decade, however, there has been a decline in the bifurcation of research traditions between the fields of family sociology and criminology. Family sociologists have become more aware of criminological findings challenging the notion of offense specialization, and criminologists have begun to study domestic violence. Research to date suggests that the criminological perspective on partner violence holds promise. The remainder of this section provides a brief overview of the evidence supporting the perspective. First, we will present the results of studies concerned with the relationship between partner violence and other types of antisocial behavior. Second, we will review research regarding the extent to which a general pattern of antisocial behavior mediates or explains the relationship between growing up in a violent family and engaging in partner abuse. Finally, we will discuss research on typologies of wife batterers in order to account for those instances in which the criminological perspective does not appear to apply.

In recent years, several studies have investigated the extent to which abusive spouses engage in other types of deviance as well. Much of this research has focused on the question of whether spouse batterers also engage in violence toward nonintimates. Reviews of this literature find substantial overlap between the two types of violence (Fagan and Browne, 1994; Felson, 2000; Holtzworth-Monroe and Stuart, 1994; Hotaling, Straus, and Lincoln, 1990; Marvell and Moody, 1999). Instead of limiting their focus to violent crime, other researchers have examined the extent to which spouse abuse is associated with a deviant lifestyle. Findings from these studies indicate that this tends to be the case. This research shows, for example, that perpetrators of domestic assault often have had contact with the police for a variety of criminal behaviors (Dunford, Huizinga, and Elliott, 1990; Hotaling, Straus, and Lincoln, 1990; Sherman et al., 1991), self-report involvement in general crime (Moffitt et al., 2000), and have a history of participation in delinquent and antisocial behavior (Simons et al., 1995; Simons and Johnson, 1998). Although the degree of co-occurrence is not 100 percent, these studies find considerable overlap between spouse abuse and other types of deviant and criminal behavior. Further, this pattern holds for females as well as males (Hotaling, Straus, and Lincoln, 1990; McNeely and Mann, 1990; Moffitt et al., 2000; Simons et al., 1995; Simons and Johnson, 1998).

These findings challenge the oft-made assertion that perpetrators of spouse abuse have few distinguishing characteristics (Pagelow, 1984). They are often depicted as ordinary citizens in all respects except for their abusive behavior. This view may well be accurate for individuals who only occasionally engage in family violence. In large part, such common couple violence is probably a function of situational factors such as economic pressure, emotional distress, and marital conflict. Many, if not most, individuals who engage in severe, recurrent spouse assault (i.e., intimate terrorists), on the other hand, appear to be distinctive in that they participate in other forms of deviant behavior as well. In other words, severe partner abuse is often an expression of a more general antisocial orientation.

If this is true, the theories of delinquent and criminal behavior discussed in earlier chapters (e.g., social and self-control, social learning) provide another view of why childhood exposure to family violence predicts adult partner abuse. These theories posit that an antisocial orientation is fostered by ineffective parenting practices such as inadequate monitoring, inconsistent discipline, and the absence of warmth and support. Harsh, explosive punishment is highly correlated with these dimensions of inept parenting (Patterson, 1982; Patterson, Reid, and Dishion, 1992). Thus, it may be ineffective parenting in general, rather than abusive discipline per se, that increases the chances of engaging in spouse abuse. And rather than lessons regarding the legitimacy of marital violence, it may be commitment to involvement in an antisocial lifestyle that links growing up in a violent family to partner abuse.

Unfortunately, only a handful of studies have investigated this possibility. These studies have focused on both adolescent dating violence (Riggs and O'Leary, 1996; Simons, Lin, and Gordon, 1998) and partner assault by adults (Simons et al., 1995; Simons and Johnson, 1998; Swinford et al., 2000; White and Widom, 2003). In all cases, the results indicate that commitment to a general antisocial orientation explains much of the relationship between growing up in a violent family and partner abuse. This finding suggests that the family processes that have been shown to predict general crime and delinquency may go a long way toward accounting for partner violence as well.

Although research indicates that many spouse abusers manifest an antisocial lifestyle and that this lifestyle is rooted in their experiences as part of a dysfunctional family, these studies also show that there are many exceptions to this tendency. Some individuals are intimate terrorists but they rarely, if ever, engage in other types of criminal or antisocial behavior. Greater understanding of this point is provided by scholars who have attempted to develop typologies of men who engage in severe and persistent abuse of their wives (Dutton, 1998; Holtzworth-Monroe and Stuart, 1994; Jacobson and Gottman, 1998). All of these typologies identify a group of batterers who are generally antisocial. They fit the profile described by the research we have reviewed in this section. In addition, however, the typologies also distinguish a second group of batterers, who have no history of antisocial behavior.

This category of batterers is usually labeled dysphoric/borderline or borderline/dependent, as they tend to show the characteristics of persons diagnosed with borderline personality disorder (Dutton, 1998; Holtzworth-Monroe and Stuart, 1994; Johnson and Ferraro, 2000). These individuals tend to be emotionally dependent and harbor strong fears of abandonment. Further, they have low self-esteem and feel unloveable. As a consequence, they are very controlling in intimate relationships and become threatened, jealous, and angry if they perceive that their partner is exercising independence or developing outside interests and activities. In the midst of this rage and anxiety, the person resorts to verbal abuse or physical violence in an effort to reestablish control and avoid abandonment. Thus, the violence of these individuals tends to be specific to intimate relationships, as this behavior is an expression of fear and anger regarding rejection, rather than a component of a more general antisocial orientation.

Donald Dutton (1998) has completed a series of studies in an attempt to identify the childhood factors that foster such an orientation. His results indicate that borderline/dependent abusers usually have grown up in a family characterized by emotional and physical abuse. The child's desperate attempts to obtain parental approval and acceptance were met with criticism and rejection. These experiences gave rise to feelings of anger, loneliness, and worthlessness. They also fostered a cynical, distrustful view of people and relationships. As adults, these individuals enter romantic relationships with intense needs for support, acceptance, and approval. This emotional dependency is coupled, however, with a strong sense of mistrust and fear of abandonment. Even subtle indications of rejection or disinterest on the part of the wife feed into these fears and concerns, triggering old childhood feelings of frustration and rage. Rather than communicating his feelings in a constructive fashion, the abuser attempts to coerce his partner into meeting his needs by engaging in the emotionally and physically abusive actions that he saw modeled by his parents. This alienates the wife, and her disapproval further threatens her borderline/dependent husband, leading to an escalation in his use of violence to exercise control.

Thus, research to date indicates that inept parenting is implicated in the etiology of both the borderline/dependent batterer and the generally antisocial abuser. It is yet to be established, however, how the parenting characteristics that place a child at risk for becoming an antisocial batterer differ from those that increase his chances of becoming a borderline/dependent batterer. Past research suggests two explanations.

The first explanation emphasizes parental differences in monitoring and discipline. In previous chapters, we saw that a parenting style characterized by a failure to set rules, lax monitoring, and inconsistent discipline increases the chances that a child will grow up to have an antisocial orientation. Thus, it follows that these parenting practices place a child at risk for becoming an antisocial spouse abuser. In contrast, it appears to be parental rejection in the form of emotional and physical abuse that produces the psychological and behavioral traits associated with the borderline/dependent batterer. Apparently, the parents of these individuals set rules and engage in the consistent discipline necessary to produce a basically conventional lifestyle. The rejection and abuse, however, results in emotional dependence and a violent, turbulent approach to intimate relationships.

The second explanation emphasizes differences in the level or severity of abuse experienced as a child. There is evidence that antisocial batterers usually have experienced more extreme physical and emotional abuse as children than borderline/dependent batterers (Jacobson and Gottman, 1998). Thus, it may be that antisocial batterers have developed an avoidant approach to intimate relationships. Their family environment has taught them that people are untrustworthy and exploitive, so as adults they avoid emotional dependence on others. This lack of emotional involvement allows them to treat others, including romantic partners, in a callous and coercive fashion. Consistent with this view, Jacobson and Gottman (1998) reported that antisocial batterers are often quite cruel and savage in their treatment of intimate partners.

Compared with their antisocial counterparts, borderline/dependent batterers may have been subject to less severe and more episodic childhood abuse (Dutton, 1998; Jacobson and Gottman, 1998). Although their parents were often hostile and rejecting, at other times they may have been at least somewhat nurturing. Boys exposed to such parenting might be expected to develop an insecure view of intimate relationships. They want to be loved but fear rejection. Their experience of intimate relationships is likely to involve feelings of insecurity, jealousy, and paranoia. And they are likely to respond to these feelings with the violent control tactics they saw modeled in their family of origin. Given the aggression modeled in their families of origin, these men may use emotional abuse and physical intimidation to control their spouse. Given their emotional attachment to their partner, however, the severity of their emotional and physical attacks is likely to be less extreme than that of the antisocial batterer.

As we have noted, current research findings do not allow us to determine whether it is differences in monitoring and discipline or variations in severity of childhood abuse that place a child at risk for becoming an antisocial versus a borderline/dependent batterer. Indeed, it may turn out that neither of these explanations is correct and that it is some third set of factors that distinguishes the two types of spouse abusers. At this point, it is clear that there are two types of husbands that engage in intimate terrorism. We have little understanding of the childhood circumstances that foster each of the types.

This chapter has examined various avenues whereby growing up in an abusive family increases the chances that a person will engage in partner abuse. Before ending our discussion of marital violence, there is a puzzling finding that remains to be considered. Several studies have found that being physically abused during childhood increases the chances that a woman will grow up to experience violence at the hands of a boyfriend or spouse (see Stith, Rosen, and Middleton, 2000). Thus, exposure to harsh parenting as a child not only increases the probability that a person will engage in marital violence; it also raises the chance that a woman will be the *victim* of marital violence. Why might this be the case?

Explaining Women's Double Jeopardy

Ironically, women who were victims of harsh parenting as children often grow up to be the victims of violence by their romantic partners. This association has been reported in several studies, and recently Stith and colleagues (2000) corroborated this link in a meta-analysis based on 39 well-designed studies published between 1978 and 1997. This analysis showed that childhood exposure to harsh parenting was a much stronger predictor of being the victim of spouse abuse than was witnessing interparental violence. This does not mean that most abused wives were mistreated as children. Well over half of all women who experience violence as wives were not subjected to harsh treatment by parents (Bowker, 1983; Pagelow, 1981). It does appear to be the case, however, that exposure to abusive parents increases the probability of being married to an assaultive husband. Such women endure a *double jeopardy* in which they escape violence in their family of origin only to encounter further violence in their marriage.

The most widely accepted account for the double jeopardy phenomenon is based on the theoretical writings of Straus and Gelles discussed earlier in this chapter (Straus and Gelles, 1990; Straus, Gelles, and Steinmetz, 1980). This perspective was formulated to explain the finding that family violence tends to be transmitted across generations. It argues that children subject to harsh parenting learn that family violence is normal and to be expected, that sometimes it is necessary, or at least acceptable, to hit those you love (Straus and Smith, 1990a; 1990b). Using this perspective, Gelles (1976, 1979) argued that there are two reasons why women who experienced harsh treatment as children are prone to be victims of spouse abuse as adults.

First, he noted that, just as family aggression provides a role model for perpetrators, so it may furnish a role model for victims. Thus, women who were exposed to family violence as children may develop the expectation that "husbands are 'supposed' to hit wives, and this role expectation may in turn become the motivator for her husband to use violence on her" (Gelles, 1979, 102). Simons, Johnson, et al. (1993) contend that this explanation for the double jeopardy phenomenon is problematic on several counts. They note that a girl might learn that men hit women as a consequence of repeated exposure to corporal punishment by her father, but studies have generally found that harsh treatment by either the mother or father increases a woman's chances of being the victim of spouse abuse. Further, Simons and colleagues argue that even if a woman was socialized to believe that it is legitimate for husbands to hit their wives, it seems unlikely that this idea could somehow evoke violence from her husband. How would she communicate this expectation to her husband, and why would he respond with violence simply because she believed such behavior was legitimate?

The second explanation offered by Gelles seems more plausible. Citing the homogamy theory of selection, he argued that the relationship between abuse during childhood and victimization by husbands may be a function of an assortative mating process whereby women who grew up in an environment of family violence are apt to marry men from similar backgrounds. This point of view raises a question concerning the attributes that persons raised in a milieu of family violence have in common. If men and women engage in assortative mating based on shared attributes acquired in an atmosphere of family violence, what are these attributes?

The theories and research presented in earlier chapters suggest an answer to this question. We saw that children exposed to harsh, explosive, and inconsistent parenting are at risk for behavior and adjustment problems. They often grow up to be noncompliant and defiant, and engage in a wide variety of deviant behaviors. Further, we noted that individuals with such an orientation tend to affiliate with persons who possess similar characteristics. This pattern of findings suggests the following explanation for the double jeopardy phenomenon: Women who were subjected to harsh parenting are at greater risk for aggressive/deviant behavior than those who were raised by authoritative parents. Antisocial women are likely to meet, date, and fall in love with men who are also antisocial. Several studies support this idea (Cairns and Cairns, 1994; Rowe and Farrington, 1997; Simons, Stewart, et al., 2002). Unfortunately, antisocial males are more apt to strike their romantic partners than are their more conventional counterparts. This explanation for women's double jeopardy is simply an extension of the control, social learning, and life course theories discussed earlier.

We are aware of only two studies that test this argument. In a study of divorced women, Simons and colleagues (1993) found that a general antisocial orientation and assortative mating explain the association between childhood exposure to harsh corporal punishment and adult victimization by a romantic partner. Similarly, Swinford and colleagues (2000) found that the relationship between having had an abusive childhood and being the victim of intimate violence was explained by involvement in an antisocial lifestyle and involvement with an antisocial partner. There is certainly a need for more investigation of this issue. But the evidence that exists provides support for an assortative mating explanation for the phenomenon of double jeopardy.

Summary and Conclusions

Many couples sometimes hit each other in the midst of an argument. Although it is morally and socially undesirable, we saw that such common couple violence occurs infrequently, does not escalate over time, and rarely results in physical injury or psychological trauma. This is not the type of violence that most human-service workers, policy makers, or everyday citizens have in mind when they refer to spouse abuse or battering. Rather, it is the phenomenon of intimate terrorism that concerns society. This type of violence is frequent, persistent, and severe, and it results in physical injury and emotional trauma. It is in response to this social problem that we have established shelters, strengthened restraining orders, instituted mandatory arrest policies, and implemented treatment programs. This assaultive behavior is relatively rare and is usually committed by a man against a woman.

Past research indicates that two types of men tend to engage in intimate terrorism. The first group consists of men who engage in a wide variety of antisocial behaviors in addition to spouse abuse. For these individuals, severe partner abuse is an expression of a more general antisocial orientation. Their antisocial behavior appears to be, in large measure, a consequence of having grown up in a disorganized, violent family. In contrast, the second category of batterers displays the characteristics of borderline personality disorder and engages in little antisocial behavior outside of the couple's relationship. Their intimate violence appears to be an expression of fear and anger regarding rejection, rather than a component of a more general antisocial orientation. There is some evidence to suggest that these abusers often have grown up in a family characterized by emotional and physical abuse. Apparently, the parents of these individuals set rules and engage in the consistent discipline necessary to produce a basically conventional lifestyle. The rejection and abuse, however, results in a violent, turbulent approach to intimate relationships.

There is still much to be learned about the types of men who engage in severe partner abuse and the childhood factors that give rise to such behavior. Given its low base rate, it is difficult to generate samples of intimate terrorists. As a result, most studies have focused on common couple violence. Thus, we know much more about minor acts of partner violence than we do about more extreme forms of assault. We hope that future studies will devote more attention to serious cases of abuse. ✦

Chapter Nine

Child Maltreatment: Inept Parenting or Expression of a General Antisocial Orientation?

Child maltreatment is widely recognized as a major social problem in the United States and, increasingly, abroad. Kempe and his colleagues broke ground in the medical world with their 1962 publication describing the "battered child syndrome" (Kempe et al., 1962). Since then, several measures have been taken to protect children from maltreatment, the most prominent being the enactment of state and federal laws requiring the reporting of suspected maltreatment, and the creation of a nationwide child protective service system. During the past 15 years, the National Child Abuse and Neglect Data System (NCANDS) has collected important data on the incidence of child abuse and neglect in the United States. Additionally, the research community has come to a greater awareness of this social issue. Social scientists have initiated groundbreaking studies of the incidence, etiology, and consequences of child maltreatment. The present chapter provides an overview of much of this research.

We will begin by defining child abuse and neglect and by briefly describing the methodological and conceptual issues encountered when attempting to establish estimates of the incidence and prevalence of these two phenomena. We will then turn to the primary concern of the chapter—the factors that increase the chances that parents will engage in child maltreatment. Past research has consistently found that exposure to abusive parenting during childhood significantly increases the probability that a person will grow up to mistreat his or her own child (Heyman and Slep, 2002). Further, these studies indicate that this is a powerful risk factor, as it produces a several-fold increase in the chances that an individual will mistreat a child.

There are basically two theoretical perspectives on this link between exposure to maltreatment and subsequently engaging in abusive parenting. Usually, this relationship is explained in terms of lessons learned during childhood regarding the nature of parenting. It is assumed that abused children learn that harsh, punitive measures are the proper approach to parenting. They then utilize this parenting style in raising their own children. Proponents of this perspective usually assume that child abusers are conventional, often quite successful individuals, who display this singular deviant behavior in the privacy of their homes. The theories presented in earlier chapters, however, suggest an alternative perspective. In Chapter Four, we saw that exposure to abusive parenting tends to foster a general antisocial orientation that gives rise to a wide variety of deviant behaviors. This suggests that child maltreatment may be part of a more general antisocial lifestyle. Rather than simply providing dysfunctional lessons regarding the nature of parenting, it may be that abused children are at risk for engaging in an array of adult criminal acts, including child abuse. Evidence will be examined regarding the validity of these two competing points of view.

The causes of child sexual abuse differ from those of other forms of physical abuse. We will therefore treat sexual abuse as a separate topic in the latter part of the chapter. Information is provided regarding the prevalence and incidence of this form of maltreatment, focusing on risk factors and types of offenders. We will briefly review literature showing a link between having been sexually abused as a child and perpetration of this behavior as an adult.

How Common Is Child Maltreatment?

We need to clarify what we mean by child maltreatment prior to discussing its incidence. *Child abuse* is usually defined legally and medically as intentional physical injury of a minor child by a caretaker. It involves a deliberate act calculated to harm the child. This includes acts of commission (e.g., hitting the child with an object, burning the child with a cigarette) as well as those of omission (e.g., withholding water, food, sleep, or medical care).

Child neglect, on the other hand, involves negligence by a caretaker that threatens the physical and emotional well-being of the child. The caretaker unintentionally jeopardizes the child's welfare by failing to provide the conditions necessary for normal physical, psychological, and social development. For example, the child may not be properly clothed, fed, or supervised. Although it is the most common form of maltreatment, neglect receives far less attention than physical abuse, perhaps because neglect is much more difficult to define or recognize than abuse.

What is the incidence of child maltreatment in the United States? The answer to this question depends on the source of data one uses. Basically, there are two types of data: information from official records prepared by governmental agencies and self-report survey data collected by social scientists. NCANDS has collected annual reports from child-protection services in the 50 states since 1990. These data revealed an estimated 903,000 victims of abuse and neglect in 2001, yielding an incidence rate of 12.4 per 1,000 children. More than half of the children were under the age of 7, and in the vast majority of cases (81 percent), the abuse was perpetrated by a parent. Most cases involved neglect (57.2 percent), 18.6 percent were physical abuse cases, 10 percent were charges of sexual abuse, with the remainder involving other kinds of maltreatment (6.8 percent were emotional abuse cases) or more than one type of abuse. Rates were similar for boys and girls, with the exception of sexual abuse, for which the rate was 1.7 per 1,000 girls and .4 per 1,000 boys (U.S. Department of Health and Human Services, 2002).

Statistics such as these are very useful, but they are limited by the fact that abuse not brought to the attention of agencies is not a part of this data set. Therefore, rates of child abuse based on "official" statistics necessarily underestimate the incidence and prevalence of child abuse in the United States. Another crucial consideration when using official data is the issue of what behaviors, conditions, and situations are included in these statistics. Most cases or incidents reported to law enforcement or social services are designated as "unsubstantiated," "unfounded," or "not indicated." Each of these terms indicates that no action was taken because there was not enough evidence of abuse to proceed, but this does not mean that abuse or neglect did not take place. In addition to cases of malicious or false reports, this classification includes cases in which the maltreatment is mild or warrants other intervention, such as services to the family, as well as a myriad of other situations, including cases in which there are no witnesses or the family cannot be found. In 2001, 59.2 percent of all investigated cases nationwide were found to be "unsubstantiated" (U.S. Department of Health and Human Services, 2002).

In order to remedy the methodological weakness of official records and obtain a more complete record of child abuse, social scientists have conducted interview studies that ask parents to report on their parenting behaviors, including harsh measures that might be considered abusive. These self-report surveys of child maltreatment usually produce vastly larger rates than those based on cases reported to law enforcement or child protection agencies. These studies not only include the large number of cases that go unreported to official agencies; they also tend to use a somewhat broader set of criteria for defining abuse than is specified in legal definitions.

Given the difficulty of defining neglect or emotional abuse, self-report surveys have largely concentrated on physical abuse. The most widely acclaimed studies of this type are the National Family Violence Surveys completed by Murray Straus and his colleagues. In the mid-1970s (Straus, Gelles, and Steinmetz, 1980) and again in the mid-1980s (Straus and Gelles, 1986), these researchers conducted general population surveys in an attempt to determine the incidence of parents' physical abuse of their children. Both studies used the Conflict Tactics Scale (which includes a wide range of aggressive and violent behaviors) to measure violence in families. Straus and Gelles found that 3.6 percent of parents had engaged in violence toward children aged 3 to 17 in 1975, and approximately 2 percent of parents reported having done so in the 1985 survey. These rates are much higher than official report statistics, and they undoubtedly underestimate the problem, as many respondents were probably unwilling to admit to engaging in violence toward their children. The good news, however, is that the rate of abuse appears to have declined significantly during the 10-year period between the two surveys. One hopes that this trend is continuing, and fewer parents are resorting to physically abusive tactics to control their children.

Intergenerational Transmission of Child Maltreatment

One of the most popular ideas regarding child abuse is that it is transmitted across generations. Exposure to abusive parenting during childhood is seen as significantly increasing the probability that individuals will grow up to mistreat their own children. This view has been labeled the "cycle of violence" hypothesis. Unfortunately, many well-meaning experts have overgeneralized the strength of this association (Gelles and Conte, 1990; Schwartz, Rendon, and Hsieh, 1994; Kaufman and Zigler, 1993). Schwartz and his colleagues cite several examples from the 1980s and 1990s of witnesses overstating the negative impact of abuse on children to lawmakers. In 1992, for instance, a state senator from New York testified before a U.S. House subcommittee that 70 to 75 percent of seriously abused children become abusers or violent criminals. And Kaufman and Zigler (1993) relate a case in which a woman who was abused as a child refrained from having children of her own on the advice of a mental health professional.

In recent years, several studies have attempted to quantify the extent to which child abuse is transmitted across generations. Due in part to dissimilarities in methodology, these studies have yielded differing estimates of the intergenerational effect (Egeland, Jacobvitz, and Papatola, 1988; Kaufman and Zigler, 1987). Reviews of this research conclude, however, that a reasonable estimate of child maltreatment among parents who were themselves abused is 30 percent (Kaufman and Zigler, 1987). This may sound like a modest proportion, but only 2 percent of parents in the general population abuse their children (Straus and Gelles, 1986). Thus, parents who were abused as children are approximately 15 times more likely to abuse their offspring than parents in general. Health risk factors identified in medical research usually do not even double a person's odds of contracting a particular disease (e.g., high cholesterol and the risk of heart disease). Thus, it is apparent that childhood maltreatment is a potent risk factor for becoming an abusive parent. Recent research continues to find a clear relationship between being abused as a child and perpetrating abuse as an adult (Heyman and Slep, 2002).

Having established that there is a tendency for adults to repeat the abuse they experienced as a child, the question naturally arises as to what accounts for this cycle. Social scientists have provided two explanations for this phenomenon. The first is based on social learning theory (Bandura, 1977) and argues that children learn how to parent by observing the behavior of their parents (Simons, Beaman, et al., 1993a; Simons et al., 1991; Steinmetz, 1987; Straus, Gelles, and Steinmetz, 1980). In the course of growing up, a child is subject to countless repetitions of particular patterns of parental behavior. Children might be expected to possess only a superficial understanding of the routine parenting practices used in families other than their own. Hence, the behavior displayed by their parents is apt to be accepted as a model of normal or typical parental behavior. Later, when the individual achieves adulthood, she is likely to employ these parenting scripts in a reflexive, rather unthinking fashion when parenting her own children.

This idea is consistent with reports from family therapists that parents often have little awareness regarding their behavior toward their children. Thus, individuals raised by authoritative parents utilize authoritative parenting techniques with their own children, whereas those who were subject to harsh, explosive parenting during childhood grow up to repeat this parenting style with their offspring (Herrenkohl, Herrenkohl, and Toedter, 1983; Simons et al., 1991; Steinmetz, 1987; Straus, Gelles, and Steinmetz, 1980). This perspective tends to assume that abusive parents are conventional members of society who display this one type of deviant behavior in the privacy of their homes.

The second point of view on the link between childhood and adult abuse takes a very different position. This perspective builds on the criminological theories discussed in Chapters Two and Three, and is consistent with the arguments developed in Chapter Eight regarding marital violence as an expression of a more general antisocial orientation. In those chapters, we reviewed research showing that individuals who engage in one type of deviant behavior tend to participate in other types as well, and that antisocial behavior is relatively stable across the life course. Those who manifest high levels of antisocial behavior at an early age are at risk for chronic delinquency during adolescence and continued reckless and irresponsible behavior during adulthood. This body of research suggests that abusive parenting may be an expression of a more general antisocial pattern of behavior. It indicates that persons who are persistently aggressive and explosive with their children may have a history of involvement in a variety of other antisocial behaviors as well.

If abusive parenting is an expression of a general antisocial lifestyle, how does such an orientation develop? Theory and research reviewed in prior chapters suggested that antisocial tendencies tend to emerge in childhood as a result of ineffective parenting practices such as low supervision, rejection, and inconsistent discipline. Further, this research indicated that there is an increased probability that parents will engage in ineffective parenting if they have antisocial tendencies such as excessive drinking, erratic work performance, and altercations with peers. These antisocial tendencies often include domestic violence. Thus, antisocial parents are likely to hit each other and their children, and to engage in ineffective parenting. This ineffective parenting, in turn, increases the probability that their children will grow up to engage in antisocial behavior of all sorts, including violence toward romantic partners. In other words, it is a general pattern of antisocial behavior, rather than specific lessons about parenting, that is transmitted across generations in violent families (Newcomb, 1993; Newcomb and Loeb, 1999; Simons and Johnson, 1998; Simons et al., 1995).

There are several pieces of evidence that support this antisocial orientation explanation. First, studies show that exposure to abusive parenting increases the chances that a person will grow up to engage in a wide variety of criminal and deviant behaviors as an adult (Maxfield and Widom, 1996; Smith and Thornberry, 1995; Widom, 1989; Widom and Maxfield, 2001; Zingraff et al., 1993). This suggests that abusive parenting fosters a general antisocial orientation rather than simply teaches an inept approach to parenting. Second, the few studies that have examined the issue find that parents who engage in abusive parenting tend to also assault their spouses as well as nonfamily members (Hotaling, Straus, and Lincoln, 1990; Newcomb and Loeb, 1999; Shields, McCall, and Hanneke, 1988; Simons and Johnson, 1998; Simons et al., 1995). These findings support the idea that abusive parenting is often part of a more general antisocial lifestyle. Finally, Simons et al. (1995) and Simons and Johnson (1998) found that the association between exposure to harsh parenting during childhood and subsequently engaging in abusive parenting is mediated by involvement in a general antisocial life orientation. These findings are consistent with the view that child abuse is part of a deviant lifestyle, while they contradict the role modeling hypothesis. If the parental role modeling idea is correct, the association between having been the victim of maltreatment and later engaging in abusive parenting should remain after controlling for commitment to a general antisocial orientation.

Together, these results provide rather strong support for the idea that childhood exposure to abusive parenting increases the chances that a person will grow up to manifest a deviant lifestyle that includes harsh treatment of one's children. The child abuse literature often portrays perpetrators as having few distinguishing characteristics (Pagelow, 1984). They are depicted as ordinary citizens in all respects except for their abusive behavior. This view may well be accurate regarding parents who are strict and authoritarian, or who sometimes use corporal punishment to discipline their children. Their approach to parenting probably reflects the practices modeled by their parents. Or their harsh parenting may be a function of situational factors such as economic pressure, emotional distress, and marital conflict, as past research has shown that aversive circumstances such as these have a disruptive effect on parenting (Belsky, 1993; Boney-McCoy and Finkelhor, 1996; Conger et al., 1992; Pears and Capaldi, 2001; Simons, Lorenz, et al., 1993).

We are concerned, however, with the small proportion of parents who persistently engage in practices that endanger the physical and mental health of their children. These individuals beat up their children, burn them with cigarettes, tie them with cords, deny them food, and so forth. It is unlikely that these parenting practices were modeled in their family of origin. The evidence we have reviewed suggests that this 2 to 3 percent of the population does not comprise persons who would be considered ordinary citizens. Rather, they often have a history of involvement in a wide variety of criminal and deviant behaviors.

The finding that abusive parenting tends to be part of a general antisocial orientation is important because of the treatment implications that it suggests. Effective intervention for any difficulty requires an accurate understanding of the factors that serve to foster and maintain the problem. Many programs for abusive parents are built on the assumption that such behavior is a function of distorted beliefs (learned in the family of origin) regarding the role of parent. Based on this premise, treatment programs for abusive parents usually involve teaching more constructive strategies for managing children's behavior.

Although such approaches may have some value, treatment is likely to have a limited long-term effect to the extent that it ignores the fact that, at least in many cases, the person's behavior is indicative of a more general antisocial approach to life. The perpetrator is apt to revert to violent and explosive parenting practices if he continues to use substances, get into fights, miss work, mismanage family finances, and so on. A truly effective treatment would involve assisting the perpetrator to develop a more responsible lifestyle. Such interventions are likely to be costly in terms of both time and money. Indeed, it is not clear that current treatment technologies are able to produce such pervasive changes in a person's lifestyle, especially if he is resistant to change.

We should not allow ourselves to get too pessimistic about the possibility of such persons changing their approach to life, however, as we saw in Chapter Seven that many individuals with a troubled childhood and a history of antisocial behavior are able to transition to a conventional lifestyle at some point during adulthood. Likewise, we noted earlier in this chapter that the majority of abused children do not go on to abuse their own children. Research has revealed specific environmental circumstances that enable mothers who were abused as children to break the cycle of violence. These studies show that abused mothers who do not mistreat their own children either had access to a supportive, nonabusive adult as a child or are in a stable, satisfying romantic relationship as an adult (Egeland, Jacobvitz, and Papatola, 1987; Quinton and Rutter, 1988).

In the previous chapter, we saw that children discontinued involvement in antisocial behavior when their parents adopted more competent parenting practices, and adults often desisted from crime when they became involved romantically with a conventional partner. It appears that similar factors break the cycle of abuse. Abused children often avoid the negative consequences of abuse if they receive supportive parenting from a second caregiver. Apparently, the love and nurturance received from this caregiver is able to compensate for the potentially destructive behavior of the abusive parent. All is not lost, however, even if such a caregiver is not available, as involvement with a caring romantic partner can also break the cycle of abuse. Such partners probably produce this effect by providing a stake in conformity and by modeling appropriate parenting practices. Regardless of the mechanisms, however, research shows that abused persons often grow up to be conscientious, effective parents. And the availability of a concerned and caring caregiver or romantic partner increases the chances that this will occur.

Sexual Abuse of Children

As we noted in the introduction, the causes of child sexual abuse are quite different from physical abuse or neglect. There is little evidence, for example, that it is part of a more general antisocial orientation. Individuals who engage in sexual abuse do not necessarily engage in other types of deviant behavior as well. This distinctiveness requires that we discuss this topic separately from other forms of child abuse.

Broadly defined, *child sexual abuse* refers to sexual interaction between a child and either an adult or an older, more knowledgeable child. It includes behaviors such as kissing, touching, and fondling the child's body, oral-genital contact, penetration of the child's vagina or anus with fingers or objects, vaginal and anal intercourse, exposing one's genitals, and having children pose unclothed while being watched, filmed, or photographed (McAnulty and Burnette, 2001). Most abusers do not employ physical force. Rather, they exploit their authority over the child, offer rewards, portray the activity as "fun" or "educational," or threaten untoward consequences if the child tells. When sexual abuse involves a relative, it is considered *incest*. The relative may be a parent, stepparent, or sibling, or a more distant relative such as an uncle, cousin, or grandparent.

Only rarely are children abused by strangers. More than 80 percent of sex abusers are either relatives or acquaintances. The perpetrator is a family member, however, in only one third to one half of cases involving female victims and 10 to 20 percent of cases with male victims (McAnulty and Burnette, 2001). Thus, in the majority of cases, perpetrators of sexual abuse are neither strangers nor family members. Rather, they are neighbors, teachers, priests, coaches, family friends, or someone else that the child knows (McAnulty and Burnette, 2001). Roughly 90 percent of child molesters are male (Finkelhor, 1994).

Children often engage in voluntary sexual exploration with each other (e.g., playing doctor), and this is not defined as abuse. Such interaction does constitute abuse, however, if the children differ in age by five or more years (Finkelhor, 1986). Approximately one third of all sex abuse is committed by juveniles (Finkelhor, 1994). Past research indicates that 6 to 33 percent of incest cases involve siblings (Pierce and Pierce, 1985; Thomas and Rogers, 1983) and that 2 to 3 percent of all women are sexually abused by a sibling prior to age 18 (Leder, 1991).

As we have noted at several points in this book, deviant behaviors tend to be correlated. Individuals who engage in one type of antisocial behavior tend to engage in others types as well. Thus, deviance is usually part of a general pattern of antisocial behavior. Child sexual abuse is a unique antisocial behavior, as it is usually an exception to this rule. Unlike those who engage in physical abuse, perpetrators of sexual abuse are often ordinary citizens except for their participation in this aberrant behavior.

So, what explains sexual molestation of children? Unfortunately, past research has not been very helpful in answering this question. Sexual abusers are often portrayed as suffering from *pedophilia*, a psychiatric disorder in which an adult has a strong sexual attraction to prepubescent children (American Psychiatric Association, 1994). Although this condition is often applied to nonfamily abusers, it is rarely invoked in discussions of incest. Indeed, two distinct literatures have developed based on the idea that familial sexual abuse and extrafamilial sexual abuse have different etiologies. Social work and family therapy textbooks address these types of abuse separately, with incest depicted as a problem in family dynamics and extrafamilial abuse portrayed as pedophilia. However, recent studies question this conceptual distinction between incest and pedophilia. Research attempting to identify personality and sexual arousal differences between perpetrators of incest and pedophilia has been inconclusive (Gelles and Conte, 1990). Further, a large number of incestuous fathers are also pedophiles (49 percent), and a significant number of child molesters (18 percent) also abuse adult women (Abel et al., 1988). This comorbidity suggests that sexual abuse may be part of a more general tendency toward sexual aberration, rather than a specific, isolated inclination.

Throughout this text, we have been concerned with the manner in which childhood family experiences increase the chances of deviant and criminal behavior during adolescence and adulthood. We have seen that antisocial behavior often develops when parents fail to provide warmth, support, monitoring, inductive reasoning, and consistent discipline. There is no evidence that these parenting practices increase the probability that a child will grow up to commit child sexual abuse. There is one childhood factor, however, that has been related to engaging in such behavior. Several studies have found that men who perpetrate child molestation were often themselves sexually abused as children. O'Brien (1991), for example, found that 42 percent of adolescent incestuous offenders had been sexually abused, and a recent study by Glasser and colleagues (2001) reported that this was the case for one third of adult abusers.

It is not clear what conclusions might be drawn from this link between being a victim and becoming a victimizer. Perhaps being the victim of child sexual abuse fosters an aberrant understanding of what types of sexual behavior are normal and acceptable. Or perhaps such experiences promote perverse sexual fantasies and desires. We hope that future research will be able to identify the mechanisms that account for the cycle of sexual abuse.

An even more puzzling finding involves what appears to be a cycle of victimization across generations. Past studies report that mothers of sexually abused girls often have been sexually abused themselves (O'Brien, 1991). In one study, daughters were 12 times more likely to be sexually abused if their mother had been molested as a child. The mothers did not perpetrate the abuse, but they somehow contributed to their daughter's vulnerability. Ambert (2001) refers to this pattern as the "intergenerational transmission of victimization." Although studies have documented this cycle, they have yet to provide an explanation. We know that sexually abused children are at risk for emotional and behavioral problems. So, it may be that mothers who have been sexually molested grow up to be less conscientious parents than those with a less troubled past. Or childhood abuse may foster a liberal view of sex that includes tolerance of aberrant sexual behavior by husbands and boyfriends. Again, we will have to wait for future research to clarify the causal processes at work.

Summary and Conclusions

Past research has established that there is a tendency for adults to repeat the abuse they experienced as a child. This phenomenon is often labeled "the cycle of violence." Although most victims of childhood abuse do not go on to abuse their offspring, they are 10 to

15 times more likely to be abusive parents than persons who were not exposed to abusive parenting. The most popular explanation for this finding involves the idea of modeling from social learning theory. It is assumed that children observe the behavior of their parents and consider it to be normal or typical parental behavior. Later, when they achieve adulthood, they are likely to employ these parenting scripts in a reflexive, rather unthinking fashion when parenting their own children.

Recently, based largely on work by criminologists, arguments have been made for an alternative explanation for the cycle of violence phenomenon. These researchers argue that abusive parenting fosters a general antisocial orientation, rather than simply teaching a dysfunctional approach to parenting. Abusive parenting is seen as increasing the chances that a person will grow up to engage in a wide variety of criminal and deviant behaviors, including harsh and abusive parenting practices.

These two points of view suggest very different images of the abusive parent. The modeling perspective portrays perpetrators as having few distinguishing characteristics. They are depicted as ordinary citizens, conventional in all respects except for their abusive behavior. Those who support the antisocial orientation point of view, on the other hand, argue that most abusive parents are far from ordinary. Rather, parents who engage in abusive practices such as burning children with a cigarette, tying them with cords, or denying them food are likely to have a history of involvement in a wide variety of criminal and deviant behaviors as well. We will have to wait for future research to establish which viewpoint is more correct.

Although physical abuse of children may be part of a more general antisocial orientation, this is clearly not the case for child sexual abusers. There is strong evidence that perpetrators of child sexual abuse are usually conventional members of society except for their participation in this aberrant behavior. Several studies have found, however, that men who perpetrate child molestation were often themselves sexually abused as children. It is not clear what conclusions might be drawn from this link between being a victim and becoming a victimizer. We hope that future research will be able to identify the mechanisms that account for this cycle of sexual abuse. ✦

Chapter Ten

Conclusions and Observations

The previous chapters reviewed a vast array of theories and research findings regarding the link between the family and deviant behavior. We examined the contributions and limitations of various theoretical perspectives, discussed several hotly contested debates and controversies, and considered the methodological strengths and weaknesses of an assortment of studies. Although our investigation focused on a wide range of topics, it provided clear and consistent support for a simple but important thesis: Exposure to inept parenting practices increases an individual's risk for childhood conduct problems, adolescent delinquency, and adult antisocial behavior, including marital violence and child abuse. We also saw, however, that factors such as educational success, a conventional friendship network, a happy marriage, and a satisfying job can moderate this risk. Unfortunately, individuals exposed to inept parenting often possess antisocial characteristics that reduce their probability of acquiring or gaining access to these moderators.

We observed that theory and research on parenting indicates that effective parents are both responsive and demanding. Responsiveness refers to the extent to which parents are approachable, warm, supportive, and attuned to the needs of their child. Demandingness, on the other hand, refers to the extent to which parents set standards, explain moral principles, and exercise control over their child through supervision, disciplinary efforts, and a willingness to confront disobedience. We noted in Chapter Two that this parenting style is often labeled authoritative parenting. We also observed that this characterization of effective parents implies three types of deficient or inept parenting. Authoritarian parents are very demanding but not very responsive. Permissive parents are quite responsive but not very demanding. Finally, neglectful/rejecting parents show little responsiveness or demandingness.

Interestingly enough, there appears to have been a shift in the type of inept parenting most prevalent in our society. As we saw in Chapter Nine, only a small proportion of parents are neglectful and abusive, and the incidence of such parental behavior seems to have remained roughly the same over the past several years. The proportion of parents who are either authoritarian or permissive, however, has changed considerably (Baumrind, 1991b; Bronfrenbrenner, 1985). Historically, America has been a land of immigrants strongly committed to work and achievement. Life was hard and parents often stressed obedience and harsh discipline, while providing little warmth and support. Social scientists viewed this authoritarian parenting style as dysfunctional and for decades, but most notably during the 1960s and 1970s, argued that such parenting was a major cause of child behavioral and emotional problems.

Although authoritarian parenting was once the primary concern of family researchers, this inept parenting style has been eclipsed by permissive parenting (Baumrind, 1991b; Bronfrenbrenner, 1985). Increasingly, the problem is not harsh disciplinarians who lack warmth, but indulgent parents who fail to exercise control. A recent doctoral dissertation, for example, used parent report, child report, and observational data to categorize parenting styles (Gordon, 1999). Regardless of the type of data used, only a small proportion of parents were authoritarian, whereas there were nearly as many permissive parents as there were authoritative parents. Permissive parents tend to be warm and supportive, often to the point of indulging their child's every want. Unfortunately, however, they rarely set rules, explain moral principles, engage in monitoring, or confront disobedience.

We saw in earlier chapters that this approach to parenting places the child at risk for self-centeredness and behavior problems. Indeed, this parenting style may be more harmful to children today than in the past. Both Bronfrenbrenner (1985) and Baumrind (1991b) have argued that the optimal ratio of parental control to freedom increases as the other institutions of society become more lax. They note that in recent decades, there has been a decline in the amount of social control that social institutions such as the school, church, and neighborhood have exercised over children. Permissive parenting is less consequential when other social institutions are strong and pick up the slack. However, as Baumrind observes, "because the social fabric in which families are embedded has become increasingly unstable over the past 40 years, there has been a correspondingly increased need for family structure, engagement, and discipline" (1991b, 114). This is probably particularly true in impoverished inner-city areas, where social institutions are quite weak whereas crime and other deviant behaviors are widely prevalent.

Permissive parents often say that they are reluctant to enforce rules or administer discipline because their child becomes distressed and angry. They want to be their child's friends, and this bond appears to be threatened when the child becomes upset with them. Further, they believe that the role of parent involves enhancing the happiness of their child, and thwarting the child's wants seems antithetical to this charge. Unfortunately, this is a rather distorted view of the role of parent.

A parent's primary charge is not to become their child's best friend, but rather to provide an environment conducive to the child's cognitive, emotional, and social development (Rutter, 1985). This involves more than showing warmth and support. It also entails explaining rules, monitoring the child's actions, and confronting and punishing misbehavior. Virtually all theories of socialization assert that social control is necessary in order to teach self-control. This is true of criminological theories such as Gottfredson and Hirschi's (1990) general theory of crime, and of more general social psychological theories such as social learning (Bandura, 1977, 1986) and symbolic interactionism (Mead, 1934).

Given this strong association between social control and self-control, psychologist Phillip C. McGraw, host of the popular daytime talk show *Dr. Phil*, often asserts that "over-indulgence by parents is one of the most insidious and destructive forms of child abuse." These parents are reinforcing their children for being selfish and inconsiderate, while failing to teach them patience, responsibility, and sensitivity to others. As a result, he emphasizes, the child may be doomed to an unhappy life of unfulfilled desires, unstable work, and stormy relationships. After all, who wants a friend, a romantic partner, or an employee whose primary preoccupation involves satisfying his or her own wants and desires? Although it may be an exaggeration to state that permissive parents are guilty of child maltreatment, Dr. Phil's point is well taken. Although often well-intentioned, permissive parents fail to provide the conditions necessary for their children's emotional and social development.

Although parents miss the mark when they set out to be their child's best friend, it is, of course, appropriate and desirable for parents to strive for a positive relationship with their child. Parents need not worry, however, that exercising control will undermine their relationship with their child so long as they combine their demandingness with responsiveness. Children may become frustrated and angry in response to parental monitoring and discipline, but they will develop an overall attitude of love and respect for the parent if control is administered within the context of a loving, caring relationship.

Throughout this book we have stressed the importance of parental behavior. We have discussed several theories and hundreds of studies all suggesting that inept parenting increases the chances of child conduct problems, adolescent delinquency, and adult crime. Although the previous chapters have provided strong evidence in support of this thesis, we want to be careful not to overstate the case. On the one hand, it is true that the roots of an adult antisocial lifestyle appear to be planted during a person's formative years, and parenting has much to do with the formation of these roots. We reviewed evidence indicating that it is extremely rare that a person who was a model child and adolescent suddenly begins to engage in criminal behavior as an adult. On the other hand, the relationship between childhood conduct problems and adult antisocial behavior is far from perfect. Indeed, the majority of delinquent children grow up to be conventional adults!

It is not clear why so many individuals age out or mature out of antisocial lifestyles, but we saw that social factors such as school commitment, a conventional social network, a good job, and a loving romantic partner all increase the probability that this will occur. Thus, although the ancient Greek aphorism "character dictates destiny" contains an element of truth, it is important to remember how often exceptions occur. Apparently, either character sometimes changes, or social circumstances constrain a person's antisocial tendencies. In our view, some of the most exciting research during the next few years will investigate the factors that lead seriously delinquent individuals to adopt a conventional lifestyle during adulthood.

It is also important to remember that other factors besides parenting have been shown to influence involvement in delinquent and criminal behavior. This book has been concerned with family factors that increase the chances of involvement in deviant behavior. Research has shown, however, that factors such as lack of occupational opportunity (Sullivan, 1989), living in a disadvantaged neighborhood (Anderson, 1999), stressful events (Agnew, 2001), religiosity (Baier and Wright, 2001), and racial discrimination (McCord and Ensminger, 2002; Simons, Chen, et al., 2003) are associated with crime and delinquency. We believe that it is imperative that research on family processes not result in a narrow, socially conservative perspective that ignores these broader social forces that also contribute to crime. If society is to address the problems of crime and delinquency, it must pursue policies that address the full range of factors that influence participation in such behavior. In our opinion, life course theories, such as that of Sampson and Laub, are exciting because they provide a framework for merging family processes with these broader social influences.

Although we fully support policies designed to address broad criminogenic factors such as poverty and discrimination, we also believe that it is important that social scientists and policy makers not overlook the family. Indeed, the effects of many of the social factors just mentioned may be mediated by family processes. Family religiosity, for example, appears to reduce delinquency, at least in part, because religious parents tend to engage in high levels of monitoring and consistent discipline (Simons et al., in press). And there is evidence that part of the association between community disadvantage and delinquency is explained by the disruptive effect that such community conditions have on parental behavior (Brody et al., 2001, in press; Simons et al., 1996; Tolan, Gorman-Smith, and Henry, 2003). In the past, criminologists and sociologists have often ignored findings regarding a link between parenting and delinquency, treating such findings as narrow and socially conservative. Findings are not socially conservative, however, if they lead to social change.

Rather than simply blaming parents for not doing a better job of raising their children, society needs to pursue social policies that strengthen families and enhance quality of child care. For example, states should be encouraged to support programs that promote early childhood development such as parenting classes and Head

Start, and to sponsor child-care programs that ensure high-quality providers and offer financial assistance to families needing child care. Such programs have been shown to be successful in reducing child and adolescent problem behavior (Karoly et al., 1998). A few states mandate classes regarding the importance of coparenting for parents who are undergoing a divorce. Although there is great variability in the quality of these programs, they have the potential to reduce the adjustment problems that children often display following the dissolution of their parents' marriage. Other family-friendly policies include universal health insurance, a guaranteed living wage, paid maternal/paternal leave at childbirth, and flexibility in the time and place of work to reduce the work/family tension faced by many parents. Most European countries have such policies, whereas they are viewed as provocative in the United States.

Our point is not so much that the United States should adopt any particular policy, but that social scientists and policy makers should think systematically about steps that might be taken to enhance the quality of care provided to children, especially during the formative years. Unlike criminological theories concerned with economic and community factors, theories of deviant behavior that focus on family processes are often seen as having few policy implications. In our view, this is simply not the case. It is probably no more difficult to formulate policies that enhance quality of parenting and child care than it is to design policies that increase access to jobs or reduce poverty and discrimination. Although it will require a good bit of effort and creativity, there is much we can do to strengthen families and further the well-being of children in this country. To a great extent, the character of our fellow citizens, and therefore our society, depends on the success of this effort. ✦

References

Abel, G. G., Becker, J., Cunningham-Rathner, J., Mittleman, M., and Rouleau, J. L. (1988). Multiple paraphiliac diagnoses among sex offenders. *Bulletin of the American Academy of Psychiatry and the Law, 16,* 153–168.

Abramson, L. Y., Seligman, M. E., and Teasdale, J. D. (1978). Learned helplessness in humans: Critique and reformulation. *Journal of Abnormal Psychology, 87(1),* 49–74.

Acock, A. C., and Demo, D. H. (1994). *Family diversity and well-being.* Thousand Oaks, CA: Sage Publications.

Agnew, R. (1985). A revised strain theory of delinquency. *Social Forces, 64,* 151–167.

——. (1991). A longitudinal test of social control theory and delinquency. *Journal of Research in Crime and Delinquency, 28,* 126–156.

——. (2001). Building on the foundation of general strain theory: Specifying the types of strain most likely to lead to crime and delinquency. *Journal of Research in Crime and Delinquency, 38,* 319–361.

Agnew, R., and White, H. R. (1992). An empirical study of general strain theory. *Criminology, 30,* 475–499.

Akers, R. L. (1973). *Deviant behavior: A social learning approach.* Belmont, CA: Wadsworth.

——. (1977). *Deviant behavior: A social learning approach* (2nd edition). Belmont, CA: Wadsworth.

——. (1985). *Deviant behavior: A social learning approach* (3rd edition). Belmont, CA: Wadsworth.

——. (1998). *Social learning and social structure: A general theory of crime and deviance.* Boston: Northeastern University Press.

——. (2000). *Criminological theories: Introduction, evaluation, and application* (3rd edition). Los Angeles: Roxbury Publishing Company.

Akers, R. L., and Sellers, C. S. (2004). *Criminological theories: Introduction, evaluation, and application* (4th edition). Los Angeles: Roxbury Publishing Company.

Allport, G. W. (1937). *Personality: A psychological interpretation.* New York: Holt, Rinehart & Winston.

Amato, P. R. (1987). Family processes in intact, one-parent, and step-parent families: The child's point of view. *Journal of Marriage and the Family, 49,* 327–337.

——. (1994). The implications of research findings on children in stepfamilies. In A. Booth and J. Dunn (Eds.), *Stepfamilies: Who benefits? Who does not?* (pp. 81–88). Hillsdale, NJ: Lawrence Erlbaum Associates.

——. (2000). The consequences of divorce for adults and children. *Journal of Marriage and the Family, 62,* 1269–1287.

Amato, P. R., and Gilbreth, J. G. (1999). Nonresident fathers and children's well-being: A meta-analysis. *Journal of Marriage and the Family, 61,* 557–573.

Ambert, A. (1997). *Parents, children and adolescents: Interactive relationships and development in context.* New York: Haworth.

——. (1999). The effect of male delinquency on mothers and fathers: A heuristic study. *Sociological Inquiry, 69,* 621–640.

——. (2001). *Families in the new millennium.* Boston: Allyn & Bacon.

American Academy of Pediatrics. (1998). Guidance for effective discipline. *Pediatrics, 101,* 723–728.

American Psychiatric Association. (1994). *Diagnostic and statistical manual of mental disorders* (4th edition) (DSM-IV). Washington, DC: American Psychiatric Association.

Anderson, E. (1999). *Code of the street.* New York: Norton & Company.

Aneshensel, C. S., Rutter, C. M., and Lachenbruch, P. A. (1991). Social structure, stress, and mental health: Competing conceptual and analytic models. *American Sociological Review, 56,* 166–178.

Archer, J. (1994). Power and male violence. In J. Archer (Ed.), *Male violence* (pp. 310–331). London: Routledge.

——. (2000). Sex differences in aggression between heterosexual partners: A meta-analytic review. *Psychological Review, 126(5),* 651–721.

Arendell, T. (1997). Divorce and remarriage. In T. Arendell (Ed.), *Contemporary parenting: Challenges and issues* (pp. 154–195). Thousand Oaks, CA: Sage Publications.

Arneklev, B., Grasmick, H. G., Tittle, C. R., and Bursik, R. J., Jr. (1993). Low self-control and imprudent behavior. *Journal of Quantitative Criminology, 9,* 225–247.

Astone, N. M., and McLanahan, S. S. (1991). Family structure, parental practices and high school completion. *American Sociological Review, 56(3),* 309–320.

Baier, C., and Wright, R. E. (2001). 'If you love me, keep my commandments': A meta-analysis of the effect of religion on crime. *Journal of Research on Crime and Delinquency, 38,* 3–21.

Baldwin, A. L., Baldwin, C., and Cole, R. E. (1990). Stress-resistant families and stress-resistant children. In J. Rolf, A. S. Masten, D. Cicchetti, K. H.

Nuechterlein, and S. Weintraub (Eds.), *Risk and protective factors in the development of psychopathology* (pp. 257–280). New York: Cambridge University Press.

Bandura, A. (1969). *Principles of behavior modification.* New York: Holt, Rinehart, & Winston.

——. (1977). *Social learning theory.* Englewood Cliffs, NJ: Prentice-Hall.

——. (1986). *Social foundations of thought and action: A social cognitive theory.* Englewood Cliffs, NJ: Prentice-Hall.

Barbarin, O. A. (1993). Coping and resilience: Exploring the inner lives of African American children. *Journal of Black Psychology, 19,* 478–492.

Baumrind, D. (1966). Effects of authoritative parental control on child behavior. *Child Development, 37,* 887–907.

——. (1971). Current patterns of parental control. *Developmental Psychology, 4,* 12.

——. (1972). An exploratory study of socialization effects on black children: Some black-white comparisons. *Child Development, 43,* 261–267.

——. (1991a). The influence of parenting style on adolescent competence and substance abuse. *Journal of Early Adolescence, 11,* 56–95.

——. (1991b). Effective parenting during the early adolescent transition. In P. A. Cowan and M. Hetherington (Eds.), *Family transitions* (pp. 111–164). Hillsdale, NJ: Lawrence Erlbaum Associates.

——. (1996). Parenting: The discipline controversy revisited. *Family Relations, 45,* 405–414.

Baumrind, D., Larzelere, R. E., and Cowan, P. A. (2002). Ordinary physical punishment: Is it harmful? *Psychological Bulletin, 128,* 580–589.

Bean, A. W., and Roberts, M. W. (1981). The effect of time-out release contingencies on changes in the child noncompliance. *Journal of Abnormal Psychology, 9,* 95–105.

Belsky, J. (1993). Etiology of child maltreatment: A developmental-ecological analysis. *Psychological Bulletin, 114,* 413–434.

Berkowitz, L. (1989). Frustration-aggression hypothesis: Examination and reformulation. *Psychological Bulletin, 106,* 59–73.

Bernal, E., Duryee, J. S., Pruett, H. L., and Burns, B. J. (1968). Behavior modification and the brat syndrome. *Journal of Consulting and Clinical Psychology, 32,* 477–485.

Bernstein, A. C. (1997). Stepfamilies from siblings' perspectives. In I. Levin and M. B. Sussman (Eds.), *Stepfamilies: History, research, and policy* (pp. 153–175). New York: Haworth.

Block, J., and Gjerde, P. (1990). Depressive symptoms in late adolescence: A longitudinal perspective on personality antecedents. In J. Rolf, A. S. Masten, D. Cicchetti, K. H. Nuechterlein, and S. Weintraub (Eds.), *Risk and protective factors in the development of psychopathology* (pp. 334–360). New York: Cambridge University Press.

Bograd, M. (1988). Feminist perspectives on wife abuse: An introduction. In M. Bograd and K. A. Yllo (Eds.), *Feminist perspectives on wife abuse* (pp. 11–26). Beverly Hills, CA: Sage Publications.

Boney-McCoy, S., and Finkelhor, D. (1996). Is youth victimization related to trauma symptoms and depression after controlling for prior symptoms and family relationships? A longitudinal, prospective study. *Journal of Consulting and Clinical Psychology, 64,* 1406–1416.

Bowker, L. H. (1983). Battered wives, lawyers, and district attorneys: An examination of law in action. *Journal of Criminal Justice, 11(5),* 403–412.

Bramlett, M. D., and Mosher, W. D. (2001). First marriage dissolution, divorce, and remarriage: United States, advance data from vital and health statistics, no. 323. Hyattsville, MD: National Center for Health Statistics.

Bray, J. H. (1999). From marriage to remarriage and beyond. In E. M. Hetherington (Ed.), *Coping with divorce, single parenting and remarriage* (pp. 253–271). Mahwah, NJ: Lawrence Erlbaum Associates.

Brody, G. H., and Flor, D. L. (1998). Maternal resources, parenting practices, and child competence in rural, single-parent African American families. *Child Development, 69,* 803–816.

Brody, G. H., and Forehand, R. (1988). Multiple determinants of parenting: Research findings and implications for the divorce process. In E. M. Hetherington and J. D. Arasteh (Eds.), *Impact of divorce, single parenting, and stepparenting on children* (pp. 117–133). Hillsdale, NJ: Lawrence Erlbaum Associates.

——. (1993). Prospective associations among family form, family processes, and adolescents' alcohol and drug use. *Behavior Research and Therapy, 31,* 587–593.

Brody, G. H., Ge, X., Conger, R., Gibbons, F. X., McBride Murry, V., Gerrard, M., and Simons, R. L. (2001). The influence of neighborhood disadvantage, collective socialization, and parenting on African American children's affiliation with deviant peers. *Child Development, 72(4),* 1231–1246.

——. (in press). The influence of disadvantage, collective socialization, and parenting on African American children's affiliation with deviant peers. *Journal of Consulting and Clinical Psychology.*

Bronfenbrenner, U. (1979). *The ecology of human development.* Cambridge, MA: Harvard University Press.

——. (1985). Freedom and discipline across the decades. In G. Becker, H. Becker, and L. Huber (Eds.), *Ordnung and Unordnung* (pp. 326–339). Berlin: Beltz.

Brown, B. B., Mounts, N., Lamborn, S. D., and Steinberg, L. (1993). Parenting practices and group affiliation in adolescence. *Child Development, 64,* 467–482.

Browne, A. (1992). *Are women as violent as men?* Unpublished manuscript, University of Massachusetts, Worcester.

——. (1993). Violence against women by male partners: Prevalence, outcomes and policy implications. *American Psychologist, 48,* 1077–1090.

Bryant, B. (1985). The neighborhood walk: Sources of support in middle childhood. *Monographs of the society for research in child development, 50,* no. 210.

Bumpass, L., and Lu, H.-H. (2000). Trends in cohabitation and implications for children's family contexts in the United States. *Population Studies, 54,* 29–41.

Bureau of Justice Statistics. (1997). *Sex differences in violent victimization.* Washington, DC: U.S. Department of Justice.

Burgess, R. L., and Akers, R. L. (1966). A differential association-reinforcement theory of criminal behavior. *Social Problems, 14,* 128–147.

Bursik, R. J. (1988). Social disorganization and theories of crime and delinquency: Problems and prospects. *Criminology, 26,* 519–552.

Burton, L. M. (1991). Caring for children: Drug shifts and impact on families. *American Enterprise, 2,* 34–37.

Burton, L. M., and Jarrett, R. L. (2000). In the mix, yet on the margins: The place of families in urban neighborhoods and child development research. *Journal of Marriage and the Family, 63,* 1114–1135.

Byarn, J. W., and Freed, F. W. (1982). Corporal punishment: Normative data and sociological and psychological correlates in a community college population. *Journal of Youth and Adolescents, 11,* 77–87.

Caesar, P. L. (1988). Exposure to violence in the families-of-origin among wife-abusers and maritally nonviolent men. *Violence and Victims, 3,* 49–63.

Cairns, R. B., and Cairns, S. G. (1994). *Lifelines and Risks: Pathways of Youth in Our Time.* New York: Cambridge University Press.

Capaldi, D. M., Chamberlain, P., and Patterson, G. R. (1997). Ineffective discipline and conduct problems in males: Association, late adolescent outcomes, and prevention. *Aggressive and Violent Behavior, 2,* 343–353.

Capaldi, D. M., and Patterson, G. R. (1991). Relations of parental transitions to boys' adjustment problems: I. A linear hypothesis. II. Mothers at risk for transitions and unskilled parenting. *Developmental Psychology, 27,* 489–504.

Caroll, J. C. (1997). The intergenerational transmission of family violence: The long term effects of aggressive behavior. *Aggressive Behavior, 3,* 289–299.

Caspi, A., and Moffitt, T. E. (1995). The continuity of maladaptive behavior: From description to understanding in the study of antisocial behavior. In D. Cicchetti and D. J. Cohen (Eds.), *Manual of developmental psychopathology.* New York: Wiley.

Castro, J. (1993, March 29). Disposable workers. *Time,* 43–47.

Cernkovich, S. A., and Giordano, P. C. (1992). School bonding, race and delinquency. *Criminology, 30,* 261–291.

——. (2001). Stability and change in antisocial behavior: The transition from adolescence to early adulthood. *Criminology, 39(2),* 371–410.

Chafel, J. A. (1993). *Child poverty and public policy.* Washington, DC: Urban Institute.

Chao, R. K. (1994). Beyond parental control and authoritarian parenting style: Understanding Chinese parenting through the cultural notion of training. *Child Development, 65,* 1111–1119.

Chassin, L., Pillow, D. R., Curran, P. J., Molina, B. S. G., and Barrea, M., Jr. (1993). Relations of parental alcoholism to early adolescent substance use: A test of three mediation mechanisms. *Journal of Abnormal Psychology, 102,* 3–19.

Cherlin, A. J. (1978). Remarriage as an incomplete institution. *American Journal of Sociology, 84,* 634–650.

——. (2002). *Public & Private Families.* New York: McGraw-Hill.

Chiu, L. H. (1987). Child rearing attitudes of Chinese, Chinese-American, and Anglo-American mothers. *International Journal of Psychology, 22,* 409–419.

Clark, R. (1983). *Family life and school achievement: Why poor black children succeed or fail?* Chicago: University of Chicago Press.

Claxton-Oldfield, S. (1992). Perceptions of stepfather. *Journal of Family Issues, 13(3),* 378–389.

Cochran, J. K., Wood, P. B., Sellers, C. S., Wilderson, W., and Chamlin, M. B. (1998). Academic dishonesty and low self-control: An empirical test of a general theory of crime. *Deviant Behavior, 19,* 227–255.

Cohen, P., and Brooks, J. S. (1987). Family factors related to the persistence of psychopathology in childhood and adolescence. *Psychiatry, 50,* 332–345.

——. (1994). The reciprocal influence of punishment and child disorder. In J. McCord (Ed.), *Coercion and punishment in long-term perspectives.* New York: Cambridge University Press.

Coleman, J. S. (1990). *Foundations of social theory.* Cambridge: Harvard University Press.

Coleman, M., and Ganong, L. H. (1997). Stepfamilies from the stepfamily's perspective. In I. Levine and M. B. Sussman (Eds.), *Stepfamilies: History, research and policy* (pp. 107–122). New York: Haworth.

Coleman, M., Ganong, L. H., and Fine, M. (2000). Reinvestigating remarriage: Another decade of progress. *Journal of Marriage and the Family, 62,* 507–526.

Collins, R. (1988). *Sociology of marriage and the family: Gender, love, and property.* Chicago: Nelson-Hall.

Colvin, M. (2000). *Crime and coercion: An integrated theory of chronic criminality.* New York: St. Martins.

Colvin, M., and Pauly, J. (1983). A critique of criminology: Toward an integrated structural-Marxist theory of delinquency production. *American Journal of Sociology, 89,* 513–551.

Conger, R. D. (1976). Social control and social learning models of delinquency: A synthesis. *Criminology, 14,* 17–40.

Conger, R. D., Conger, K. J., Elder, G. H., Lorenz, F. O., Simons, R. L., and Whitbeck, L. B. (1992). A family process model of economic hardship and influences on adjustment of early adolescent boys. *Child Development, 63,* 526–541.

Conger, R. D., Ge, X., Elder, G. H., Lorenz, F. O., and Simons, R. L. (1994). Economic stress, coercive family process, and developmental problems of adolescents. *Child Development, 65,* 541–561.

Conger, R. D., Patterson, G. R., and Ge, X. (1995). It takes two to replicate: A mediational model for the impact of parents' stress on adolescent adjustment. *Child Development, 66(1),* 80–97.

Conger, R. D., and Rueter, M. A. (1995). Siblings, parents, and peers: A longitudinal study of social influences in adolescent risk for alcohol use and abuse. In G. Brody (Ed.), *Sibling relationships: Their causes and consequences.* Norwood, NJ: Ablex.

Conger, R. D., Rueter, M. A., and Conger, K. J. (1994). The family context of adolescent vulnerability and resilience to alcohol use and abuse. *Sociological Studies of Children, 6,* 55–86.

Conger, R. D., and Simons, R. L. (1997). Life course contingencies in the development of adolescent antisocial behavior: A matching law approach. In T. Thornberry (Ed.), *Developmental theories of crime and delinquency.* New Brunswick, NJ: Transaction.

Conger, R. D., Wallace, L. E., Sun, Y., Simons, R. L., McLoyd, V. C., and Brody, G. H. (2002). Economic pressure in African-American families: A replication and extension of the family stress model. *Developmental Psychology, 38(2),* 179–193.

Conrad, P., and Schneider, J. W. (1992). *Deviance and medicalization: From badness to sickness.* Philadelphia: Temple University Press.

Cook, D. A., and Fine, M. (1995). Motherwit: Childbearing lessons from African-American mothers of low-income. In B. B. Wadener and S. Lubeck (Eds.), *Children and families 'at promise.'* (pp. 118–142). Albany: State University of New York Press.

Cooley, C. H. (1902). *Human nature and the social order.* New York: Scribner.

Daly, K., and Bordt, R. L. (1995). Sex effects and sentencing: An analysis of the statistical literature. *Justice Quarterly, 12,* 141–169.

Davidson, A. L. (1996). *Making and molding identity in schools: Student narratives on race, gender, and academic engagement.* Albany: State University of New Press.

Davis, K. (1949). *Human society.* New York: Macmillan.

Day, R. D., Peterson, G. W., and McCracken, C. (1998). Predicting spanking of younger and older children by mothers and fathers. *Journal of Marriage and the Family, 60,* 79–94.

Deater-Deckard, K., and Dodge, K. A. (1997). Externalizing behavior problems and discipline revisited: Nonlinear effects and variation by culture, context, and gender. *Psychological Inquiry, 8,* 161–175.

Deater-Deckard, K., Dodge, K. A., Bates, J. E., and Pettit, G. S. (1996). Physical discipline among African American and European American mothers: Links to children's externalizing behaviors. *Developmental Psychology, 32,* 1065–1072.

Deleire, T., and Kalil, A. (2002). Good things come in threes: Single-parent multigenerational family structure and adolescent adjustment. *Demography, 39(2),* 393–414.

Dembo, R., Getreu, A., Williams, L., Berry, E., La Voie, L., Genung, L., Schmeilder, J., Wish, E. D., and Ker, J. (1990). A longitudinal study of the relationship among alcohol use, marijuana/hashish use, cocaine use, and emotional/psychological functioning problems in a cohort of high-risk youths. *International Journal of the Addictions, 25,* 131–138.

Dembo, R., Williams, L., Schmeilder, J., Berry, E., Wothke, W., Getreu, A., Walsh, E. D., and Christensen, C. (1992). A structural model examining the relationship between physical child abuse, sexual victimization, and marijuana/hashish use in delinquent youth: A longitudinal study. *Violence and Victims, 1,* 41–62.

Demuth, S., and Brown, S. L. (2004). Family structure, family processes, and adolescent delinquency: The significance of parental absence versus parental gender. *Journal of Research in Crime and Delinquency, 41,* 58–81.

Devine, J. A., and Wright, J. D. (1993). *The greatest of evils: Urban poverty and the American underclass.* New York: Aldine de Gruyter.

Dishion, T. J., McCord, J., and Poulin, F. (1999). When interventions harm: Peer groups and problem behavior. *American Psychologist, 54,* 755–764.

Dobash, R. E., and Dobash, R. P. (1979). *Violence against wives: A case against the patriarchy.* New York: Free Press.

——. (1992). *Women, violence and social change.* New York: Routledge.

Dodge, K. A. (1980). Social cognition and children's aggressive behavior. *Child Development, 51,* 162–170.

——. (1986). A social information processing model of social competence in children. In M. Perlmutter (Ed.), *Aggression and antisocial behavior in childhood and adolescence.* Oxford: Plenum.

——. (1991). The structure and function of reactive and proactive aggression. In D. J. Pepler and K. H. Rubin (Eds.), *The development and treatment of childhood aggression* (pp. 201–218). Hillsdale, NJ: Lawrence Erlbaum Associates.

Dodge, K. A., Bates, J. E., and Pettit, G. S. (1990). Mechanisms in the cycle of violence. *Science, 250,* 1678–1683.

Dodge, K. A., and Newman, J. P. (1981). Biased decision-making processes in aggressive boys. *Journal of Abnormal Psychology, 90,* 375–379.

Dodge, K. A., Pettit, G. S., Bates, J. E., and Valente, E. (1995). Social information processing patterns partially mediate the effect of early physical abuse on later conduct problems. *Abnormal Psychology, 104,* 632–643.

Donovan, J. E., and Jessor, R. (1985). Structure of problem behavior in adolescence and adulthood. *Journal of Consulting and Clinical Psychology, 53,* 890–904.

Dornbusch, S. M., Carlsmith, J. M., Bushwall, S. J., Ritter, P. L., Leiderman, H., Hastorf, A. H., and Gross, R. T. (1985). Single parents, extended households, and the control of adolescents. *Child Development, 56,* 326–341.

Dornbusch, S. M., Ritter, P., Leiderman H., Roberts, D. F., and Fraliegh, M. (1987). The relationship of parenting style to adolescent school performance. *Child Development, 58,* 1244–1257.

Duncan, G. J., Brooks-Gunn, J., and Klebanov, P. K. (1994). Economic deprivation and early childhood development. *Child Development, 65(2),* 296–318.

Duncan, G. J., Yeung, W. J., Brooks-Gunn, J., and Smith, J. R. (1998). How much does childhood poverty affect the life chances of children? *American Sociological Review, 63,* 406–423.

Dunford, F., Huizinga, D., and Elliot, D. S. (1990). The role of arrest in domestic assault: The Omaha experiment. *Criminology, 28,* 183–206.

Dutton, D. G. (1995). *The batterer: A psychological profile* (with Susan K. Golant). New York: Basic Books.

——. (1998). *The abusive personality: Violence and control in intimate relationships.* New York: Guilford.

Ebata, A. T., Petersen, A. C., and Conger, J. J. (1990). The development of psychopathology in adolescence. In J. Rolf, A. S. Masten, D. Cicchetti, K. H. Nuechterlein, and S. Weintraub (Eds.), *Risk and protective factors in the development of psychopathology* (pp. 308–333). New York: Cambridge University Press.

Egeland, B., Jacobvitz, D., and Papatola, K. (1987). Intergenerational continuity of abuse. In R. J. Gelles and J. B. Lancaster (Eds.), *Child abuse and neglect: Biosocial dimensions.* Hawthorne, NY: Aldine de Gruyter.

Egeland, B., Jacobvitz, D., and Sroufe, A. (1988). Breaking the cycle of abuse. *Child Development, 59(4),* 1080–1089.

Elder, G. H., Jr. (1974). *Children of the great depression.* Chicago: University of Chicago Press.

——. (1992). The life course. In E. F. Borgatta and M. L. Borgatta (Eds.), *The encyclopedia of sociology.* New York: Macmillan.

Elder, G. H., Jr., and Caspi, A. (1988). Economic stress in lives: Developmental perspectives. *Journal of Social Issues, 44,* 25–45.

Elliott, D. S. (1993). Serious violent offenders: Onset, developmental course, and termination. *Criminology, 32,* 1–23.

Elliott, D. S., Huizinga, D., and Ageton, S. S. (1985). *Explaining delinquency and drug use.* Beverly Hills, CA: Sage Publications.

Elliott, D. S., Huizinga, D., and Menard, S. (1989). *Multiple problem youth: Delinquency, substance use, and mental health problems.* New York: Springer-Verlag.

Elliott, D. S., and Menard, S. (1996). Delinquent friends and delinquent behavior: Temporal and developmental patterns. In J. D. Hawkins (Ed.), *Delinquency and crime: Current theories.* New York: Cambridge University Press.

Elliott, D., Wilson, W. J., Huizinga, D., Sampson, R. J., Elliott, A., and Rankin, B. (1996). Effects of neighborhood disadvantage on adolescent development. *Journal of Research in Crime and Delinquency, 33,* 389–426.

Ellison, C. G., and Skerkat, D. E. (1992). Conservative Protestantism and support for corporal punishment. *American Sociological Review, 58,* 131–144.

Entwisle, D. R., and Alexander, K. L. (1996). Family type and children's growth in reading and math over the primary grades. *Journal of Marriage and the Family, 58(2),* 341–355.

EPOCH-USA. (2000). *Legal reforms: Corporal punishment of children in the family.* Retrieved from <http://www.stophitting.com/legalReform.php>.

Evans, T. D., Cullen, F. T., Burton, V. S., Dunaway, R. G., and Benson, M. L. (1997). The social consequences of self-control: Testing the general theory of crime. *Criminology, 35,* 475–501.

Fagan, J. A., and Browne, A. (1994). Violence between spouses and intimates: Physical aggression between women and men in intimate relationships. In A. J. Reiss, Jr., and J. A. Roth (Eds.), *Understanding and preventing violence: Vol. 3. Social influences.* Washington, DC: National Academy Press.

Fagan, J. A., Stewart, D. K., and Hansen, K. V. (1983). Violent men or violent husbands? Background factors and situational correlates. In D. Finkelhor, R. J. Gelles, G. T. Hotaling, and M. A. Straus (Eds.), *The dark side of families: Current family violence research* (pp. 49–67). Beverly Hills, CA: Sage Publications.

Farrington, D. P. (1991). Childhood aggression and adult violence: Early precursors and later life outcomes. In D. J. Pepler and K. H. Rubin (Eds.), *The development and treatment of childhood aggression* (pp. 5–30). Hillsdale, NJ: Lawrence Erlbaum Associates.

Federman, M., Garner, T. I., Short, K., Cutter, W. B., IV, and Kiely, J. (1996, May). What does it mean to be poor in America? *Monthly Labor Review*, 3–17.

Felson, R. B. (2000). The normative protection of women. *Sociological Forum, 15*, 91–116.

——. (2002). *Violence and gender reexamined.* Washington, DC: American Psychological Association.

Felson, M., and Gottfredson, M. (1984). Social indicators of adolescent activities near peers and parents. *Journal of Marriage and the Family, 46*, 709–714.

Ferster, C. B., and Perrott, M. C. (1968). *Behavior principles.* New York: New Century.

Finkelhor, D. (1986). Sexual abuse: Beyond the family systems approach. *Journal of Psychotherapy and the Family, 2*, 53–64.

——. (1994). The international epidemiology of child sexual abuse. *Child Abuse Neglect, 17*, 67–70.

Flanagan, T., and Maguire, K. (Eds.). (1990). *Sourcebook of criminal justice statistics: 1989.* Washington, DC: Government Printing Office.

Flynn, C. P. (1998). To spank or not to spank: The effect of situation and age of child on support for corporal punishment. *Journal of Family Violence, 13*, 21–37.

Fox, J. A. (2001). Uniform Crime Reports [United States]: Supplementary Homicide Reports, 1976–1999 [computer file]. ICPSR version. Ann Arbor, MI: Inter-University Consortium for Political and Social Research.

Freeman, R. (1991). *Crime and the employment of disadvantaged youth.* Cambridge, MA: Harvard University, National Bureau of Economic Research.

Friedman, S. B., and Schonberg, S. K. (1996a). Consensus Statements. *Pediatrics, 98*, 853.

——. (1996b). The short- and long-term consequences of corporal punishment (Supplement). *Pediatrics, 98* (4, pt. 2).

Furstenberg, F. F., Jr., and Cherlin, A. J. (1991). *Divided families.* Cambridge, MA: Harvard University Press.

Furstenberg, F. F., Jr., Cook, T., Eccles, J., Elder, G. H., and Sameroff, A. (1998). *Managing to make it: Urban families in high-risk neighborhoods.* Chicago: University of Chicago Press.

Furstenberg, F. F., Jr., Morgan, S. P., and Allison, P. D. (1987). Parental participation and children's well-being after marital dissolution. *American Sociological Review, 52,* 695–701.

Furstenberg, F. F., Jr., and Nord, C. W. (1985). Parenting apart: Patterns of childbearing after marital disruption. *Journal of Marriage and the Family, 47,* 893–904.

Ganong, L. H., and Coleman, M. (2000). Remarried families. In C. Hendrick and S. C. Hendrick (Eds.), *Close relationships: A sourcebook* (pp. 155–168). Thousand Oaks, CA: Sage Publications.

Garfinkel, I., McLanahan, S. S., and Robins, P. K. (Eds.). *Child support and child well-being* (pp. 285–316). Washington, DC: Urban Institute.

Gelles, R. J. (1976). Abused wives: Why do they stay? *Journal of Marriage and the Family, 38,* 659–685.

——. (1979). *Family violence.* Beverly Hills, CA: Sage Publications.

Gelles, R. J., and Conte, J. R. (1990). Domestic violence and sexual abuse of children: A review of research in the eighties. *Journal of Marriage and the Family, 52,* 1045–1058.

Gelles, R. J., and Straus, M. A. (1979). Violence in the American family. *Journal of Social Issues, 35,* 15–30.

Gershoff, E. T. (2002). Corporal punishment by parents and associated child behaviors and experiences: A meta-analytic and theoretical review. *Psychological Bulletin, 128,* 539–579.

Gibbs, J. J., Giever, D., and Martin, J. S. (1998). Parental management and self-control: An empirical test of Gottfredson and Hirschi's general theory. *Journal of Research in Crime and Delinquency, 35,* 40–71.

Giordano, P. C., Cernkovich, S. A., and Pugh, M. D. (1986). Friendships and delinquency. *American Journal of Sociology, 91,* 1170–1202.

Glasser, M., Kolvin, I., Campbell, D., Glasser, A., Leitch, I., and Farrelly, S. (2001). Cycle of child sexual abuse: Links between being a victim and becoming a perpetrator. *British Journal of Psychiatry, 179,* 482–494.

Glick, J. E., Bean, F. D., and Van Hook, J. (1997). Immigration and changing patterns of extended family household structure in the United States: 1970–1990. *Journal of Marriage and the Family, 59,* 177–191.

Glueck, S., and Glueck, E. (1950). *Unraveling juvenile delinquency.* New York: Commonwealth Fund.

——. (1968). *Delinquents and non-delinquents in perspective.* Cambridge, MA: Harvard University Press.

Goffman, E. (1963). *Behavior in public places.* New York: Free Press.

——. (1974). *Frame analysis: An essay on the organization of experience.* New York: Harper & Row.

Gonzales, N. A., Cauce, A. M., Freidman, R. J., and Mason, C. A. (1996). Family, peer, and neighborhood influences on academic achievement among African American adolescents: One-year prospective effects. *American Journal of Community Psychology, 24,* 365–387.

Goode, E. (2001). *Deviant dehavior* (6th edition). Upper Saddle River, NJ: Prentice Hall.

Goodman, C. C., and Silverstein, M. (2001). Grandmothers who parent their grandchildren. *Journal of Family Issues, 22(5),* 557–578.

Goodman, S. H., Hoven, C. W., Narrow, W. E., Cohen, P., Fielding, B., Alegria, M., Leaf, P. J., Kandel, D., Horwitz, S. M., Bravo, M., Moore, R., and Duncan, M. K. (1998). Measurement of risk for mental disorders and competence in a psychiatric epidemiologic community survey: The National Institute of Mental Health methods for the epidemiology of child and adolescent mental disorders (MECA) study. *Social Psychiatry and Psychiatric Epidemiology, 33,* 162–173.

Gordon, L. C. (1999). Linking gender differences in parenting to a typology of family parenting styles and adolescent developmental outcomes. Doctoral dissertation. Iowa State University.

Gottfredson, M., and Hirschi, T. (1990). *A general theory of crime.* Stanford, CA: Stanford University Press.

Graham, J. W., Beller, A. H., and Hernandez, P. M. (1994). The effects of child support on educational attainment. In I. Garfinkel, S. S. McLanahan, and P.K. Robins (Eds.), *Child support and child well-being* (pp. 317–354). Washington, DC: Urban Institute.

Graham, P. (1979). Epidemiological studies. In H. C. Quay and J. S. Werry (Eds.), *Psychopathological disorders of childhood* (2nd edition, pp. 185–209). New York: Academic.

Grall, T. (2000). *Child support for custodial mothers and fathers.* Washington, DC: U.S. Census Bureau.

Gray, M. R., and Steinberg, L. (1999). Unpacking authoritative parenting: Reassessing a multidimensional construct. *Journal of Marriage and the Family, 61,* 574–587.

Grizzle, G. L. (1998). Institutionalization and family unity: An exploratory study of Cherlin's (1978) views. *Journal of Divorce and Remarriage, 30(3/4),* 125–142.

Gunnoe, M. L., and Mariner, C. L. (1997). Toward development-contextual model of the effects of parental spanking on children's aggression. *Archives of Pediatric and Adolescent Medicine, 151,* 768–775.

Gutierrez, J., and Sameroff, A. (1990). Determinants of complexity in Mexican-American mothers' conceptions of child development. *Child Development, 61,* 384–394.

Hagan, J. (1989). Micro and macro structures of delinquency causation and a power control theory of gender and delinquency. In S. F. Messner, M. D. Krohn, and A. E. Liska (Eds.), *Theoretical integration in the study of de-*

viance and crime (pp. 213–228). Albany: State University of New York Press.

Hagan, J., Gillis, A. R., and Simpson, J. (1985). The class structure of gender and delinquency: Toward a power-control theory of common delinquent behavior. *American Journal of Sociology, 90,* 1151–1178.

——. (1987). Class in the household: A power-control theory of gender and delinquency. *American Journal of Sociology, 92,* 788–816.

——. (1990). Clarifying and extending power-control theory. *American Journal of Sociology, 95,* 1024–1037.

——. (1993). The power of control in sociological theories. In F. Adler and W. S. Laufer (Eds.), *New directions in criminological theory: Advances in criminological theory* (Vol. 4) (pp. 381–398). New Brunswick, NJ: Transaction.

Hagan, J., and Kay, F. (1990). Gender and delinquency in white-collar families: A power-control perspective. *Crime and delinquency, 36,* 391–407.

Hanson, T. L., McLanahan, S., and Thomson, E. (1996). Double jeopardy: Parental conflict and stepfamily outcomes for children. *Journal of Marriage and the Family, 58(1),* 141–154.

Hareven, T. K. (1994). Continuity and change in American family life. In A. S. Skolnick and J. H. Skolnick (Eds.), *Family in transition* (8th edition, pp. 40–46). New York: Harper Collins.

Hays, C. (2001). Parenting, self-control, and delinquency: A test of self-control theory. *Criminology, 39,* 707–736.

Heffer, R. W., and Kelley, M. L. (1987). Mothers' acceptance of behavioral interventions: The influence of parent race and income. *Behavior Therapy, 18,* 153–163.

Hemenway, D., Solnick S., and Carter, J. (1994). Childrearing violence. *Child Abuse and Neglect, 18,* 1011–1020.

Herrenkohl, E. C., Herrenkohl, R. C., and Toedter, L. J. (1983). Perspectives on the intergenerational transmission of abuse. In D. Finkelhor, R. J. Gelles, G. T. Hotaling, and M. A. Straus (Eds.), *The dark side of families: Current family violence research* (pp. 305–316). Thousand Oaks, CA: Sage Publications.

Hetherington, E. M. (1987). Family relations six years after divorce. In K. Pasley and M. Ihinger-Tallman (Eds.), *Remarriage and stepparenting: Current research and theory* (pp. 185–205). New York: Guilford Press.

——. (1993). An overview of the Virginia longitudinal study of divorce and remarriage with a focus on early adolescence. *Journal of Family Psychology, 7,* 39–56.

——. (1999). *Coping with divorce, single parenting, and remarriage: A risk and resiliency perspective.* Mahwah, NJ: Lawrence Erlbaum Associates.

Hetherington, E. M., Cox, M., and Cox, R. (1982). Effects of divorce on parents and children. In M. E. Lamb (Ed.), *Nontraditional families: Parenting and child development* (pp. 233–285). Hillsdale, NJ: Lawrence Erlbaum Associates.

Hetherington, E. M., and Stanley-Hagan, M. M. (1999). Stepfamilies. In M. E. Lamb (Ed.), *Parenting and child development in 'nontraditional' families* (pp. 137–159). Mahwah, NJ: Lawrence Erlbaum Associates.

Hewitt, J. P. (1991). *Self and society: A symbolic interactionist social psychology* (5th edition). Boston: Allyn & Bacon.

Heyman, R. E., and Slep, A. M. S. (2002). Do child abuse and interparental violence lead to adulthood family violence? *Journal of Marriage and the Family, 64,* 864–870.

Hill, S. A. (1999). *African American children: Socialization and development in families.* Thousand Oaks, CA: Sage Publications.

Hipple, S. (1998). Contingent work: Results from the second survey. *Monthly Labor Review, 124,* no. 11.

Hirschi, T. (1969). *Causes of delinquency.* Berkeley: University of California Press.

Hirschi, T., and Gottfredson, M. (1983). Age and the explanation of crime. *American Journal of Sociology, 89,* 552–584.

——. (1994). The generality of deviance. In T. Hirschi and M. Gottfredson (Eds.), *The generality of deviance.* New Brunswick, NJ: Transaction.

Holmes, S. J., and Robins, L. N. (1988). The role of parental disciplinary experience on the development of depression and alcoholism. *Psychiatry, 51,* 24–35.

Holtzworth-Monroe, A., and Stuart, G. L. (1994). Typologies of male batterers: Three subtypes and the differences among them. *Psychological Bulletin, 116,* 476–497.

Homans, G. E. (1974). *Social behavior: Its elementary forms.* New York: Harcourt, Brace, and World.

Hotaling, G. T., Straus, M. A., and Lincoln, A. J. (1990). Intrafamily violence and crime and violence outside the family. In M. A. Straus and R. J. Gelles (Eds.), *Physical violence in American families: Risk factors and adaptations to violence in 8,145 families.* New Brunswick, NJ: Transaction.

Hyman, I. A. (1997). *The case against spanking: How to discipline your child without hitting.* San Fransisco: Jossey-Bass.

Immershein, A. W., and Simons, R. L. (1976). Rules and exemplars in lay and professional psychiatry: An ethnomethodological comment on the Scheff-Gove controversy. *American Sociological Review, 41,* 559–563.

Ireland, T. O., Smith, C. A., and Thornberry, T. P. (2002). Developmental issues in the impact of child maltreatment on later delinquency and drug use. *Criminology, 40,* 359–402.

Ireland, T. O., and Widom, C. S. (1994). Childhood victimization and risk for alcohol and drug arrests. *The International Journal of the Addictions, 29,* 235–274.

Jacobson, N., and Gottman, J. (1998). *When men batter women: New insights into ending abusive relationships.* New York: Simon & Schuster.

Jensen, G. F., and Thompson, K. (1990). What's class go to do with it? A further examination of power control theory. *American Journal of Sociology, 95,* 1009–1023.

Jessor, R., Donovan, J. E., and Costa, F. M. (1991). *Beyond adolescence: Problem behavior and young adult development.* New York: Cambridge University Press.

Jeynes, W. (2000). A longitudinal analysis on the effects of remarriage following divorce on the academic achievement of adolescents. *Journal of Divorce and Remarriage, 33(1/2),* 131–148.

Johnson, M. P. (1995). Patriarchal terrorism and common couple violence: Two forms of violence against women. *Journal of Marriage and the Family, 57,* 283–294.

——. (1998, June). Commitment and entrapment. Paper presented at the Ninth International Conference on Personal Relationships, Saratoga Springs, NY.

——. (2000). Conflict and control: Images of symmetry and asymmetry in domestic violence. In A. Booth, A. C. Crouter, and M. Clements (Eds.), *Couples in conflict.* Hillsdale, NJ: Lawrence Erlbaum Associates.

Johnson, M. P., and Ferraro, K. J. (2000). Research on domestic violence in the 1990's: Making distinctions. *Journal of Marriage and the Family, 62(4),* 948–963.

Jones, C. L., Tepperman, L., and Wilson, S. J. (1995). *The futures of the family.* Englewood Cliffs, NJ: Prentice Hall.

Kakar, S. (1996). *Child abuse and delinquency.* New York: University Press of America.

Kandel, D. B., and Davies, M. (1991). Friendship networks, intimacy, and illicit drug use in young adulthood: A comparison of two competing theories. *Criminology, 29,* 441–469.

Karoly, L. A., Everingham, S. S., Hoube, J., Kilburn, R., Rydell, C. P., Sanders, M., and Greenwood, P. W. (1998). *Investing in our children: What we know and what we don't know about costs and benefits of early childhood intervention.* Santa Monica, CA: Rand Corporation.

Kaufman, J., and Zigler, E. (1987). Do abused children become abusive parents? *American Journal of Orthopsychiatry, 57,* 186–192.

——. (1993). The intergenerational transmission of abuse is overstated. In R. J. Gelles and D. R. Loseke (Eds.), *Current controversies on family violence.* New York: Sage Publications.

Kelley, M. L., Power, T. G., and Wimbush, D. D. (1992). Determinants of disciplinary practices in low-income black mothers. *Child Development, 63,* 573–582.

Kelley, M. L., Sanchez-Hucles, J., and Walker, R. R. (1993). Correlates of disciplinary practices in working- to middle-class African-American mothers. *Merrill-Palmer Quarterly, 39,* 252–264.

Kempe, C. H., Silverman, F. N. Steele, B. F., Droegemuller, W., and Silver, H. K. (1962). The battered child syndrome. *Journal of the American Medical Association, 181,* 17–24.

King, V. (1994). Nonresident father involvement and child well-being: Can dads make a difference? *Journal of Family Issues, 15,* 78–96.

Knox, V. W., and Bane, M. J. (1994). Child support and schooling. In I. Garfinkel, S. S. McLanahan, and P. K. Robins (Eds.), *Child support and child well-being* (pp. 285–316). Washington, DC: Urban Institute.

Kohn, M. L. (1977). *Class and conformity: A study in values* (2nd edition). Chicago: University of Chicago Press.

Kohn, M. L., Kazimierz, M., Slomczynski, M., and Schoenbach, C. (1986). Social stratification and the transmission of values in the family: A cross-national assessment. *Sociological Forum, 1,* 73–102.

Kohn, M. L., and Schooler, C. (1982). Job conditions and personality: A longitudinal assessment of their reciprocal effects. *American Journal of Sociolology, 87,* 1257–1286.

——. (1983). *Work and personality: An inquiry into the impact of social stratification.* Norwood, NJ: Ablex.

Kornhauser, R. (1978). *Social sources of delinquency.* Chicago: University of Chicago Press.

Koss, M. P., Goodman, L. A., Browne, A., Fitzgerald, L. F., Keita, G. P., and Russo, N. F. (1994). *No safe haven: Male violence against women at home, at work, and in the community* (1st edition). Washington, DC: American Psychological Association.

Kriger, S. F., and Kroes, W. H. (1972). Childrearing of Chinese, Jewish, and Protestant parents. *Child Development, 23,* 726–729.

Ladd, G. W., Profilet, S. M., and Hart, C. H. (1992). Parents' management of children's peer relations: Facilitating and supervising children's activities in the peer culture. In R. D. Parke and G. W. Ladd (Eds.), *Family-peer relationships: Modes of linkage.* Hillsdale, NJ: Lawrence Erlbaum Associates.

Lamanna, M. A., and Riedmann, A. (2003). *Marriages and families: Making choices in a diverse society* (8th edition). Belmont, CA: Wadsworth.

Lamborn, S. D., Mounts, N. S., Steinberg, L., and Dornbusch, S. M. (1991). Patterns of competence and adjustment among adolescents from authoritative, authoritarian, indulgent, and neglectful families. *Child Development, 62,* 1049–1065.

Larzelere, R. E. (1996). A review of the outcomes of parental use of nonabusive or customary physical punishment. *Pediatrics, 98,* 824–828.

Larzelere, R. E., and Merenda, J. A. (1994). The effectiveness of parental discipline for toddler misbehavior at different levels of child distress. *Family Relations, 43,* 480–488.

Larzelere, R. E., and Patterson, G. R. (1990). Parental management: Mediator of the effect of socioeconomic status on early delinquency. *Criminology, 28,* 301–324.

Larzelere, R. E., Schneider, W., Larson, D. B., and Pike, P. L. (1995). The effects of disciplinary responses in delaying toddler misbehavior recurrences. *Child and Family Behavior Therapy, 18,* 35–37.

Laub, J. H., Nagin, D. S., and Sampson, R. J. (1998). Good marriages and trajectories of change in criminal offending. *American Sociological Review, 63,* 225–238.

Laub, J. H., and Sampson, R. J. (1988). Unraveling Families and Delinquency: A reanalysis of the Gluecks' data. *Criminology, 26,* 355–380.

——. (1991). The Sutherland-Glueck debate: On the sociology of criminological knowledge. *American Sociological Review, 96,* 1402–1440.

——. (1993). Turning points in the life course: Why change matters in the study of crime. *Criminology, 31,* 301–326.

——. (1994). Unemployment, marital discord, and deviant behavior: The long-term correlates of childhood misbehavior. In T. Hirschi and M. R. Gottfredson (Eds.), *The generality of deviance* (pp. 235–252). New Brunswick, NJ: Transaction.

Lauer, R. H., and Handel, W. H. (1977). *Social psychology: The theory and application of symbolic interactionism.* Boston: Houghton Mifflin.

Leder, J. M. (1991). *Brothers and sisters: How they shape our lives.* New York: St. Martin's Press.

Lemmon, J. H. (1999). How child maltreatment affects dimensions of juvenile delinquency in a cohort of low-income urban youths. *Justice Quarterly, 16,* 357–376.

Levinson, D. (1989). *Family violence in cross-cultural perspective.* Newbury Park, CA: Sage Publications.

Lichter, D. T. (1997). Poverty and inequality among children. *Annual Review of Sociology, 23,* 121–145.

Lie, G.-Y., Schilit, R., Bush, J., Montagne, M., and Reyes, L. (1991). Lesbians in currently aggressive relationships: How frequently do they report aggressive past relationships? *Violence and Victims, 6,* 121–135.

Lieh-Mak, F., Chung S. Y., and Liv Y. W. (1983). Characteristics of child battering in Hong Kong: A controlled study. *British Journal of Psychiatry, 14,* 89–94.

Lin, C. C., and Fu, V. R. (1990). A comparison of child-rearing practices among Chinese, immigrant Chinese, and Caucasian-American parents. *Child Development, 61,* 429–433.

Linden, E., and Hackler, J. (1973). Affective ties and delinquency. *Pacific Sociological Review, 16,* 27–46.

Liska, A. E., and Messner, S. F. (1999). *Perspectives on crime and deviance* (3rd edition). Upper Saddle River, NJ: Prentice Hall.

Loeber, R. (1982). The stability of antisocial child behavior: A review. *Child Development, 53,* 1431–1436.

Loeber, R., Farrington, D. P., Stouthamer-Loeber, M., and Van Kammen, W. B. (1998). *Antisocial behavior and mental health problems: Explanatory factors in childhood and adolescence.* Mahwah, NJ: Lawrence Erlbaum Associates.

Loeber, R., and Le Blanc, M. (1990). Toward a developmental criminology. In M. Tonry and N. Morris (Eds.), *Crime and justice: A review of research* (Vol. 12) (pp. 375–473). Chicago: University of Chicago Press.

Loeber, R., and Stouthamer-Loeber, M. (1986). Family factors as correlates and predictors of juvenile conduct problems and delinquency. In M. Tonry and N. Morris (Eds.), *Crime and justice* (Vol. 7). Chicago: University of Chicago Press.

Lytton, H. (1990). Child and parent effects in boys' conduct disorder: A reinterpretation. *Developmental Psychology, 26,* 683–697.

Maccoby, E. E. (1992). The role of parents in the socialization of children: An historical overview. *Developmental Psychology, 28,* 1006–1017.

Maccoby, E. E., and Martin, J. A. (1983). Socialization in the context of the family: Parent-child interaction. In P. Mussen (Ed.), *Handbook of child psychology* (pp. 1–101). New York: Wiley.

MacIntyre, D. I., and Cantrell, P. J. (1995). Punishment history and adult attitudes towards violence and aggression in men and women. *Social Behavior and Personality, 23,* 23–28.

Mahoney, A., Donnelly, W. O., Lewis, T., and Maynard, C. (2000). Mother and father self-reports of corporal punishment and severe physical aggression toward clinic-referred youth. *Journal of Clinical Child Psychology, 26,* 266–281.

Marsiglio, W., Amato, P., Day, R. D., and Lamb, M. E. (2000). Scholarship on fatherhood in the 1990's and beyond. *Journal of Marriage and the Family, 62,* 1173–1191.

Marvell, T. B., and Moody, C. E. (1999). Female and male homicide victimization rates: Comparing trends and regressors. *Criminology, 37,* 879–900.

Mason, C. A., Cauce, A. M., Gonzalez, N., and Hiraga, Y. (1996). Neither too sweet nor too sour: Problem peers, maternal control, and problem behavior in African American adolescents. *Child Development, 67,* 2115–2130.

Maxfield, M. G., and Widom, C. S. (1996). The cycle of violence: Revisited six years later. *Archives of Pediatrics and Adolescent Medicine, 150,* 390–395.

McAnulty, R. D., and Burnette, M. M. (2001). *Exploring human sexuality.* Needham Heights, MA: Allyn & Bacon.

McCarthy, B., Hagan, J., and Woodward, T. S. (1999). In the company of women: Stucture and agency in a revised power-control theory of gender and delinquency. *Criminology, 26,* 627–648.

McCord, J. (1988). Parental behavior in the cycle of aggression. *Psychiatry, 51,* 14–23.

——. (1991a). Family relationships, juvenile delinquency, and adult criminality. *Criminology, 29,* 397–417.

——. (1991b). Questioning the value of punishment. *Social Problems, 38,* 167–179.

——. (1997). On discipline. *Psychological Inquiry, 8,* 215–217.

McCord, J., and Ensminger, M. E. (2002). Racial discrimination and violence: A longitudinal perspective. In D. Hawkins (Ed.), *Violent crime: Assessing race and ethnic differences* (pp. 319–330). New York: Cambridge University Press.

McCord, W., and McCord, J. (1959). *Origins of crime.* New York: Columbia University Press.

McLanahan, S. S., and Sandefur, G. (1994). *Growing up with a single parent.* Cambridge, MA: Harvard University Press.

McLanahan, S. S., Seltzer, J. A., Hanson, T. L., and Thompson, E. (1994). Child support enforcement and child well-being: Greater security or greater conflict? In I. Garfinkel, S. S. McLanahan, and P. K. Robins (Eds.), *Child support and child well-being* (pp. 239–256). Washington, DC: Urban Institute Press.

McLeod, J. D., and Shanahan, M. J. (1993). Poverty, parenting, and children's mental health. *American Sociological Review, 58(3),* 351–366.

McLoyd, V. C. (1990). Minority children: Introduction to the special issue. *Child Development, 61,* 263–266.

——. (1998). Socioeconomic disadvantage and child development. *American Psychologist, 53(2),* 185–204.

McNeely, R. L., and Mann, C. R. (1990). Domestic violence is a human issue. *Journal of Interpersonal Violence, 5,* 129–132.

Mead, G. H. (1934). *Mind, self, and society.* Chicago: University of Chicago Press.

Messner, S., and Krohn, M. (1990). Class compliance structures and delinquency: Assessing integrated structural Marxist theory. *American Journal of Sociology, 96,* 300–328.

Messner, S., and Tardiff, K. (1986). Economic inequality and levels of homicide: An analysis of urban neighborhoods. *Criminology, 24,* 297–318.

Moffitt, T. E. (1993a). Adolescent-limited and life-course persistent antisocial behavior: A developmental taxonomy. *Psychological Review, 100,* 674–701.

——. (1993b). 'Life-course persistent' and 'adolescent-limited' antisocial behavior: A developmental taxonomy. *Development and Psychopathology, 5,* 133–151.

——. (1997). Adolescent-limited and life-course persistent offending: A complementary pair of developmental theories. In T. P. Thornberry (Ed.), *Developmental theories of crime and delinquency.* New Brunswick, NJ: Transaction.

Moffitt, T. E., Begg, D., Caspi, A., Dickson, N., Langley, J., McGee, R., Paul, C., Silva, P., Stanton, W., and Stevenson, P. (1996). Childhood-onset versus adolescent-onset antisocial conduct in males: Natural history from age 3 to age 18. *Development and Psychopathology, 32,* 1–9.

Moffitt, T. E., Krueger, R. F., Caspi, A., and Fagan, J. (2000). Partner abuse and general crime: How are they the same? How are they different? *Criminology, 38,* 199–232.

Morash, M., and Chesney-Lind, M. (1991). A reformulation and partial test of the power-control theory of delinquency. *Justice Quarterly, 8,* 347–378.

Morrow, L. (1993, March 29). The temping of America. *Time,* 40–41.

Nagin, D. S., and Farrington, D. P. (1992). The stability of criminal potential from childhood to adulthood. *Criminology, 30,* 253–260.

Nagin, D. S., Farrington, D. P., and Moffitt, T. E. (1995). Life-course trajectories of different types of offenders. *Criminology, 33,* 111–139.

——. (2001). Life-course trajectories of different types of offenders. In A. Piquero and P. Mazerolle (Eds.), *Life-course criminology: Contemporary and classic readings* (pp. 173–198). Belmont, CA: Wadsworth/Thomson Learning.

Nagin, D. S., and Paternoster, R. (1991). On the relationship of past and future participation in delinquency. *Criminology, 29,* 163–190.

Nagin, D. S., and Waldfogel, J. (1992). The effects of criminality and conviction on the labor market status of young British offenders. Unpublished manuscript, Pittsburgh: Carnegie Mellon University.

Nasby, W., Hayden, B., and DePaulo, B. M. (1980). Attributional bias among aggressive boys to interpret unambiguous social stimuli as displays of hostility. *Journal of Abnormal Psychology, 89,* 450–468.

Newcomb, M. D. (1993). Problem behavior theory and perhaps a little beyond. *Contemporary Psychology, 38,* 895–898.

Newcomb, M. D., and Loeb, T. B. (1999). Poor parenting as an adult problem behavior: General deviance, deviant attitudes, inadequate family support and bonding, or just bad parents? *Journal of Family Psychology, 13(2),* 175–193.

Newman, G. (1976). *Comparative deviance: Perception and law in six cultures.* New York: McGraw-Hill.

Nye, F. I. (1958). *Family relationships and delinquent behavior.* New York: Wiley.

O'Brien, M. J. (1991). Taking sibling incest seriously. In M. Q. Patton (Ed.), *Family sexual abuse: Frontline research and evaluation* (pp. 75–92). Newbury Park, CA: Sage Publications.

Osgood, D. W., Johnston, L. D., O'Malley, P. M., and Buchman, J. G. (1988). The generality of deviance in late adolescence and early adulthood. *American Sociological Review, 53,* 81–93.

Pagelow, M. D. (1981). *Wife-battering: Victims and their experiences.* Beverly Hills, CA: Sage Publications.

——. (1984). *Family violence.* New York: Praeger.

Parcel, T. L., and Menaghan, E. G. (1994). Early parental work, family social capital, and early childhood outcomes. *American Journal of Sociology, 99,* 972–1009.

Parke, R. D., and Bhavnagri, N. P. (1989). Parents as managers of children's peer relationships. In D. Belle (Ed.), *Children's social networks and social supports.* New York: Wiley & Sons.

Paternoster, R., and Brame, R. (1997). Multiple routes to delinquency? A test of developmental and general theories of crime. *Criminology, 35,* 49–84.

Paternoster, R., Dean, C. W., Piquero, A., Mazerolle, P., and Brame, R. (1997). Generality, continuity, and change in offending. *Journal of Quantitative Criminology, 13,* 231–266.

Paternoster, R., and Tittle, C. R. (1990). Parental work control and delinquency: A theoretical and empirical critique. In W. S. Laufer and F. Adler (Eds.), *Advances in criminological theory* (Vol. 2) (pp. 39–70). New Brunswick, NJ: Transaction.

Patterson, G. R. (1982). *A social learning approach: 3. Coercive family process.* Eugene, OR: Castalia.

Patterson, G. R., Debaryshe, B. D., and Ramsey, E. (1989). A developmental perspective on antisocial behavior. *American Psychologist, 44,* 329–335.

Patterson, G. R., Reid, J. B., and Dishion, T. J. (1992). *Antisocial boys: A social interactional approach.* Eugene, OR: Castalia.

Patterson, G. R., and Yoerger, K. (1993). Development models for delinquent behavior. In S. Hodgins (Ed.), *Mental disorder and crime* (pp. 140–172). Newbury Park, CA: Sage Publications.

Pears, K. C., and Capaldi, D. M. (2001). Intergenerational transmission of abuse: A two-generation prospective study of an at-risk sample. *Child Abuse and Neglect, 25,* 1439–1461.

Perry, D. G., Perry, L. C., and Rassmussen, P. (1986). Cognitive social learning mediators of aggression. *Child Development, 57,* 700–711.

Pierce, R., and Pierce, L. (1985). Analysis of sexual abuse hotline reports. *Child Abuse and Neglect, 9,* 37–45.

Piquero, A. R., and Brezina, T. (2001). Testing Moffitt's account of adolescent-limited delinquency. *Criminology, 39,* 353–370.

Polakowski, M. (1994). Linking self- and social control with deviance: Illuminating the structure underlying a general theory of crime and its relation to deviant activity. *Journal of Quantitative Criminology, 10,* 41–78.

Pratt, T. C., and Cullen, F. T. (2000). The empirical status of Gottfredson and Hirschi's general theory of crime: A meta-analysis. *Criminology, 38,* 931–964.

Presser, H., and Cox, A. G. (1997). The employment schedules of low-educated American women and implications for welfare reform. Paper presented at the meeting of the American Sociological Association, Toronto, Canada.

Puntenney, D. L. (1997). The impact of gang violence on the decisions of everyday life: Disjunctions between policy assumptions and community conditions. *Journal of Urban Affairs, 19,* 143–161.

Quinton, D., and Rutter, M. (1988). *Parenting breakdown: The making and breaking of inter-generational links.* Aldershot: Avebury.

Reckless, W. (1961). A new theory of delinquency and crime. *Federal Probation, 25,* 42–46.

——. (1967). *The crime problem.* New York: Appleton-Century-Crofts.

Reese, L., Goldenberg, C., Loucky, J., and Gallimore, R. (1995). Ecocultural context, cultural activity and emergent literacy: Sources of variation in home literacy experiences of Spanish-speaking children. In S. W. Rothstein (Ed.), *Class, culture, and race in American schools: A handbook* (pp. 199–224). Westport, CT: Greenwood Press.

Reiss, A. J. (1951). Delinquency as the failure of personal and social controls. *American Sociological Review, 16,* 196–207.

Renzetti, C. M. (1992). *Violent betrayal: Partner abuse in lesbian relationships.* Thousand Oaks, CA: Sage Publications.

Rey, J. M., and Walter, G. (1999). Oppositional Defiant Disorder. In D. O. Hendren (Ed.), *Disruptive behavior disorders in children and adolescents* (pp. 99–126). Washington, DC: American Psychiatric Association.

Riggs, D. S., and O'Leary, K. D. (1996). Aggression between heterosexual dating partners: An examination of a causal model of courtship aggression. *Journal of Interpersonal Violence, 11,* 519–540.

Roberts, M. W. (1982). Resistance to timeout: Some normative data. *Behavior Assessment, 4,* 239–248.

——. (1988). Enforcing chair timeouts with room timeouts. *Behavior Assessment, 12,* 353–370.

Roberts, M. W., and Powers, S. W. (1990). Adjusting chair time-out enforcement procedures for oppositional children. *Behavior Therapy, 21,* 257–271.

Robins, L. N. (1978). Sturdy predictors of adult antisocial behavior, replications from longitudinal studies. *Psychological Medicine, 8,* 611–622.

Roe, K. M., and Minkler, M. (1998). Grandparents raising grandchildren: Challenges and responses. *Generations, 22,* 25–32.

Roncek, D. (1981). Dangerous places: Crime and residential environment. *Social Forces, 60,* 74–96.

Rosenbaum, A., and O'Leary, K. D. (1981). Marital violence: Characteristics of abusive couples. *Journal of Consulting and Clinical Psychology, 49,* 63–71.

Rothbaum, F., and Weisz, J. R. (1994). Parental caregiving and child externalizing behavior in non-clinical samples: A meta-analysis. *Psychological Bulletin, 116,* 55–74.

Rowe, D. C. (1994). *The limits of family influence: Genes, experience, and behavior.* New York: Guiford.

Rowe, D. C., and Farrington, D. P. (1997). The familial transmission of criminal convictions. *Criminology, 35,* 177–201.

Rutter, M. (1985). Family and school influences on behavioral development. *Journal of Child Psychology and Psychiatry, 26,* 349–368.

Sampson, R. J. (1985). Neighborhood and crime: The structural determinants of personal victimization. *Journal of Research in Crime and Delinquency, 22,* 7–40.

——. (1986). Neighborhood family structure and the risk of criminal victimization. In J. M. Byrne and R. J. Sampson (Eds.), *The social ecology of crime* (pp. 25–46). New York: Springer-Verlag.

——. (1992). Family management and child development: Insights from social disorganization theory. In J. McCord (Ed.), *Facts, frameworks, and forecasts,* Vol. 3 of *Advances in criminological theory.* New Brunswick, NJ: Transaction.

——. (1997). The embeddedness of child and adolescent development: A community-level perspective on urban violence. In J. McCord (Ed.), *Violence and childhood in the inner city* (pp. 31–77). New York: Cambridge University Press.

Sampson, R. J., and Groves, W. B. (1989). Community structure and crime: Testing social-disorganization theory. *American Journal of Sociology, 94,* 774–802.

Sampson, R. J., and Laub, J. H. (1990). Crime and deviance over the life course: The salience of adult social bonds. *American Sociological Review, 55,* 609–627.

——. (1993). *Crime in the making: Pathways and turning points through the life course.* Cambridge, MA: Harvard University Press.

——. (1994). Urban poverty and the family context of delinquency: A new look at structure and process in a classic study. *Child Development, 55,* 523–540.

——. (1997). A life course theory of cumulative disadvantage and the stability of delinquency. In T. P. Thornberry (Ed.), *Development theories of crime and delinquency* (pp. 133–161). New Brunswick, NJ: Transaction.

Sampson, R. J., Raudenbush, S. W., and Earls, F. (1997). Neighborhoods and violent crime: A multilevel study of collective efficacy. *Science, 277,* 918–924.

Sather, P. (1992). Side effects of parental punishment of toddlers. Doctoral diss. La Mirada, CA: Biola University.

Scaramella, L. V., Conger, L. D., Spoth, R., and Simons, R. L. (2002). Evaluation of a social contextual model of delinquency: A cross-study replication. *Child Development, 73,* 175–195.

Scheff, T. J. (1984). *Being mentally ill: A sociological theory* (2nd edition). New York: Aldine Publishing.

Schuerman, L., and Korbin, S. (1986). Community careers in crime. In A. J. Reiss, Jr. and M. Tonry (Eds.), *Communities and crime* (pp. 67–100). Chicago: University of Chicago Press.

Schutz, A. (1964). *Collected papers II: Studies in social theory.* The Hague: Martinus Nijhoff.

Schwartz, I. M., Rendon, J. A., and Hsieh, C. M. (1994). Is child treatment a leading cause of delinquency? *Child Welfare, 73,* 639–655.

Seccombe, K. (2000). Families in poverty in the 1990's: Trends, causes, consequences, and lessons learned. *Journal of Marriage and the Family, 62(4),* 1094–1113.

Seltzer, J. A. (2000). Families formed outside of marriage. *Journal of Marriage and the Family, 62,* 1247–1268.

Sherman, L. W., Schmidt, J. D., Rogan, D. P., Gartin, P. R., Cohn, E. G., Dean, J. C., and Bacich, A. R. (1991). From initial deterrence to long-term escalation: Short-term custody arrest for poverty ghetto domestic violence. *Criminology, 29,* 821–850.

Shields, N. M., McCall, G. J., and Hanneke, C. R. (1988). Patterns of family and nonfamily violence: Violent husbands and violent men. *Violence and Victims, 3(2),* 83–97.

Shoemaker, D. J. (2000). *Theories of delinquency: An examination of explanations of delinquent behavior* (4th edition). New York: Oxford University Press.

Simcha-Fagan, O., and Schwartz, J. E. (1986). Neighborhood and delinquency: An assessment of contextual effects. *Criminology, 24,* 667–704.

Simons, L. G., Simons, R. L., Brody, G. H., and Conger, R. D. (2003). Collective socialization and child conduct problems: A multi-level analysis with an African American sample. *Youth and Society.* In press.

Simons, L. G., Simons, R. L., and Conger, R. D. (in press). Identifying the mechanisms whereby family religiosity influences the probability of adolescent antisocial behavior. *Journal of Comparative Family Studies.*

Simons, R. L., and Associates. (1996). *Understanding differences between divorced and two-biological-parent families: Stress, interaction, and child outcome.* Thousand Oaks, CA: Sage Publications.

Simons, R. L., Beaman, J., Conger, R. D., and Chao, W. (1993a). Childhood experience, conceptions of parenting, and attitudes of spouse as determinants of parental behavior. *Journal of Marriage and the Family, 55,* 91–106.

——. (1993b). Stress, support, and antisocial behavior trait as determinants of emotional well-being and parenting practices among single mothers. *Journal of Marriage and the Family, 55,* 385–398.

Simons, R. L., Chao, W., Conger, R. D., and Elder, G. H. (2001). Quality of parenting as mediator of the effect of childhood defiance on adolescent friendship choices and delinquency: A growth curve analysis. *Journal of Marriage and the Family, 63,* 63–79.

Simons, R. L., Chen, Y.-F., Stewart, E., and Brody, G. H. (2003). Incidents of discrimination and risk for delinquency: A longitudinal test of strain theory with an African American sample. *Justice Quarterly, 20,* 502–528.

Simons, R. L., and Johnson, C. (1998). An examination of competing explanations for the intergenerational transmission of domestic violence. In Y. Danieli (Ed.), *Multigenerational legacies of trauma: An international handbook.* New York: Plenum.

Simons, R. L., Johnson, C., Beaman, J., and Conger, R. D. (1993). Explaining women's double jeopardy: Factors that mediate the association between harsh treatment as a child and violence by a husband. *Journal of Marriage and the Family, 55,* 713–723.

Simons, R. L., Johnson, C., Beaman, J., Conger, R. D. and Whitbeck, L. B. (1996). Parents and peer groups as mediators of the effect of community structure on adolescent problem behavior. *American Journal of Community Psychology, 24,* 145–171 (special issue on methodology).

Simons, R. L., Johnson, C., and Conger, R. D. (1994). Harsh corporal punishment versus quality of parental involvement as an explanation of adolescents' maladjustment. *Journal of Marriage and the Family, 56,* 591–607.

Simons, R. L., Johnson, C., Conger, R. D., and Elder, G. H., Jr. (1998). A test of latent trait versus life course perspectives on the stability of adolescent antisocial behavior. *Criminology, 36,* 217–244.

Simons, R. L., Lin, K.-H., and Gordon, L. C. (1998). Socialization in the family of origin and male dating violence: A prospective study. *Journal of Marriage and the Family, 60,* 467–478.

Simons, R. L., Lin, K., Gordon, L. C., Brody, G. H., Murry, V., and Conger, R. D. (2002). Community differences in the association between parenting practices and child conduct problems. *Journal of Marriage and the Family, 64(2),* 331–345.

Simons, R. L., Lin, K., Gordon, L. C., Conger, R. D., and Lorenz, F. O. (1999). Explaining the higher incidence of adjustment problems among children of divorce compared to those in intact families. *Journal of Marriage and the Family, 61,* 1020–1033.

Simons, R. L., Lorenz, F. O., Conger, R. D., and Wu, C. (1992). Support from spouse as mediator and moderator of the disruptive influence of economic strain on parenting. *Child Development, 63,* 1282–1301.

Simons, R. L., Lorenz, F. O., Wu, C., and Conger, R. D. (1993). Social network and marital support as mediators and moderators of the impact of stress and depression on parental behavior. *Developmental Psychology, 29(2),* 368–381.

Simons, R. L., Murry, V., McLoyd, V., Lin, K., Cutrona, C., and Conger, R. D. (2002). Discrimination, crime, ethnic identity, and parenting as correlates of depressive symptoms among African American children: A multilevel analysis. *Development and Psychopathology, 14,* 371–393.

Simons, R. L., Simons, L. G., Stewart, E., and Chen, Y. (2003). Incidents of discrimination and risk for delinquency: A longitudinal test of strain theory with an African American sample. *Justice Quarterly, 20,* 827–854.

Simons, R. L., Stewart, E., Gordon, L. C., and Conger, R. D. (2002). A test of life-course explanations for stability and change in antisocial behavior from adolescence to young adulthood. *Criminology, 40,* 401–434.

Simons, R. L., Whitbeck, L. B., Beaman, J., and Conger, R. D. (1994). The impact of mothers' parenting, involvement by nonresidential fathers, and parental conflict on the adjustment of adolescent children. *Journal of Marriage and the Family, 56,* 356–374.

Simons, R. L., Whitbeck, L. B., Conger, R. D., and Wu, C. (1991). Intergenerational transmission of harsh parenting. *Developmental Psychology, 27,* 159–171.

Simons, R. L., Whitbeck, L. B., Melby, J. N., and Wu, C. (1994). Economic pressure and harsh parenting. In R. D. Conger and G. H. Elder (Eds.), *Families in troubled times* (pp. 207–222). New York: Aldine.

Simons, R. L., Whitbeck, L. B., and Wu, C. (1994). Resilient and vulnerable adolescents. In R. D. Conger and G. H. Elder (Eds.), *Families in troubled times: Adapting to change in rural America* (pp. 223–234). New York: Aldine de Gruyter.

Simons, R. L., Wu, C., Conger, R. D., and Lorenz, F. O. (1994). Two routes to delinquency: Differences between early and late starters in the impact of parenting and deviant peers. *Criminology, 32,* 247–275.

Simons, R. L., Wu, C. I., Johnson, C., and Conger, R. D. (1995). A test of various perspectives on the intergenerational transmission of domestic violence. *Criminology, 33,* 141–171.

Simons, R. L., Wu, C., Lin, K., Gordon, L., and Conger, R. D. (2000). A cross-cultural examination of the link between corporal punishment and adolescent antisocial behavior. *Criminology, 38,* 47–74.

Simpson, S. S., and Ellis, L. (1994). Is gender subordinate to class? An empirical assessment of Colvin and Pauly's structural Marxist theory of delinquency. *Journal of Criminal Law and Criminology, 85,* 453–480.

Singer, S. I., and Levine, M. (1988). Power-control theory, gender, and delinquency: A partial replication with additional evidence on the effects of peers. *Criminology, 26,* 627–648.

Skolnick, A. S., and Skolnick, J. H. (2001). Introduction: Family in transition. In A. S. Skolnick and J. H. Skolnick (Eds.), *Family in transition* (11th edition, pp. 1–13). Boston: Allyn and Bacon.

Slaby, R. G., and Guerra, N. G. (1988). Cognitive mediators of aggression in adolescent offenders: 1. Assessment. *Developmental Psychology, 24,* 580–588.

Smith, C., and Thornberry, T. P. (1995). The relationship between childhood maltreatment and adolescent involvement in delinquency. *Criminology, 33,* 451–477.

Smith, D. R., and Jarjourna, G. R. (1988). Social structure and criminal victimization. *Journal of Research in Crime and Delinquency, 25,* 27–52.

Smith, P. K., and Drew, L. M. (2002). Grandparenthood. In M. H. Bornstein (Ed.), *Handbook of parenting, volume 3: Being and becoming a parent* (2nd edition). Mahwah, NJ: Lawrence Erlbaum Associates.

Stacey, J. and Biblarz, T. J. (2001). (How) Does the sexual orientation of parents matter? *American Sociological Review, 66,* 159–183.

Steinberg, L., Dornbusch, S., and Brown, B. B. (1992). Ethnic differences in adolescent achievement: An ecological perspective. *American Psychologist, 47,* 723–729.

Steinberg, L., Elmen, J., and Mounts, N. S. (1989). Authoritative parenting, psychosocial maturity, and academic success among adolescents. *Child Development, 60,* 1424–1436.

Steinberg, L., Lamborn, S., Dornbusch, S., and Darling, N. (1992). Impact of parenting practices on adolescent achievement: Authoritative parenting, school involvement, and encouragement to succeed. *Child Development, 63,* 1266–1281.

Steinberg, L., Mounts, N., Lamborn, S., and Dornbusch, S. (1991). Authoritative parenting and adolescent adjustment across various ecological niches. *Journal of Reseach on Adolescence, 1,* 19–36.

Steiner, H. (1997). Practice parameters for the assessment and treatment of children and adolescents with conduct disorder. *Journal of the American Academy of Child and Adolescent Psychiatry, 36 (supplement),* S1–S18.

Steiner, H., and Wilson, J. (1999). Conduct disorder. In D. O. Hendren (Ed.), *Disruptive behavior disorders in children and adolescents* (pp. 47–92). Washington, DC: American Psychiatric Association Press.

Steinmetz, S. K. (1987). Family violence. In M. B. Sussman and S. K. Steinmetz (Eds.), *Handbook of marriage and the family* (pp. 725–765). New York: Plenum Press.

Stewart, E., Simons, R. L., and Conger, R. D. (2000). The effects of delinquency and legal sanctions on parenting behaviors. In L. F. Greer and M. L. Benson (Eds.), *Families and crime* (pp. 257–279). Samford, CT: JAI.

——. (2002). Assessing neighborhood and social psychological influences on childhood violence in an African American sample. *Criminology, 40,* 801–830.

Stith, S. M., Rosen, K. H., and Middleton, K. A. (2000). The intergenerational transmission of spouse abuse: A meta-analysis. *Journal of Marriage and the Family, 62(3),* 640–654.

Stitt, B. G., and Giacopassi, D. J. (1992). Trends in the connectivity of theory and research in criminology. *Criminologist, 17,* 3–6.

Straus, M. A. (1990). Social stress and marital violence in a national sample of American families. In M. A. Straus and R. J. Gelles (Eds.), *Physical violence in American families: Risk factors and adaptations to violence in 8,145 families.* New Brunswick, NJ: Transaction Publishers.

——. (1991). Discipline and deviance: Physical punishment of children and violence and other crime in adulthood. *Social Problems, 38,* 133–154.

——. (1994). Should the use of corporal punishment by parents be considered child abuse? Yes. In M. A. Mason and E. Gambrill (Eds.), *Debating children's lives: Current controversies on children and adolescents.* Newbury Park, CA: Sage Publications.

——. (1999). Is it time to ban corporal punishment of children? *Canadian Medical Association Journal, 161,* 821–822.

——. (2001). New evidence for the benefits of never spanking. *Society, 38(6),* 52–61.

Straus, M. A., and Donnelly, D. A. (1994). *Beating the devil out of them: Corporal punishment in American families.* New York: Lexington Books.

Straus, M. A., and Gelles, R. J. (1986). Social change and change in family violence from 1975 to 1985 as revealed by two national surveys. *Journal of Marriage and the Family, 48,* 465–479.

——. (1990). Societal change and change in family violence from 1975 to 1985 as revealed by two national surveys. In M. A. Straus and R. J. Gelles (Eds.), *Physical violence in American families: Risk factors and adaptations to violence in 8,145 families.* New Brunswick, NJ: Transaction.

Straus, M. A., Gelles, R. J., and Steinmetz, S. K. (1980). *Behind closed doors: Violence in the American family*. Beverly Hills, CA: Sage Publications.

Straus, M. A., and Smith, C. (1990a). Family patterns and primary prevention of family violence. In M. A. Straus and R. J. Gelles (Eds.), *Physical violence in American families* (pp. 507–528). New Brunswick, NJ: Transaction.

——. (1990b). Family patterns and child abuse. In M. A. Straus and R. J. Gelles (Eds.), *Physical violence in American families* (pp. 245–260). New Brunswick, NJ: Transaction.

Straus, M. A., and Stewart, J. H. (1999). Corporal punishment by American parents: National data on prevalence, chronicity, severity, and duration, in the relation to child and family characteristics. *Clinical Child and Family Psychology Review, 2*, 55–70.

Straus, M. A., Sugarman, D. B., and Giles-Sims, J. (1997). Spanking by parents and subsequent antisocial behavior of children. *Archives of Pediatric and Adolescent Medicine, 151*, 761–767.

Sullivan, M. (1989). *'Getting paid': Youth crime and work in the inner city.* Ithaca, NY: Cornell University Press.

Sutherland, E. H. (1947). *Principles of criminology* (4th edition). Philadelphia: J. B. Lippincott.

Swinford, S. P., DeMaris, A., Cernkovich, S. A., and Giordano, P. C. (2000). Harsh physical discipline in childhood and violence in later romantic involvements: The mediating role of problem behaviors. *Journal of Marriage and the Family, 62(2)*, 508–520.

Targ, D. B., and Brintnall-Peterson, M. (2001). Grandparents raising grandchildren. *Journal of Family Issues, 22(5)*, 579–593.

Taylor, R. B., Gottfredson, S., and Brower, S. (1984). Block crime and fear: Defensible space, local social ties, and territorial functioning. *Journal of Research in Crime and Delinquency, 21*, 303–331.

Teachman, J. D. (2000). Diversity of family structure: Economic and social influences. In D. H. Demo, K. R. Allen, and M. A. Fine (Eds.), *Handbook of family diversity* (pp. 32–58). New York: Oxford.

Teachman, J. D., Tedrow, L. M., and Crowder, K. D. (2000). The changing demography of America's families. *Journal of Marriage and the Family, 62*, 1234–1246.

Tennant, F. S., Jr., Detels, R., and Clark, V. (1975). Some childhood antecedents of drug and alcohol use. *American Journal of Epidemiology, 102*, 377–385.

Thomas, J., and Rogers, C. (1983). A treatment program for interfamily juvenile sexual offenders. In J. Greer and I. Stuart (Eds.), *The sexual aggressor: Current perspectives on treatment* (pp. 127–143). New York: Van Nostrand Reinhold.

Thomson, E., McLanahan, S. S., and Curtin, B. B. (1992). Family structure, gender, and parental socialization. *Journal of Marriage and the Family, 54,* 368–378.

Tjaden, P., and Thoennes, N. (1999). *Extent, nature, and consequences of intimate partner violence: Findings from the national violence against women survey.* Washington, DC: National Institute of Justice/Centers for Disease Control and Prevention.

Toby, J. (1957). Social disorganization and stake in conformity: Complementary factors in the predatory behavior of hoodlums. *Journal of Criminal Law, Criminology, and Police Science, 48,* 12–17.

Tolan, P. H., Gorman-Smith, D., and Henry, D. B. (2003). The developmental ecology of urban males' youth violence. *Developmental Psychology, 39(2),* 274–291.

Turrel, S. C. (2000). A descriptive analysis of same-sex relationship violence for a diverse sample. *Journal of Family Violence, 15,* 281–293.

U.S. Census Bureau. (1999, September). *Poverty in the United States, 1998.* Washington, DC: U.S. Printing Office.

——. (2000a). *Statistical abstracts of the United States,* Table 144. Washington, DC: U.S. Printing Office.

——. (2000b). *Current population reports,* No. 514, pp. 1–20. Washington, DC: U.S. Printing Office.

——. (2001a). *Profile of general demographic characteristics,* Table DP-1. Washington, DC: U.S. Printing Office.

——. (2001b). *Living arrangements of children under 18 years old: 1960 to present.* Washington, DC: U.S. Printing Office.

U.S. Department of Health and Human Services, Administration on Children, Youth, and Families. (2002). *Child maltreatment 2001.* Washington, DC: U.S. Printing Office.

Volk, D. (1994). A case study of parent involvement in the homes of three Puerto Rican kindergarteners. *Journal of Educational Issues of Language Minority Students, 14,* 89–113.

Walker, L. E. (1979). *The battered woman.* New York: Harper & Row.

——. (1989). Psychology and violence against women. *American Psychologist, 44,* 659–702.

Walster, E. G., Walster, W., and Berschied, E. (1978). *Equity: Theory and research.* Boston: Allyn & Bacon.

Warr, M. (1993). Age, peers, and delinquency. *Criminology, 31,* 17–40.

——. (1998). Life-course transitions and desistence from crime. *Criminology, 36,* 1075–1108.

Warr, M., and Stafford, M. (1991). The influence of delinquent peers: What they think or what they do? *Criminology, 29,* 851–866.

Wasserman, G. A., Miller, L., Pinner, E., and Jaramillo, B. (1996). Parenting and predictors of early conduct problems in urban, high-risks boys. *Journal of the Academy of Child and Adolescent Psychiatry, 35,* 1227–1236.

Watson, J. B., and Rayner, R. (1920). Conditioned emotional reactions. *Journal of Experimental Psychology, 3,* 1–14.

Wellman, B., Wong, R. Y., Tindall, D., and Matthews, L. (1997). A decade of network change: Turnover, persistence and stability in personal communities. *Social Networks, 19,* 25–50.

Whaley, A. L. (2000). Sociocultural differences in the developmental consequences of the use of physical discipline during childhood for African Americans. *Cultural Diversity and Ethnic Minority Psychology, 6,* 5–12.

White, L. K., and Gilbreth, J. G. (2001). When children have two fathers: Effects of relationships with stepfathers and noncustodial fathers on adolescent outcomes. *Journal of Marriage and the Family, 52,* 453–462.

White, L. K., and Rogers, S. J. (2000). Economic circumstances and family outcomes: A review of the 1990's. *Journal of Marriage and the Family, 62(4),* 1035–1051.

White, R. W., and Widom, C. S. (2003). Intimate partner violence among abused and neglected children in young adulthood: The mediating effects of early aggression, antisocial personality, hostility, and alcohol problems. *Aggressive Behavior, 29,* 332–345.

Widom, C. S. (1989). Child abuse, neglect, and violent criminal behavior. *Criminology, 27,* 251–271.

——. (1991). The role of placement experiences in mediating the criminal consequences of early childhood victimization. *American Journal of Orthopsychiatry, 61,* 195–220.

Widom, C. S., and Maxfield, M. G. (2001). *An update on the 'cycle of violence.'* Washington, DC: U.S. Department of Justice.

Wilson, J. Q. (1983, October). Raising kids. *Atlantic Monthly,* 45–46.

——. (1995). Crime and public policy. In J. Q. Wilson and J. Petersilia (Eds.), *Crime* (pp. 489–510). San Francisco: ICS.

Wilson, J. Q., and Herrnstein, R. (1985). *Crime and human nature.* New York: Simon & Schuster.

Wilson, W. J. (1987). *The truly disadvantaged.* Chicago: University of Chicago.

——. (1996). *When work disappears: The world of the new urban poor.* New York: Alfred Knopf.

Wright, B. R. E., Caspi, A., Moffitt, T. E., and Silva, P. A. (2001). The effects of social ties on crime vary by criminal propensity: A life-course model of interdependence. *Criminology, 39(2),* 321–352.

Wright, J. P., and Cullen, F. T. (2001). Parental efficacy and delinquent behavior: Do control and support matter? *Criminology, 39,* 677–706.

Yee, J. H. Y. (1983). Parenting attitudes, acculturation, and social competence in the Chinese-American child. *Dissertation Abstracts International, 43,* 4166-B.

Zill, N. (1994). Understanding why children in stepfamilies have more learning and behavior problems than children in nuclear families. In A. Booth and J. Dunn (Eds.), *Stepfamilies: Who benefits? Who does not?* (pp. 97–106). Hillsdale, NJ: Lawrence Erlbaum Associates.

Zingraff, M. T., Leiter J., Myers, K. A., and Johnson, M. C. (1993). Child maltreatment and youthful problem behavior. *Criminology, 31,* 173–202. ✦

Name Index

A, B

C, D

E, F

G, H

I, J

K, L

M, N

O, P

Q, R

S, T

U, V

W, X

Y, Z

Subject Index

A, B

C, D

E, F

G, H

I, J

O, P

Q, R

S, T

U, V

W, X, Y, Z

CPSIA information can be obtained at www.ICGtesting.com
Printed in the USA
BVOW040806070912

299790BV00002B/44/P